"NO STANDING ARMIES!"

A N

ARGUMENT,

Shewing, that a

Standing Army

Is inconfiftent with

A Free Government, and abfolutely
deftrućtive to the Conftitution of
the Englifh Monarchy.

Cervus Equum pugna melior communibus herbis
Pellebat, donec minor in certamine longo
Imploravit opes hominis frænumq; recepit.
Sed poftquam victor violens difceffit ab hofte,
Non Equitem dorfo, non frænum depulit ore.

Horat. Epift. 10.

LONDON;
Printed in the Year 1697.

LOIS G. SCHWOERER

"No Standing Armies!"

THE ANTIARMY IDEOLOGY IN SEVENTEENTH-CENTURY ENGLAND

The Johns Hopkins University Press
Baltimore and London

This book has been brought to publication with assistance from the University Committee on Research of the George Washington University.

The Johns Hopkins University Press, Baltimore, Maryland 21218
The Johns Hopkins University Press Ltd., London

Library of Congress Catalog Card Number 73-19337
ISBN 0-8018-1563-0

Library of Congress Cataloging in Publication data will be found on the last printed page of this book.

The frontispiece shows the cover of John Trenchard's tract, courtesy Folger Shakespeare Library. The portraits in the text of Henry Powle and Walter Moyle, by George Vertue, and of Andrew Fletcher, by Anna Forbes, and the diagram of King James II's army are copyright British Museum. The portrait of Sir Thomas Lee is by Sir Peter Lely, courtesy Leicestershire Museum and Art Gallery.

For Frank

CONTENTS

ABBREVIATIONS

Add. Mss.	Additional Manuscripts
B.M.	British Museum
B.I.H.R.	*Bulletin Institute of Historical Research*
C.S.P.D.	*Calendar of State Papers, Domestic Series*
C.S.P.V.	*Calendar of State Papers, and manuscripts relating to English affairs existing in the archives and collections of Venice*
C.H.J.	*Cambridge Historical Journal*
C.J.	*Journals of the House of Commons*
D.N.B.	*Dictionary of National Biography*
E.H.R.	*English Historical Review*
H.M.C.	*Reports of the Historical Manuscripts Commission*
H.L.Q.	*Huntington Library Quarterly*
J.B.S.	*Journal of British Studies*
L.J.	*Journals of the House of Lords*
O.P.H.	*Old Parliamentary History*
P.R.O.	Public Record Office
T.R.H.S.	*Transactions of the Royal Historical Society*
W.M.Q.	*William and Mary Quarterly*

ACKNOWLEDGMENTS

Librarians and their staffs in the United States and England have given me expert assistance. I am especially indebted to the staff of the Folger Shakespeare Library in Washington, D.C., where the collection and the amenities are unrivaled. The Union Theological Seminary Library, in New York City, and the Houghton Library, at Harvard University, allowed me to use their rich collection of tracts and pamphlets and assisted in many ways during my visits. I am grateful, too, for the countless courtesies extended to me when I worked at the Library of Congress, the British Museum, especially the Manuscript Room, the Public Record Office, and the Bodleian Library. I thank the duke of Buccleuch and Queensberry, K.T., G.C.V.O., for permission to have copied manuscripts in his possession, now held at Delapré Abbey, Northamptonshire Record Office. Librarians at Bryn Mawr College, The George Washington University, and Georgetown University have also been cooperative.

Many scholars have offered advice and suggestions. For help in dealing with biographical problems, I am indebted to Prof. P. H. Hardacre, Prof. Basil D. Henning, editor of the History of Parliament Trust project for the Restoration period, and to Prof. Henning's colleagues in London who put unpublished biographies at my disposal. I thank the officers of the Parliament Trust, Institute of Historical Research, for permission to use that material. Prof. Mary Keeler generously shared knowledge of early Stuart bibliography and issues, while Profs. C. M. Williams and David Underdown clarified some matters in the Civil War and Cromwellian periods. The late Prof. **Douglas R.** Lacey kindly allowed me to use his photocopy of Roger Morrice, "Entr'ing Book, Being An Historical Register of Occurrences from April, Anno 1677, to April 1691." I have discussed Renaissance themes with Dr. Richard De Molen and Prof. Anthony Parrell but am most deeply obligated to Prof. Felix Gilbert, who first introduced me to the intricacies of Machiavelli's thought in a graduate seminar at Bryn Mawr College. Dr. Barbara Bradfield Taft allowed me to read the typescript of her book on English republicans. The best of scholarly friends, she painstakingly read and commented on the manuscript of this book and tirelessly discussed bibliography and problems. Above all, I am indebted to Prof. Caroline Robbins, whose work has always been a guide and inspiration. She has read everything I have written, always to my great profit.

Two graduate students have ably assisted in the research for this study. Todd White, a Ph.D. candidate at The George Washington University, helped assemble bibliographical material for eighteenth-century America. John C. R. Childs, a Ph.D. candidate at the University of London, answered questions about Charles II's army and counted the number of regular army and militia officers in the parliamentary sessions of 1675 and 1678. White's study of military ideals and practices at the time of the American Revolution and Childs' book on Charles II's army are in preparation. Dr. Isabel Kenrick, a personal friend in London, had material photocopied for me and verified certain details.

A sabbatical leave allowed me to finish the research and writing. I thank Prof. Robert P. Sharkey, then chairman of the History Department, and Prof. Calvin D. Linton, dean of Columbian College, The George Washington University, for approving my request for leave. A generous grant from the American Philosophical Society financed one of several visits to England, while short- and long-term grants from the Graduate School of Arts and Sciences at The George Washington University helped defray the costs of research and preparation of the manuscript for publication. I am grateful for these tangible testimonies of confidence and encouragement.

The editorial boards of the *Huntington Library Quarterly* and the *Journal of British Studies* kindly granted me permission to use material from three articles, which appeared in 1965, 1966, and 1971.

Special thanks are due Virginia Williams for typing successive drafts of the manuscript and Rebecca Murray for taking care of a complicated household. My husband has been a pillar of support. Our son kept all things in perspective.

"NO STANDING ARMIES!"

INTRODUCTION

"A Standing Army Is inconsistent with A Free Government, and absolutely destructive to the Constitution of the English Monarchy." This emphatic assertion, written by John Trenchard in 1697, was a central assumption in an attitude toward a permanent, paid military force that gradually emerged in England during the seventeenth century. During the entire century, but especially after the Restoration when the Stuart kings set up a standing army, successive generations of Englishmen thought, talked, and wrote about the armed forces of the realm. Between 1697 and 1699, when the question of a standing army in peacetime reached a climax, the arguments for and against a permanent, professional army, which had been offered in fragments before, were forged into coherent statements. The antistanding army arguments, and the political decisions they accompanied, seeded an intellectual tradition that remained vital for at least another one hundred years not only in England but in the American colonies, where it was carried. The arguments still speak to a troubled twentieth century, and although the context is obviously different, much that is said today in the United States about military organization and citizen responsibility echoes the passionate arguments of three hundred years ago.

The term "standing army" refers to a military force that is permanently embodied and kept "standing," even in time of peace. Standing armies are distinguished from mercenaries, who are paid, professional soldiers hired for an occasion and then dismissed, and

1

from the armies of the Tudors and early Stuarts, which were composed of men who were conscripted to defend the state, to man an expedition, or to fight a war and who were then disbanded. A standing army is also different from the local, casually trained militia, which most Englishmen approved. Properly, a standing army should not be equated with the king's Guards, but the new Guards established in 1661 served as a nucleus for an enlarged military force and were sometimes purposely denominated a "standing army" by the king's critics.

England had no standing army until the New Model Army was created in 1645 to win a revolution and was then kept on to support the government of the Commonwealth and Protectorate. The term, with reference to an English force, does not appear in the written record until 1648. But before then, the country had experienced the impact of soldiers who had been raised for expeditions, such as in the 1620s, and individuals had explored the question of military prerogative, a matter of great constitutional significance, such as in the Militia Bill controversy of 1641-42. In many respects, the New Model Army was unique, but it posed the same kinds of problems that any permanent military force did and provoked widespread hostility. Thus, a negative attitude toward soldiers and the central government's efforts to strengthen the military forces already existed in the first half of the seventeenth century, long before a standing army answerable to a legitimate monarch was established by Charles II, long before the issue of a standing army became one of the most politically and intellectually important questions of the late seventeenth century. The antistanding army ideology articulated in the late seventeenth century is illuminated when earlier episodes and expressions of protest against soldiers and the military policies of the central government are taken into account.

Opposition to standing armies had a long line of development in England. Criticism of soldiers and the government's military policies were part of every major political and constitutional confrontation between the crown, or protector during the Interregnum, and the Parliament. The Petition of Right of 1628, the Militia Bill/Ordinance of 1641-42, the criticism of the New Model Army and the major-generals during the Cromewellian interlude, the settlement at the Restoration, the contest between Charles and the parliamentary opposition during the 1670s, the Revolutionary settlement in 1689, and the controversy over William III's army from 1697 through 1699 each, in different ways, provided the framework within which the question was argued. In Parliament and press, arguments were offered to show that a standing army in peacetime under the authority of the executive was politically dangerous, economically costly, socially menacing, and morally hazardous and that the country should depend for its land defense on the local militia controlled by the upper classes. This was the English brand of antimilitarism. Persons across the political spectrum could agree on this. But the most articulate and thorough-going indictment of standing armies was made by men who had been infected by the libertarian assumptions of the seventeenth century. What was said and done in the early and middle years of the century set precedents for future attitudes and actions. Yet at each point in the century, the themes of the antiarmy argument were adapted to meet specific circumstances.

At the beginning of the seventeenth century, a predisposition, which reflected the influence of geography, England's experience, and Renaissance assumptions about military power, already existed (chapter 1). This inclination was hardened by policies of the government in the 1620s, when troops raised for the Thirty Years War were billeted in private houses and soldiers and civilians were disciplined by martial law. The local lieutenancy was bitterly criticized for implementing such policies. The Petition of Right of 1628 was, in part, a protest against the intrusion in the affairs of the local county of an armed central government using the agency of the local lieutenancy (chapter 2). In the 1630s, Charles i's efforts to reform and centralize the militia played a larger part than is sometimes recognized in the Long Parliament's indictment of the government. In 1641-42, the Militia Bill/Ordinance controversy led men in Parliament and in the press to argue that ultimate military power should be vested in Parliament, a conviction that remained central to all subsequent protests against standing armies. The most important of many polemicists was Henry Parker (chapter 3).

Men of every political persuasion expressed fear and dislike of the New Model Army and the major-generals. But the most articulate spokesmen were libertarians and radicals of one kind or another, especially republicans. The most significant among them in the press was the political philosopher, James Harrington, whose *Oceana*, heavily indebted to the thought of Niccolò Machiavelli, influenced subsequent opponents of standing armies (chapter 4). At the Restoration, the Cromwellian army was hastily disbanded. But to meet the threat of domestic insurrection, Charles ii created a body of guards that became the nucleus of the first standing army in peacetime under a legitimate monarch. As part of the military settlement at the Restoration, the militia was after much debate settled in the hands of the king. The military settlement failed to resolve the fundamental question of military authority and laid the groundwork for future confrontations (chapter 5). Antimilitary sentiment surfaced again in the 1670s when distrust of the king deepened because of policies that suggested his sympathy for absolutism, Popery, and France. In this decade, the genuine fear of Charles's forces was exploited by the Country-Whig party to discredit the king, his ministers, and his policies and to promote partisan political goals, especially the dissolution of the Cavalier Parliament. The cry "No Standing Armies" became a slogan and, like the cry "No Popery," was used as a propaganda tool. Feared as an instrument of tyranny and political corruption, the army was criticized in tracts from the first earl of Shaftesbury's circle and in *Plato Redivivus*, written by Henry Neville (chapter 6).

James II's policy of maintaining a standing army officered in part by Catholics was attacked so vigorously in the fall of 1685 that the king prorogued his only Parliament. Deepening fear of James's growing standing army played a part in the coming of the Revolution of 1688. In the settlement that followed, Article VI of the Bill of Rights, which asserted that there should be no standing army in peacetime without the consent of Parliament, was the only genuinely revolutionary principle. The Mutiny Act of 1689 was also directed toward achieving parliamentary control of the military (chapter 7). Despite these constitutional regulations, the climax in the controversy over standing armies in peacetime and the fullest expression of the antistanding army attitude came a decade later in 1697–99. Opposition to William III's plans to keep a large army after the Peace of Ryswick was led in Parliament by a new Tory-Old Whig alignment headed by Robert Harley and argued in the press by a group of radical Whigs, especially John Trenchard, Walter Moyle, and Andrew Fletcher, who summed up and elaborated upon what had already been said about the evils of standing armies. Arguments for the king's project were offered by John lord Somers. The issue was compromised by the establishment of a small permanent force dependent upon parliamentary appropriation, a principle that has lasted. Wider agreement with the idea of maintaining a permanent army was expressed than has been recognized (chapter 8).

Seventeenth-century antiarmy pamphlets and debates seeded an intellectual tradition that continued in eighteenth-century England and was carried to the English colonies in America, where it had a profound impact upon the thinking of American leaders. In both England and the United States, the tradition remained, in the United States as a constitutional issue that challenged executive power in various ways throughout the nineteenth century. Indeed in somewhat different form, the same issues are being raised today, and to those issues the tracts and debates of three hundred years ago can speak (chapter 9).

Inherent in all the successive controversies about the army was a fundamental question, the nature of the English government: whether the king or Parliament should hold ultimate sovereignty in the state, whether the government should move in the direction of an absolute monarchy based on military power as governments on the continent were doing. That military authority expresses sovereignty as no other function of government is axiomatic. The struggle for the command of the militia was, in the words of one Stuart king, the "Fittest Subject for a King's Quarrel." As profoundly as any political philosopher, Charles I recognized that without military command, royal power was "but a shadow."[1] The outcome of the controversies about standing armies by the end of the century was a genuine shift in sovereignty in England's government.

That a standing army should have been established was probably inevitable, given the technological and political changes on the continent. But it was not inevitable that the armed forces under the command of the executive should have been so persistently resisted nor that by the end of the century the standing army should have, in terms of size, pay, and discipline, been placed in peacetime under the ultimate authority of Parliament. Civilian control of the military, exercised by the legislature, was the contribution of seventy years of confrontations. This contribution and achievement, which helped to preserve free institutions and to assure a government in which Parliament dominated, must be measured, if its full significance is to be understood, in terms of the development in the seventeenth century

---

[1] *The King's Cabinet Opened: Or Certain Pacquets of Secret Letters and Papers. Written with the King's Own Hands* (London, 1645), included later in *Harleian Miscellany* (London, 1746), 7: 525. The king's papers were seized at the Battle of Naseby. For an account of the steps taken to publish them, see R. E. Maddison, " 'The King's Cabinet Opened': A Case Study in Pamphlet History," *Notes and Queries*, New Series, 13 (1966): 2–9.

of absolute monarchies based on large standing armies on the continent and in terms of its ongoing significance for both England and the United States.

Such an important subject has not gone unnoticed. Almost every political and constitutional history of the period mentions the growth of the standing army and notes the development of opposition to it. Over a century ago, Thomas lord Macaulay referred to the standing army question of the 1697 session of Parliament as "preeminent in interest and importance." Subsequently, Leopold Von Ranke, A. S. Turberville, Keith Feiling, and David Ogg, among other historians, treated the political aspects of the issue within the context of their larger interests. The institutional history of the English army has found many students, such as Charles M. Clode, J. W. Fortescue, and Colonel Clifford Walton, but they do no more than refer to the standing army issue. Interest in military history has grown, but there is still need for a study of the army that would employ demographic techniques and would answer different kinds of questions from those posed by earlier historians.[2] The local militia in the Tudor-Stuart period has also been examined, most recently by Lindsay Boynton and J. R. Western.[3] No attempt is made in the present study to contribute to the work being done on the army or militia as military institutions. During the past two decades, some aspects of the questions that do concern this book have been investigated. Zera Fink's *Classical Republicans* illuminated the relationship between the antiarmy ideology and antimonarchical concepts. Many of the men who wrote tracts against the army have been studied for other reasons by Caroline Robbins. Her *Eighteenth Century Commonwealthmen* and many articles have also contributed to understanding the ideological connections between England and the

[2]See Robin Higham, ed., *A Guide to the Sources of British Military History* (London, 1972). Chapter 3 written by C. G. Cruickshank deals with the Tudor-Stuart period. The most useful general military histories are C. M. Clode, *The Military Forces of the Crown* (London, 1896); J. W. Fortescue, *A History of the British Army* (London, 1899-1930); and C. E. Walton, *History of the British Standing Army 1660-1700* (London, 1894). For the early seventeenth century: Godfrey Davies, *The Early History of the Coldstream Guards* (Oxford, 1924), and Sir Charles Firth, *Cromwell's Army*, with a new introduction by P. H. Hardacre (London, 1961). For the Elizabethan age, C. G. Cruickshank, *Elizabeth's Army* (Oxford, 1966).

[3]Lindsay Boynton, *The Elizabethan Militia 1558-1638* (London, 1967), which covers the early seventeenth century; Gladys Scott Thomson, *Lords Lieutenants in the Sixteenth Century* (London, 1923); Joan Wake, ed., *A Copy of Papers Relating to Musters, Beacons and Subsidies, etc., in the County of Northampton 1586-1623* (Printed for Northamptonshire Record Society, 1926); and J. R. Western, *The English Militia in the Eighteenth Century* (London, 1965), which starts with the Restoration.

American colonies, as has the work of Bernard Bailyn and H. Trevor Colbourn among others. J. G. A. Pocock's article, "Machiavelli, Harrington and English Political Ideologies in the Eighteenth Century," in the *William and Mary Quarterly* in 1965 emphasized the relationship between Machiavelli, Harrington, and eighteenth-century thinkers. But no previous study has thoroughly traced the origins and expression of the antistanding army ideology in Parliament and the press in the seventeenth century and shown its continuing influence in England and the United States.

CHAPTER I

ORIGINS OF THE ENGLISH ANTIMILITARY ATTITUDE

 Long before a standing army was created in England, a predisposition to distrust the paid, professional soldier was discernible. Articulated in casual and general terms, this inclination reflected many elements: geography, the country's traditional system of military organization, social assumptions, and the influence of classical and Renaissance wisdom. The antimilitary sentiment grew from such roots as these, rather than from pacifism or Christian idealism.

The evidence of a negative attitude toward the military at the opening of the Stuart era is scattered and fragmentary. In the absence of an army and of interest, even in the militia,[1] there was little reason for a systematic airing of opinion about military matters. But some direct testimony comes from Elizabeth's reign, when a number of pamphlets were written by a small group of men who argued for a policy of military preparedness.[2] Barnabe Rich, Thomas Digges, and

---

[1] A general muster of the militia was not ordered until 1612. See Boynton, *The Elizabethan Militia*, p. 210.

[2] During Elizabeth's reign, seventy-eight books on a variety of military matters were printed. See Maurice J. D. Cockle, *A Bibliography of English Military Books up to 1642 and of Contemporary Foreign Books*, introduction by Sir Charles Oman (London, 1900). Many of the tracts are at the Folger Shakespeare Library. The best studies on them from different points of view are: Henry J. Webb, *Elizabethan Military Science: The Books and the Practice* (London, 1965); G. Geoffrey Langsam, *Martial Books and Tudor Verse* (New York, 1951); and Paul A. Jorgensen, *Shakespeare's Military World* (Berkeley, 1956).

8

Geoffrey Gates, among others, justified war as a positive contribution to national character and tried to vindicate the reputation of the soldier. Paradoxically, their tracts attest to the poor regard in which the professional soldier was held. In 1578, a writer complained that Englishmen "hath alwayes had that faute . . . of being unnatural and unthankful" to professional soldiers.[3] Gates illustrated this point by referring to an ancient literary controversy over which of the professions was the most honorable. Englishmen rated the lawyer first, the merchant second, and the soldier far down the list.[4] According to Rich, the merchant and the lawyer were the "greatest findefaults that . . . invey against soldiers," but he accused all his countrymen of being selfish, luxury-loving, and lazy.[5]

Evidence from other sources confirms the accusations of these pamphleteers. In 1603, for example, one of the men who was sentenced to die in the Essex conspiracy declared that anyone who advocated reform of the nation's military system was treated like a dog; in his view it was unlikely that the attitude would ever change.[6] Around the same time, Sir Thomas Overbury characterized the soldier in disparaging terms.[7] John Selden preserved a story that underscored the disregard in which soldiers were held. Apollo, so the tale went, was approached by a group of soldiers who petitioned that war be given the status of the eighth liberal science. Upon hearing of Apollo's agreement to this proposal, a contingent of butchers protested on the ground that they were more worthy than soldiers because the slaughter they performed was to preserve men's lives not to destory them. Persuaded by their argument, Apollo reversed his decision and made the soldier's trade a mystery instead.[8] An anonymous antifeminist of the early seventeenth century could think of no more effective way to express his dislike of women than to say that they

---

[3]Barnabe Googe's "Testimonial" appended to Barnabe Rich, *Allarme Foreshewing What Perilles Are Procured When People Live without Regarde to Martiall Lawe* (London, 1578).

[4]Geoffrey Gates, *The Defence of Militarie Profession, Wherein is Eloquently Shewed the Due Commendation of Martiall Prowesse, and Plainly Prooved How Necessary the Exercise of Armes Is for This Our Age* (London, 1579), pp. 9, 10, 12, 18.

[5]Rich, *Allarme*, pp. Cii verso, Ciii, Ai–Ai verso, Fiiii verso, Gi. Cf. *Foure Paradoxes or Politique Discourses Concerning Militarie Discipline, Written Long Since by Thomas Digges, Esq., of the Worthiness of Warre and Warriors by Dudly Digges, His Sonne* (London, 1604), pp. 96, 97, 100, 102, 111.

[6]Jorgensen, *Shakespeare's Military World*, p. 223.

[7]Edward F. Rimbault, ed., *The Miscellaneous Works in Prose and Verse of Sir Thomas Overbury, Knt, Now First Collected* (London, 1890), pp. 76–78.

[8]*The Works of John Selden, Esq.* (London, 1826), 3 (part 2): 2076.

9

were like soldiers, only worse.[9] Sir Francis Bacon, in examining what made a kingdom great, concluded that history showed that the prince who depended upon professional soldiers "may spread his feathers for a time, but he will mew them soon after."[10]

Contemporary English drama, especially Shakespeare's plays, also reflected the general disparagement of the soldier. Literary scholars have shown that the soldier was portrayed in late sixteenth- and early seventeenth-century drama either as a cipher, a reprobate, or a discontent who inevitably clashed with a peacetime society. Falstaff described his men as "slaves" or "scarecows" in *1 Henry IV* and declared they were as "ragged as Lazarus in the painted cloth." In the recruitment scene in *2 Henry IV*, Falstaff chose an old man and a feeble, emaciated fellow to serve in the army. The famous Pistol, the epitome of the common soldier, was a filthy, dirty rogue who displayed none of the martial virtues.[11]

It may be concluded that there was extant a general predisposition to disparage and condemn the military at the beginning of the seventeenth century. Why should Englishmen have been so inclined decades before they had had any direct experience with a standing army in peacetime? One consideration is the geography of the country. Surrounded by water and protected by her navy, of which almost everyone approved, the country enjoyed a sense of psychological security, which neither conquest, threat, naval disaster, nor foreign landing diminished. Examples could be readily produced to show that geography has been endlessly used to justify the idea that the nation should not depend upon a large, permanent military establishment. For example, an English pamphleteer wrote in 1579 that if the country were not an island, men would "know and value the soldier and lick the dust off the feete" of an army.[12]

A second reason for the disparagement of the military was the character of the foot soldiers with whom Englishmen had had experience. In times of emergency, during Elizabeth's reign and again in the 1620s, men from the lowest reaches of society were pressed into

[9]*Tracts Written by John Selden of the Inner-Temple, Esquire. The First Entitled Jani Anglorum Facies Altera, Rendered into English, with Large Notes Thereupon by Redman Estcot, Gent.* (London, 1683), pp. 18 (misnumbered)-21. In reporting the comment Selden seized the opportunity to call the man a "dirty fellow!"

[10]James Spedding, ed., *The Works of Sir Francis Bacon* (London, 1858), 6: 446. From "Of the True Greatness of Kingdoms and Estates."

[11]Jorgensen, *Shakespeare's Military World, passim* and pp. 120-23, 128, 133-35, 143, 208, 216, 217, 227.

[12]Gates, *The Defence of the Militarie Profession*, p. 18.

service to form the armies that were sent abroad. At the end of the hostilities, the army was disbanded and returned to the counties where they had been levied. Elizabeth herself referred to the men in her armies as "thieves [who] ought to hang."[13] A recent study of Elizabeth's army has shown that the recruitment system was riddled with corruption and graft and operated so that vagabonds, misfits, and prisoners, who traded their sentence for service in the army, filled the regiments.[14] The method of conscription operated with the same results in the 1620s.[15] When the emergency was over and the men were discharged, the responsibility for providing for them and reintegrating them in society was laid on the local shires. The indifference of local authorities to the needs of the disbanded soldier was widespread throughout England. The Privy Council was constantly dispatching scolding letters to the counties urging that the soldiers be cared for. The character of the soldiers, the cost of providing for them, and the importunities of the central government did nothing to recommend to country gentlemen the idea of creating a permanent, professional corps.

A third factor is the lack of genuine leadership from the center of government in establishing a permanent force. Although the king's military prerogatives were not spelled out in statutory form until the Restoration, in practice the crown always claimed ultimate authority over the defenses of the realm. If a step so monumental as creating a standing force was to be taken in the sixteenth century, the initiative for it would have had to come, as it did in fifteenth-century France, from the highest level. Although Elizabeth and her council considered various proposals to strengthen the nation's defenses, none was promoted.[16] The tracts on military matters, that have been mentioned, were not endorsed by the government. In a phrase grown famous, Elizabeth said that her soldiers were the "loves of her people." Sensitivity to public opinion prompted her to drop at least one scheme to strengthen the defenses of the country. Her most important advisor, William Cecil, lord Burghley, had no use for professional soldiers in peacetime, observing that "soldiers in peace are like chimneys in summer."[17] General ignorance about military affairs,

---

[13]Jorgensen, *Shakespeare's Military World*, p. 144. The law against pressing men to serve in a land army was, of course, freely ignored.

[14]Cruickshank, *Elizabeth's Army*, pp. 17–36, 130–42, 280.

[15]Stephen Stearns, "Conscription and English Society," *Journal of British Studies* 11 (1972): 1–24 (hereafter cited as *J.B.S.*).

[16]Boynton, *Elizabethan Militia*, pp. 59–62, 90.

[17]Jorgensen, *Shakespeare's Military World*, p. 220.

as a contemporary charged, may also explain Elizabeth's aversion to a permanent force.[18] As for James I he was too sincerely the pacifist, or as some observers would have had it, too much the coward to advocate a standing army. James was proud of being a "peaceable king," and towards the end of his reign reminded his Parliament, in his inimitable style, that while he ruled everyone had been able to "live quietly under his own vine and fig tree."[19] For both these monarchs, the failure to introduce an element of permanence and professionalism was because neither could have paid for an army from his own resources nor could have expected a grant from Parliament for such a purpose. The historian of Elizabeth's army confirms that the economy was simply not strong enough to support a permanent military establishment, and this was true for James I also.[20] Further, neither James nor Elizabeth (except for a few years) felt a need for a permanent establishment because of foreign obligations or threats; in fact, there was general peace between 1562 and 1588 and again from 1604 to the 1620s.

A fourth consideration in explaining the early inclination to dislike professional soldiers was that England had preserved her ancient system of military organization and obligation without fundamental change until 1645. This was in contrast to continental states, which since the middle of the fifteenth century, had been undergoing a "military revolution," including the maintenance of standing armies in peacetime.[21] The English system contained neither customary nor statutory place for a standing army. Recently scholars have argued that medieval monarchs (whatever their ambitions) depended even in war upon soldiers who were "for the most part professional and mercenary."[22] These men were always disbanded after the emergency. In the late fifteenth century, following the battle at Bosworth Field, Henry Tudor established the Yeomen of the Guard to secure his new throne. In 1539, his son added the Gentlemen Pensioners. Thus,

---

[18]M. Sutcliffe, *The Practice, Proceedings, and Lawes of Armes* (London, 1593), pp. B2 verso, B3.

[19]Wallace Notestein, Frances H. Relf, and Hartley Simpson, eds., *Common Debates, 1621* (New Haven, 1935), 2: 7.

[20]Cruickshank, *Elizabeth's Army*, p. 1.

[21]For an excellent, brief discussion of this change, see Michael Roberts, *The Military Revolution, 1560-1660* (Belfast, 1956); also Denys Hay, *Europe in the 14th and 15th Centuries* (New York, 1966), pp. 33-34.

[22]See, for example, H. G. Richardson and G. O. Sayles, *The Governance of Medieval England from the Conquest to Magna Carta* (Edinburgh, 1963), p. 72 (a controversial study), and John Schlight, *Monarchs and Mercenaries* (New York, 1968), pp. 7-10, 74-75.

there were permanent royal guards to protect the king, garrison strategic castles and forts, curb the ambitions of the great magnates, and partake in court ceremonials. A distinguished military historian has remarked that these guards contained not even the "germ" of a genuine standing army.[23] Englishmen were, of course, aware that the traditional system of military defense did not include a permanent, professional army, and this was one consideration that inclined men to an antimilitary attitude. A tract printed in 1648, whose purpose was to plead for the disbanding of the New Model Army, declared that "if there were no other argument against it, it is enough that it is a thing was never used in this Kingdome."[24] Further, the nature of the two "constitutional"[25] elements in England's military system, the citizen militia, and the feudal array predisposed men to distrust a permanent army. Both reflected hierarchical social values and the fear of arming the lower classes. The equation of military responsibility and socioeconomic status encouraged the belief that military talents were inherent in the well-to-do classes. Although the feudal array was in the early seventeenth century and before a military anachronism,[26] romantic chivalric myths and hierarchical ideas about military responsibility remained. For example, a pamphleteer wrote in 1578 that "the knowledge, and practyse of the actes and feates of armes, principallie and properlye are of the profession of noble menne, and gentlemen of great revenues."[27] Or again, Sir Edward Coke referred to feudalism as "excellent military policy" and regretted that it was now "utterly altered."[28] Lawrence Stone notes the revival of the chivalric ideal in literature with Malory's Arthurian legends and Stephen Hawes's *The Pastime of Pleasure.*[29] In a parliamentary debate on November 26, 1621, a speaker was roundly critical because so few retainers were armed.[30] At the beginning of the Civil War the

[23]Cruickshank, *Elizabeth's Army*, p. 11.

[24]*The Peaceable Militia, or the Cause and Cure of this Late and Present Warre* (London, 1648), p. 2. Cf. J. T. Rutt, ed., *Diary of Thomas Burton, Esq.* (London, 1828), 1: lxxxiii.

[25]The term is used by Francis Grose, *Military Antiquities Respecting a History of the English Army from the Conquest to the Present Time* (London, 1812), 1: 8.

[26]Lawrence Stone, *The Crisis of the Aristocracy, 1558-1641*, abridged edition (Oxford, 1967), pp. 98, 99, 101, 104-5, 107, 113-22, 129-34, for a brilliant commentary on why feudalism decayed.

[27]T. Procter, *Of the Knowledge and Conducte of Warres* (London, 1578), preface.

[28]Sir Edward Coke, *The Third Part of the Institutes* (London, 1633), p. 86; cf. Spedding, *Works of Bacon*, 6: 447; *The Works of Sir Walter Raleigh* (London, 1751), pp. 206-7.

[29]Stone, *Crisis of the Aristocracy*, p. 131.

[30]Notestein, Relf, and Simpson, *Commons Debates, 1621*, 6: 318.

chivalric ideal motivated more than one man to side with Charles I.[31] Such notions inclined the English upper classes to disdain a man who fought for pay.

In a similar way the organization of the militia predisposed men to an antimilitary attitude. Like the feudal array, the militia was a venerable institution. Although the word first appeared in the English language around 1590, the seventeenth-century militia was directly descended, if not from the old fyrd, at least from the Anglo-Saxon customary obligation that every able-bodied freeman between the ages of fifteen and sixty should defend his country.[32] Henry II's Assize of Arms (1181) and Edward I's Statute of Winchester (1285) had translated the custom into law and specified the military obligations of a subject according to his income. This early correlation between militia responsibility and social degree was akin to the hierarchical notions implicit in feudal theory. Tudor legislation, which in 1558 created a new structure for the militia and instituted the new office of lord-lieutenant of the county, was based upon the same assumptions. By it the militia was placed directly in the hands of the lord-lieutenant, who was almost always a peer, and his deputy-lieutenant, who was chosen from the gentry. Although ultimate authority over the militia remained with the king and Privy Council, the actual command was exercised by the lord-lieutenant and the deputy-lieutenant. In carrying out their militia duties, the lieutenancy regularly conferred with the country gentry, who, as a class, officered the militia and largely financed it. The administration of the militia occupied a very important place in the life of the gentry, who consequently resented any effort of the government to centralize control, to require personal service, or to insist upon payment of militia assessments.[33]

In 1573, the "trained bands" were established. These were men who had been selected for training from among the adult males in the counties. Although the "trained bands," numbering over one hundred thousand men, were not organized on a regimental basis until the Civil War, they were regarded as the "core" of the militia system.

[31]Keith Feiling, *History of the Tory Party* (London, 1923), pp. 55–58.

[32]Richardson and Sayles, *The Governance of England*, pp. 48, 50, 55, questions the connection between the fyrd and the militia. But see Boynton, *The Elizabethan Militia*, p. 7, and Wake. *Musters, Beacons and Subsidies*, p. xxx.

[33]See Wake, *Musters, Beacons and Subsidies*, pp. xxxi, xlvi; Boynton, *The Elizabethan Militia*, pp. 62–91 passim. For the militia in one county see, for example, William B. Willcox, *Gloucestershire: A Study in Local Government, 1590–1640* (New Haven, 1940).

Considerable attention was directed to assuring that the "best" men of the county were chosen by the lieutenancy at musters. Gentry or well-to-do yeomanry, not servants, were to be picked. The men were to be "well-affected" in religion and politics. Although the gentry, notwithstanding their identification with the militia, regularly evaded their military responsibilities, the notion that men of substance should compose the trained bands and should be prepared to defend the country persisted.

Elizabethan interest in strengthening the militia was dissipated in the early years of James I's reign. For example, in 1603 the Statute of 1558 was repealed, thus, legally speaking, removing the militia from the authority of the lord-lieutenant. In practice, however, no such change occurred and the militia functioned very much as it had before, with the lord-lieutenant still regarded as the military leader of the county. The repeal, it should be noted, created substantive, legal reasons for questioning the actions of the lieutenancy, which were freely exploited during Charles I's reign by the critics of the crown. Or again, James's government took no interest in mustering and training the militia and did not call for a general muster until 1612. But after then, as Lindsay Boynton has shown, interest in strengthening the militia increased. On the part of private citizens, it became the fashion to drill under the tutelage of an expert. The Privy Council sent out orders to replace weapons, train soldiers, and exact payment of the militia assessment. A sympathetic hearing was given the suggestions for reform, which were put forward by men who had served as volunteers in continental armies. A Council of War, a kind of high command over the army and navy, was created.[34]

Neither the militia nor the feudal array were viable military instruments in the early seventeenth century. They are important not for what they did but for the attitudes they encouraged. Based on socially elitist assumptions, their theoretical organization (however disparate the actual condition) encouraged Englishmen to disparage the professional soldier. Both were mythologized. The country became accustomed to a military force that was inefficient and unreliable. Efforts on the part of the crown to strengthen the militia were regarded as unjustifiable interference verging on tyranny. They came to nothing in the last years of James's reign but helped to precipitate the collapse of Charles I's government.

Another important factor in explaining the country's inclination to distrust a professional army was the influence of classical and

[34]Boynton, *The Elizabethan Militia*, pp. 205–42 *passim*.

15

humanist philosophy to which all literate men were exposed. Two lines of speculation about war, soldiers, and how a country's defenses should be organized had already been developed, one best exampled in the works of Desiderius Erasmus and Sir Thomas More, the other in the writings of Niccolò Machiavelli. Recent scholarship has shown that a large and important part of the thought of Erasmus and More was concerned with war and peace.[35] Their interest in the question was not new. Long before, classical writers such as Seneca, Plutarch, and Pliny the elder had sought to explain and condemn war. The early Christians had developed primitive ideas of nonviolence that had survived during the Middle Ages along with the Augustinian doctrine of the "just" war and had been reinvigorated later by such thinkers as John Wycliffe and the Lollards. In the early sixteenth century the Biblical scholar, John Colet, developed a critique of violence, war, and soldiers that was new both in method and insight. Erasmus, More, and Juan Luis Vives carried on and enlarged Colet's view. In their writings were such ideas as the "folly," corruptness, and destructiveness of war; the moral depravity, criminality, and incompetence of the paid soldier; and the essential baseness of the ideals of military honor and glory. More was emphatically against a country's keeping an army during peace. The history of France, Rome, Carthage, and Syria illustrated the dangers.[36] That the resources of the nation are drained, the character of the people corrupted, and the moral fiber weakened by such a system was made plain in *The Utopia*. The defense of the land should be entrusted to its own citizens. The popularity of *The Utopia* (it was reprinted four times in English in the sixteenth century)[37] spread this message. That More's attitude towards soldiers had an impact is verified since he was specifically targeted by one of the Elizabethan pamphleteers, who favored a stronger military establishment, for "most unwisely" writing that an untrained subject could defend a country better than a paid, professional soldier.[38]

Erasmus leveled biting satire against war and soldiers in his famous *In Praise of Folly*. War was depicted as a foolish game, "played by parasites, panders, bandits, assassins, peasants, sots,

---

[35]See Robert P. Adams, *The Better Part of Valor: More, Erasmus, Colet and Vives on Humanism, War and Peace, 1496–1535* (Seattle, 1962), pp. 4, 6–9, 11, 21, 24, 28, 29.

[36]Sir Thomas More, *The Utopia*, ed. Jack Hexter (New Haven, 1965), p. 13; cf. pp. 28–29, 31.

[37]See R. W. Gibson, comp., *St. Thomas More: A Preliminary Bibliography of His Works and Moreana to the Year 1750* (New Haven, 1961).

[38]Googe, "Testimonial," appended to Rich, *Allarme*.

bankrupts, and such other dregs of mankind."[39] In many treatises he stressed the bestial aspects of war. The widespread popularity of Erasmus's antiwar criticisms is shown by the fact that *The Education of a Christian Prince* was translated into English and was printed at least thirteen times before 1600, while *In Praise of Folly* appeared in English three times before 1600.[40] These works must have confirmed the *general* English predisposition to distrust the professional soldier. But it must be stressed that seventeenth-century Englishmen were a bellicose rather than a pacifistic people[41] and that as the antistanding army sentiment emerged in the seventeenth century, this strand of humanism did not have a direct influence.

The second theme inherited from the Renaissance was that mercenary soldiers were dangerous to a free government and that free states should be defended by their own citizens. This idea was advocated by Machiavelli, especially in *The Art of War, The Prince*, and *The Discourses on the First Decade of Titus Livius*, which appeared in the early sixteenth century. Machiavelli both summed up and added to a tradition that, as recent studies have shown, already enjoyed a long line of development.[42] Although Machiavelli drew freely on the work of classical and early Renaissance thinkers, he did more than reiterate their ideas about militias and mercenaries. The main difference between Machiavelli and his forerunners is that ideas of force and military organization were central considerations in Machiavelli's concept of politics and the state.[43] In brief, Machiavelli identified the professional soldier with an absolute form of government, insisted that in a free state the armed force should be a citizen militia for practical and moral reasons, and argued that a good citizen should serve his government in both a political and military capacity.[44]

---

[39]Hoyt H. Hudson, trans., *The Praise of Folly by Desiderius Erasmus* (Princeton, 1941), pp. 30-31.

[40]E. J. Devereux, *A Checklist of English Translations of Erasmus to 1700* [Oxford Bibliographical Society] (Oxford, 1968), pp. 15-17, 20-21, 26.

[41]Wallace Notestein, *The English People on the Eve of Colonization, 1603-1630* (London, 1962), pp. 13, 14, 31.

[42]See Hans Baron, *The Crisis of the Early Italian Renaissance: Civic Humanism and Republican Liberty in an Age of Classicism and Tyranny* (Princeton, 1966), pp. 430-39, 560-61, and more particularly, C. C. Bayley, *War and Society in Renaissance Florence: The De Militia of Leonardo Bruni* (Toronto, 1961).

[43]See Felix Gilbert, *Machiavelli and Guicciardini: Politics and History in Sixteenth-Century Florence* (Princeton, 1965), p. 154.

[44]Allan Gilbert, trans., *Machiavelli: The Chief Works and Others* (Durham, 1965), 1: 47 and n. 1, 48, 54 (*The Prince*); 286, 350, 381-83 (*The Discourses*), 2: 576-78, 580, 583-86 (*The Art of War*), 3: 925 (Letter to Francesco Vettori, August 26, 1513).

That Machiavelli's thought was familiar to educated Elizabethan and early Stuart Englishmen has long been established by scholars. *The Art of War* was translated into English by Peter Whitehorne in 1560 and appeared in two subsequent editions in 1573 and 1588.[45] *The Discourses* and *The Prince* were also known before their appearance in translation in 1636 and 1640 respectively. How widely read they were is impossible to say. Felix Raab believed that at the turn of the century Machiavelli "directly affected the thinking of only a small minority" but that his influence spread at the "second, third and fourth hand."[46] The "Elizabethan martialists" read and were instructed by *The Art of War*, and Bacon[47] was not alone in the interest expressed in Machiavelli's ideas. Machiavelli's writings undoubtedly contributed to the predisposition to disparage the professional soldier, but no tracts were written specifically about the evils of professional soldiers that might have revealed the extent of his influence at the beginning of the century.

A negative attitude towards the professional soldier was present in England at the opening of the seventeenth century. Justified by the security offered by geography and the absence of pressing international requirements, the sentiment was nourished by hierarchical social ideals that were implicit in the country's traditional system of military organization, the militia and the feudal array, and by classical and humanist ideas, especially those about the value of the citizen militia conveyed in the work of Niccolò Machiavelli. These were the distant origins of a viewpoint that could have remained fragmentary. It took the presence of an army in England and a deepening alienation between crown and parliamentary gentry to create a genuinely identifiable antiarmy attitude by 1628.

---

[45]See Cockle, *English Military Books up to 1642*, pp. 9–11.

[46]Felix Raab, *The English Face of Machiavelli: A Changing Interpretation 1500–1700* (London, 1964), p. 102.

[47]The classic study of Machiavelli's impact on Bacon is N. Orsini, *Bacone e Machiavelli* (Genoa, 1936). For the spread of Machiavelli's ideas see Raab, *The English Face of Machiavelli*, chapter 2. The scholarship on the Elizabethan martialists mentioned in note 2 refers to Machiavelli's influence on their treatises.

CHAPTER II

THE PETITION OF RIGHT OF 1628:
THE ANTIMILITARY SENTIMENT
HARDENS

The general antipathy toward the professional soldier which was present in England at the turn of the seventeenth century was sharpened by events of the 1620s. The outbreak of the Thirty Years War in 1618 on the continent, and England's involvement in it under the leadership of the increasingly unpopular George Villiers, the first duke of Buckingham, created circumstances within which a domestic crisis developed. The army raised for the war had to be paid, housed, and disciplined. Failing to win the cooperation of Parliaments called in 1625, 1626, and 1627, Charles I fell back upon extralegal expedients—forced loans and arbitrary imprisonment for refusers, quartering in private households, and martial law for soldiers and civilians associated with them—all implemented by the agency of the county lieutenancy or specially appointed commissions. Resentment of the government's policies and the army was expressed in protests from the counties, aired in parliamentary debate during the spring of 1628, and focused in the Petition of Right.[1] As it is well known, that Petition condemned the levying of taxes without the approval of Parliament, arbitrary imprisonment, billeting of soldiers on private householders, and the use of martial law. What has not been stressed in studies of the debates and the Petition is that the powers

---

[1]The text of the Petition of Right may be found conveniently in Samuel R. Gardiner, *The Constitutional Documents of the Puritan Revolution, 1625-1660* (Oxford, 1906), pp. 66-70.

of the lieutenancy, especially of the deputy-lieutenants, were also condemned. Thus, the antiarmy criticism that was expressed in 1628 was partly a protest against the intrusion into the affairs of the local county of an armed central government using the agency of the lieutenancy.

The circumstances of this first major protest against an army and the government's policies associated with the military require brief review. The Thirty Years War was only one of many reasons for the tension between king and Parliament. For philosophical, diplomatic, and economic reasons, King James I was reluctant to commit England to active support of the Protestant cause. By contrast, members of the Parliament of 1621 enthusiastically urged war to aid the Protestant cause, rescue the English princess (James's daughter, Elizabeth, who was queen of Bohemia), check the economic competition of Spain, win economic wealth, restore the nation's honor, and strengthen the country's character.[2] But it was a naval war, not a war involving raising an army of foot soldiers that Parliament wanted.[3] Considerations of a romantic and personal nature led James's son, Charles, who became king in 1625, and his favorite, the first duke of Buckingham, to favor an aggressive foreign policy. Despite parliamentary sentiment, an army was raised and sent off under Buckingham on a series of disastrous expeditions—against Cadiz in 1625, the Isle of Rhé in 1626, and Rochelle in 1627. From mid-1624 to the beginning of 1628, about fifty thousand men, or one percent of the population, were conscripted into the army.[4] The soldiers were billeted in many parts of England, and over two and one-half years the outcry against them mounted.

In assessing the nature of the criticism, one should bear in mind the problems Charles I confronted in maintaining a military role in the Thirty Years War as well as the difficulties experienced by his subjects. Similar problems plagued all of the Stuart kings until the end of the century. In the absence of a system of barracks or army camps, the government had no alternative, if it was to keep the army embodied for future engagements, but to quarter the soldiers in public houses or inns and, as necessary, in private households. It was the responsibility of the local lieutenancy, in practice of the deputy-

[2]Notestein, Relf, and Simpson, *Commons Debates, 1621* 3: 449; 4: 56, 436; 6: 318.

[3]William Cobbett, ed., *Parliamentary History of England. From the Norman Conquest, in 1066, to the Year 1803* (London, 1808-20), 2: 33.

[4]Stephen Stearns, "Conscription and English Society," *J.B.S.* 11 (1972): 4-5.

lieutenants, to make arrangements for the billeting of soldiers in their counties. According to regulations issued by the Privy Council, officers were to be billeted in the houses of well-to-do gentry, while ordinary soldiers were to be quartered with other householders of "competent ability," although soldiers themselves, who found their accommodations inadequate, and poor persons complained that houses of the indigent were used.[5] Thus, persons from all social classes came into contact with the soldiers and had reason to regard them as a social and moral threat and an economic burden. It should be stressed that householders were theoretically not expected to house and feed the soldiers free of charge. On the contrary, they were supposed to be reimbursed for quartering at a rate fixed by the government, which was graduated upward from the soldier to the officer. Thus, a billet did not have to be a financial hardship and could be turned to profit. Lindsay Boynton's recent study of the question, limited just to the example of the Isle of Wight where many soldiers were posted, has shown that opposition to billeting did not become pronounced until the government fell behind in reimbursing the householders. Quartered free, billeted soldiers became, from the subjects' points of view, a tax or confiscation of property. As for the government, it would have willingly reimbused householders for the billeted soldiers had funds been available.[6] But, the court had few options. Either it got money from Parliament to pay for the billets or it got money indirectly from private householders who were obliged to take in soldiers. Charles regarded billeting soldiers as part of his prerogative.[7] On a practical level, his secretary of state argued in the House of Commons, in April 1628, that unless a grant of money were immediately forthcoming, the government's hands were tied with respect to billeting. If the soldiers were to be "unbilleted" (as contemporaries put it), they had to "either be disbanded or employed; neither of which his majesty could effect without money."[8]

---

[5]Lindsay Boynton, "Billeting: The Example of the Isle of Wight," *English Historical Review* 74 (1959): 31 (hereafter cited as *E.H.R.*). For complaints about quartering in houses of the poor, see *Calendar of State Papers, Domestic Series, 1628-29*, pp. 2, 238, 465 (hereafter cited as *C.S.P.D.*); *Acts of the Privy Council of England: 1627 Sept.-1628 June* (London, 1940), p. 292.

[6]*Acts of the Privy Council of England: 1627 Sept.-1628 June*, pp. 310, 316, 317, 325, 332, 333, 336, 343-45, 352, 353, 356, 424, 425, 427-29, 434, 439, 490. The protests from local communities and the concern of the government are copiously illustrated.

[7]Thomas Birch, comp., *The Court and Times of Charles I* (London, 1848), 1: 338.

[8]*Ibid.*, p. 341.

The State Papers confirm that it was not until the spring of 1628 that billeting was seriously contested.[9] Then, outside of Parliament, in several areas, bitter complaints were expressed. For example, in Hampshire and around Winchester, flat refusals to billet soldiers and removals of men from households where they had been assigned were reported.[10] In Essex, thirty townsmen were wounded in a free-for-all involving a company of soldiers. Norwich reported "gross outages committed by the soldiers and their officers," while incidents on the Isle of Wight were described as "foul and insupportable."[11] National prejudices surfaced in the complaints about the soldiers. The inhabitants of Kent regarded themselves as "miserably afflicted" by Irish soldiers who differed from them in all respects and besides had quite "unreasonable appetites."[12] These complaints are worth noting, for the same arguments appeared in the petition against billeting which Parliament presented to the king on April 14. Throughout these months the king and his council tried urgently, but unsuccessfully, to deal with the crescendo of anger.

The army was an economic hardship to people in ways other than the cost of billeting. In 1626, Charles I, having failed to win either a grant from Parliament or a free gift from his subjects, resorted to the expedient of a forced loan to raise money for his army. Resistance to this device, the legality of which judges refused to affirm, was widespread among all classes. The most famous case involved John Hampden, Sir John Eliot, and Sir Thomas Wentworth, who were jailed for their refusal to pay. They were released in time to sit in the Parliament of 1628 and there became leaders in the effort that produced the Petition of Right which condemned forced loans. Forced loans were also exacted from many lesser gentlemen who refused to pay and suffered imprisonment.[13] The exaction of the so-called "coat-and-conduct" money was another economic grievance associated with the soldiers. Coat-and-conduct money, as the term suggests, was a tax imposed on subjects to pay for the expenses of the levy, including the cost of outfitting soldiers and defraying their travel expenses. It was not new, but, in the past, had been regarded as a loan to the government, repayable from funds in the exchequer.

[9]In the *C.S.P.D.* for the years 1625-1626 and 1627-1628, there are no entries that concern billeting, but for 1628-1629 there are at least ninety entries.

[10]*C.S.P.D., 1628-1629*, pp. 107, 113, 197; cf. pp. 76, 83, 86, 117.

[11]*Ibid.*, pp. 25, 27, 62, 109; cf. p. 78.   [12]*Ibid.*, p. 49.

[13]Samuel R. Gardiner, *History of England, 1603-1642* (London, 1884), 6: 143, 149, 155, 178, 213, 225.

The deputy-lieutenants were responsible for collecting the money and the Privy Council urged, especially from 1626 through 1628, rigorous execution of this duty. Because coat-and-conduct money was levied by the authority of the king and not by act of Parliament, it came to be regarded as confiscatory and illegal. Although the government promised reimbursement and often arranged for it, delays and failures in the repayment provoked bitterness, especially against the lieutenancy.[14] In the Short Parliament, the levying of "coat-and-conduct" money was cited as a grievance against the government. Later in the century, it was said that this tax was "one of the first things layd hold on to make . . . [Charles I] odious."[15]

The soldiers also had to be disciplined. The need was obvious; the Court as well as the subjects perceived that a system of disciplining was required.[16] However, there were no generally accepted procedures to follow. In the medieval period, the crown had issued books of rules and orders before a war to discipline the armies that were to be formed; these military orders were known as martial law.[17] Then, the Court of the Constable and Marshal had exercised jurisdiction over crimes connected with war both at home and abroad. But the powers of this medieval court had lapsed in 1521,[18] and its authority had migrated to committees of army officers and to a newly created office of provost-marshal. The provost-marshal, established by the Tudors under the lord-lieutenant and empowered to use martial law against both soldiers and civilians, had become by the 1620s a kind of local police.[19] In the absence of war in the early seventeenth century, there had been no need to regularize the discipline of the army. All during

[14]*Acts of the Privy Council, 1625-1626*, p. 210; *ibid., 27 Sept. 1627-1628 June*, pp. 61, 94, 153, 166, 180, 247, 362, 373; *C.S.P.D., 1625-1626*, pp. 235, 277, 382, 397, 478. For two local reactions to "coat and conduct" money before 1628, see Willcox, *Gloucestershire A Study in Local Government 1590-1640*, pp. 103-6, and T. G. Barnes, *Somerset 1625-1640 a County's Government during the "Personal Rule"* (Cambridge, Mass., 1961), pp. 109, 204.

[15]Quoted in Western, *The English Militia in the Eighteenth Century*, p. 23; cf. Gladys Thomson, ed., *The Twysden Lieutenancy Papers, 1583-1668* [Kent Archaeological Society, Records Branch] (London, 1926), pp. 55-56.

[16]Lindsay Boynton, "Martial Law and the Petition of Right," *E.H.R.* 79 (1964): 256-61, 263, 277, offers evidence to show that men involved with billeting soldiers "clamoured for martial law."

[17]Sir William Holdsworth, "Martial Law Historically Considered," *Essays in Law and History* (Oxford, 1946), p. 4.

[18]Williams S. Holdsworth, *A History of English Law* (London, 1922), 1: 573-75; Charles M. Clode, *The Administration of Justice under Military and Martial Law* (London, 1872), pp. 25-26.

[19]Lindsay Boynton, "The Tudor Provost-Marshal," *E.H.R.* 77 (1962): 437-55.

this time, moreover, no real distinction[20] had developed between "martial law"—the summary power exercised by a government over all its subjects, civilian and military, in time of an emergency—and "military law"—a canon of laws to regulate the army internally.

When soldiers were raised in the 1620s, commissions for martial law, which failed to distinguish between "martial law" and "military law," were issued by the king "with the advice of the Council of War." The first was dated December 30, 1624 and was issued when James I was still alive to discipline soldiers in Kent who were waiting to embark. Many times thereafter, to 1628, commissions were issued to discipline soldiers who were billeted in various parts of the country.[21] All of the commissions empowered the appointed commissioners (almost always the lieutenancy of the county, particularly the deputy-lieutenants,) to proceed "according to the justice of martial law," against soldiers and "other dissolute persons joining with them," that is, civilians. They were authorized to bring to trial and sentence to death persons involved in any "robberies, felonies, mutinies, or other outrages or misdemeanors." Boynton has pointed out that inclusion of the words "other outrages and misdemeanors" enabled the commissioners to extend their jurisdiction to disputes connected with billeting soldiers. Thus, many civilians were involved in the martial-law process.[22]

The public reaction to these commissions is difficult to assess. There is almost no readily available evidence. The printed calendars for 1625 through 1628, which teem with petitions and comments protesting the billeting of soldiers, contain no specific references to the commissions for martial law. Boynton's study, based largely on Hampshire, has demonstrated that the commissioners for martial law there did not impose a bloody tyranny. In fact, he suggests that very few soldiers anywhere were tried and executed by martial law and that probably no civilians were executed.[23]

Charles I called a Parliament for the spring of 1628. His purpose was to get a supply so that England might strengthen her defenses

---

[20]Clode, *The Administration of Justice*, p. 20, points out that the two terms were used synonymously.

[21]For the commission of December 30, 1624, see T. Rymer, *Foedera* (London, 1704-1735), 17: 647-48; for other commissions, *ibid.*, 18: 245 (ordering the troops not to disband), 254-55, 262-63, 751-72, 763-64; *Acts of the Privy Council, 1625-1626*, pp. 276, 290, 298, 306; *ibid.*, *1626, June–Dec.*, pp. 101, 221, 224-25, 291.

[22]Boynton, "Martial Law and the Petition of Right," *E.H.R.* 79 (1964): 258, 268, 269, 269. n. 2.

[23]*Ibid.*, pp. 266-73 *passim*, 277.

at home, encourage her allies abroad, and help restrain the aggression of Catholic forces on the continent.[24] Instead of granting a supply, members of this very full House introduced, on March 22, complaints from "all parts of the kingdom" for the House of Commons to investigate and reform.[25] All of the major complaints were related in one way or another to the soldiers. For the purposes of this study, the complaints about forced loans and arbitrary imprisonment may be put aside. They were at the heart of the effort to protect the subject in his fundamental rights of person and property and were handled, at Sir Edward Coke's suggestion, separately from other grievances. They have been, rightly so, the focus of studies on the Petition of Right.[26] Less thoroughly examined by historians, but yet of near equal importance to members of the House, was the protest over billeting of soldiers. Directly related and the object of contention for other reasons, too, was the power of the local lieutenancies, especially that of the deputy-lieutenants. Grievances about martial law were not mentioned until April 8.[27] Comments in debate, and the procedure followed in the appointment of committees[28] to deal with the grievances show the importance in the minds of members of the complaints about billeting and the lieutenancy.

Parliament opened on March 17. On March 20 general committees were appointed, among them a committee for grievances. At the same time "petty committees" were also appointed, one of which was to examine some letters that William Coriton, M.P. for Cornwall, had brought to the House. These letters purported to show that the deputy-lieutenants of Cornwall had put pressure on him not to stand for election to Parliament because he had been a recusant to the forced loan. There were a "dozen at least" of such letters which demonstrated that the lieutenancies of other counties as well had tried to disrupt the normal election process.[29] On March 22, the first debate about grievances was held. Forced loans, arbitrary imprisonment, billeting of soldiers and the local lieutenancies were vigorously

[24]Cobbett, *Parliamentary History* 2: 218-22.

[25]*Ibid.*, p. 238; for the large attendance, see Birch, *The Court and Times of Charles I* 1: 331.

[26]The most complete study is still Frances H. Relf, *The Petition of Right* (Minneapolis, 1917). For special aspects, see E. R. Adair, "The Petition of Right," *History* 5 (1920): 99-103; H. Hulme, "Opinion in the House of Commons on the Proposal for a Petition of Right," *E.H.R.* 50 (1935): 302-6.

[27]*Journals of the House of Commons* 1: 880 (hereafter cited as *C.J.*). In this detail, Boynton may be corrected.

[28]A thorough study of the committees in this session is needed.

[29]Birch, *Court and Times of Charles I* 1: 332; *C.J.* 1: 873.

25

criticized. As for billeting, the leading spokesman was Sir Francis Seymour. His point was that the House of Commons need not give the king a supply, if the king takes whatever he wants. "That this hath been done," Seymour continued, "appeareth by the Billeting of Soldiers." That is, billeting of soldiers is a violation of the right the subject has in his property. Seymour also criticized the forced loan and arbitrary imprisonment and urged that a committee take all three matters under consideration.[30]

As for the power of the lieutenancies, it was reported that the deputy-lieutenants were like "janizaries."[31] The most impassioned speaker, the irascible Sir Robert Phelips of Somerset (who, it must be noted, had personal reasons for his animus),[32] stressed that the "strange, vast and unlimited power of our lieutenants and their deputies," in billeting and taxing, was a gross violation of law. He declared that the deputy-lieutenants are "the most insupportable burdens that, at this present, afflict our poor country; and the most cruel oppression that ever yet the kingdom of England endured." He was exasperated at the intrusion in local affairs of deputy-lieutenants who carried out the "violent and unlawful" policies of the court.[33] The point was echoed by Sir Thomas Wentworth, who tried to shift the blame for billeting from the king to royal ministers and the local lieutenancies. It was they who extended the "prerogative of the king beyond its just limits."[34] Two days later, before anything was done about billeting, a special committee was appointed to bring in a bill for "regulating the power of the lieutenants and deputy-lieutenants."[35] This committee was composed of all the privy councillors who sat in the House of Commons and included Sir Edward Coke, Sir Dudley Digges, and John Selden.

On March 26, a "great complaint" was received about the insolence of soldiers in Surrey and the actions of a constable there respecting the billeting of soldiers.[36] On March 28, interrogation of John Moulden, the constable in Surrey, revealed that he had billeted soldiers on householders who had refused to pay billeting money, and, aided by eighty to one hundred soldiers, he had extorted money from men on the threat of pulling down and firing their houses. His defense was a warrant from the earl of Nottingham. The deputy-lieutenants

---

[30]Cobbett, *Parliamentary History* 2: 231–32.
[31]Whitelocke, *Memorials of English Affairs* 1: 24.
[32]For Sir Robert Phelips, see Barnes, *Somerset*, pp. 36–39, 281–82, 286–87, 289–92 and *passim*.
[33]Cobbett, *Parliamentary History* 2: 233.   [34]*Ibid.*, p. 236.   [35]*C.J.* 1: 874–75.
[36]*Ibid.*, p. 875.

of the county denied that they had issued any warrant for billeting soldiers or paying money.[37] After hearing all this, members appointed a committee of twenty-nine men to investigate the situation in Surrey. The committee was empowered to call for warrants, letters, and witnesses. No deputy-lieutenants were to sit on the committee, but they were to appear before it upon call. Nine of the members had, two days before, been appointed to the committee (already mentioned) to frame legislation for regulating the lieutenancies.

This "Surrey Committee" is of uncommon importance. It became the central committee for investigating all the complaints about billeting and the lieutenancy. On April 3, the House ordered that all complaints against the deputy-lieutenants about billeting *"or any other Charges"* should be referred to it. The knights and burgesses of the county from which the complaint came, except deputy-lieutenants, were "to have Voice in the Committee."[38] On April 9, the House showed its interest in the committee by ordering that it might itself set up subcommittees to look into "any particular Complaints."[39] All during April and May, members of this committee investigated complaints about the soldiers from such places as Taunton, Lincoln, and Chichester, reported to the House and surely took part in the debates in committee of the whole on this subject.[40] Although there is no specific evidence, it seems likely that its members helped draw up the Petition on Billeting that was presented to the King on April 14. There is evidence that three of the six-man committee appointed to draft "heads" for the Speaker's speech to accompany the Petition on Billeting were members of the Surrey Committee.

One question that these details pose is why was the responsibility for investigating complaints against the deputy-lieutenants referred to the Surrey Committee and not to the committee appointed on March 24 to frame legislation to regulate the lieutenancy? In the absence of direct evidence, one may speculate that members felt more comfortable attacking the lieutenancy through the issue of billeting and, as the days passed, through the issue of martial law (as Boynton has theorized) than criticizing it directly. The lieutenancy was so close to the crown that criticism of it was tantamount to criticism of the king. In effect, this is what Phelips did in the debate on March 22. It should be recalled that Wentworth, a more cautious critic of the king, sought then to blunt Phelips's point by shifting

[37]*Ibid.*, p. 876.   [38]*Ibid.*, p. 879. Italics supplied.   [39]*Ibid.*, p. 880.
[40]*Ibid.*, pp. 881, 886, 894, 902.

the blame away from the king. Further, there were many deputy-lieutenants serving in the House of Commons.[41] It is possible that these men did all they could to deflect the criticism from fellow deputy-lieutenants.[42] Although all the grievances the Surrey Committee looked into concerned the deputy-lieutenants, the lieutenancies were not directly mentioned in the Petition on Billeting of April 14. By condemning the actions of the lieutenancy in billeting rather than by condemning the lieutenancy itself or by bringing in a bill to regulate the deputy-lieutenants, the House implied criticism of the lieutenancy without provoking so much animosity.

The Petition on Billeting rested on the assertion that "by the fundamental laws of this realm, every freeman hath a full and absolute property in his goods and estate."[43] Billeting of soldiers on an unwilling householder was, therefore, illegal. No specific statute could be cited as a precedent, for there was none. However, a long list of inconveniences was recited. Among them were that religion was harmed (for people feared to leave their houses unprotected while they attended church), and local government and the normal processes of justice were interrupted. (This may have been a veiled reference to the powers exercised by the deputy-lieutenants.) Economic and social hardships which touched every class were mentioned. The soldiers were blamed for the decrease in rents for the gentry, idleness among husbandmen, neglect of markets, decay of trade, and innumerable crimes and outrages. The last part of the petition argued that billeting of soldiers endangered the government: Subjects were so impoverished that they were unable to meet the king's financial needs. The poor were apt to join the soldiers in rebellion; "some such mischief will shortly ensue," it was warned. The soldiers were labeled a menace to the king's government. Many were said to be Catholic. The loyalty of "popishly affected" commanders was impugned, and it was said that they would rather serve England's enemies.[44] The charge that the army was riddled with Catholics was to be repeated often after the Restoration.

Charles's reply to the Petition on Billeting underscored what an impasse had been reached. He urged the House of Commons to give

[41]The precise number of deputy-lieutenants in this Parliament is not readily available; a study of the membership is desirable. But the word "many" is used advisedly. Twelve years later, in the Long Parliament, there were between seventy and eighty deputy-lieutenants; in the fall session of 1678 there were 241.

[42]For example, *C.J.* 1: 898.   [43]Cobbett, *Parliamentary History* 2: 283.

[44]*Ibid.*, p. 284.

him a supply and promised that he would answer their petition "in a convenient time."[45]

Plainly, the issue of billeting was not resolved by the petition of April 14. Indeed, on May 3, the duke of Buckingham, in the presence of the king, told the lord mayor and aldermen of London that if they did not lend Charles £15,000 six hundred soldiers would be billeted on the city.[46] On May 5, in the debate on the king's message urging the House to trust him, Sir Nathaniel Rich pointed out that laws continued to be violated, "by more frequent billeting of soldiers than ever."[47] Rich wanted to "hear the King say hee may not by lawe billet soldiers."[48] Such reassurance was not forthcoming. Throughout May, familiar complaints about the deputy-lieutenants and billeting continued to be presented to the House of Commons.[49] Fear that Charles would dissolve Parliament moved members to add the grievance of billeting to the Petition of Right.

Along with the discussion of complaints about billeting and the deputy-lieutenants in Parliament, criticism was also leveled at the commissions for martial law. Martial law was first mentioned on April 8 and was debated on April 11 and four times thereafter during the month. The commissions were voted illegal on May 7, and on May 8 an article condemning martial law as exercised by the commissions was added to the Petition of Right.[50] This chronology suggests that members of Parliament, alarmed by the complaints about the deputy-lieutenants in billeting soldiers, sought to discredit the lieutenancy further by denouncing the commissions for martial law. As already noted, there is no evidence that complaints about the commissions were presented to Parliament. Further investigation of county records is needed before a firm conclusion may be drawn, but it seems true that the criticism of martial law voiced in Parliament in the spring of 1628 was largely manufactured for political reasons, as noted, and on theoretical legal grounds. A great legalist like Selden could find much to condemn in the commission for martial law. There was, indisputably, a potential danger to the individual, whether

---

[45]*Ibid.*, pp. 285–86.

[46]Birch, *Court and Times of Charles I* 1: 350.

[47]*Ibid.*, p. 353.

[48]Quoted in Relf, *The Petition of Right*, p. 38.

[49]*C.J.* 1: 894, 895, 898, 902; Birch, *Court and Times of Charles I* 1: 343; Gardiner, *History of England, 1603–1642* 6: 274.

[50]*C.J.* 1: 880, 893; Cobbett, *Parliamentary History* 2: 350. Rushworth, *Historical Collections* 1: 545 reported that the House in Grand Committee "spent most of its time" from April 14 to the end of the month on the issue.

civilian or military, in allowing the central government to use martial law without a strict definition of its jurisdiction and procedures. Selden said in one debate that the issue was "of the greatest consequence of any that we have yet meddled with, [because it] concerns our lives."[51] This thought was echoed in a contemporary comment on the debates which explained that Parliament aimed to protect the subjects' "life and limb against lawless violence, especially in time of peace."[52]

Consistent with the restraint with which the question of royal prerogative was handled throughout the debates,[53] Selden admitted that the king had power to use martial law.[54] His objection was thus not to the principle of martial law but to the manner in which it was being executed; that is, through commissions issued by the king and his council to deputy-lieutenants who "were not soldiers or lawyers."[55] Selden argued that the jurisdiction and authority of the commissioners for martial law could not extend beyond that exercised by the Court of the Constable and Marshal.[56] Furthermore, martial law could not apply in time of peace, except for certain crimes.[57] According to Selden, the sitting of the courts at Westminster were a "badge of peace," and further, any place where the "sheriff in the county may execute the king's writ" should be regarded as a place of peace. In time of war, martial law was "known to the common law," and "that kind of commission is confirmed by act of parliament."[58] Implicit was the thought that Parliament should have a role in imposing martial law.[59] It was further argued by Selden and others that the commissions for martial law violated the terms of specific statutes, for example Magna Charta, 28 Edward III. c.3 (which held that no one should be adjudged of life and limb except by the laws of the land), and laws guaranteeing the right of an Englishman to trial by jury. In the final Petition of Right, these specific statutes were cited in support of the contention that the commissions of martial law were illegal.

---

[51]Quoted in Boynton, "Martial Law and the Petition of Right," *E.H.R.* 79 (1964): 273.

[52]Birch, *The Court and Times of Charles I* 1: 341.

[53]For the whole question of the way in which the king's prerogative was handled, see the excellent discussion in Margaret Judson, *The Crisis of the Constitution: An Essay in Constitutional and Political Thought in England, 1603–1645* (New Brunswick, N. J., 1949), especially pp. 236–37, 239, 253–63.

[54]John Selden, *Opera Omnia, tam Edita quam Inedita* (London, 1726), 3 (part 2): 1985.

[55]*Ibid.*, p. 1986.   [56]*Ibid.*, pp. 1986, 1987, 1990.   [57]*Ibid.*, p. 1987.

[58]*Ibid.*, p. 1990.   [59]*Ibid.*, p. 1989.

The House of Lords did not immediately accept the article on martial law that the House of Commons sent up on May 8. On May 10, the Lords amended the section to allow the use of martial law over soldiers and mariners in peacetime but not over civilians.[60] On May 19, the House of Commons rejected the Lord's changes, arguing that unless the article stood as they had framed it, martial law might be extended to the Trained Bands.[61] The House of Lords were persuaded, and on May 26, agreed to the entire Petition of Right, including the clause declaring the commissions on martial law illegal.[62]

The deputy-lieutenants were not singled out for comment in a separate article in the Petition of Right, but they were cited in connection with forced loans and arbitrary imprisonment in Article I and with the illegality of the commissions of martial law in Article IV. Curiously, they were not mentioned in the section about billeting, but as previously discussed, no member of Parliament who attended the meetings in the spring of 1628 could have been unaware of the charges against the lieutenancy investigated by the Surrey Committee and reported to the House. That both Houses took the matter very seriously is underscored by the fact that, in signifying the Lords' assent to the Petition of Right on May 26, the Lord Keeper moved that the House of Commons prepare a bill respecting the power of the lieutenancy over mustering and assessing rates.[63]

The response to the first sizable army raised in England in the early-seventeenth century was vigorous protest. The criticism of the soldiers and the government's military policies reflected not only the dislike of the army, but also the deepening estrangement bewteen Charles I and his politically conscious subjects. If the king had been trusted and his policies in other areas approved, it is possible that the burden of the soldiers might have been tolerated. But the parliamentary gentry did not trust Charles. They also had little understanding of the problems the central government confronted in pursuing an aggressive foreign policy, which they themselves had recommended, but the cost of which they were unwilling to bear. Their criticism of the army revealed parochial, elitist, isolationist, and self-interested considerations. But there was more than self-interest in their insistence upon a confirmation of the subjects' rights.

---

[60] *Journal of the House of Lords* 3: 788 (hereafter cited as *L.J.*).
[61] *Ibid.*, pp. 803, 813.   [62] *Ibid.*, p. 824
[63] *Ibid.*; Rushworth, *Historical Collections* 1: 576.

They were also concerned to protect the law from what they regarded as a revolutionary violation by the central government and its agents. Underlying their criticism was alarm over the intrusive authority of the central government through the agency of the deputy-lieutenants, whose arbitrary actions were implicitly (sometimes explicitly) backed by soldiers. If the provisions in the Petition of Right had been implemented, the practical effect would have been a diminution of the royal prerogative in military affairs: the king could not have raised an army without Parliament's consent. The Petition made it illegal for him to billet soldiers on unwilling subjects and to discipline the army in peacetime by martial law. Charles I, however, did not take the Petition of Right seriously[64] and continued in the 1630s to exercise the military prerogatives which the crown had always assumed. The Petition of Right, however, served as a precedent throughout the century in criticism of the army.

[64]Angry concern was expressed in 1629 that the Petition had been violated. See, for example, Wallace Notestein and F. H. Relf, eds., *Commons Debates for 1629* (Minneapolis, 1921), pp. 4, 5, 6, 245.

CHAPTER III

THEORY OF PARLIAMENTARY COMMAND OF THE MILITIA: 1641-1642

 The question of the king's military prerogative was inherent in the criticism of Charles I during the 1630s, but it was not debated seriously until the Militia Bill was introduced in Parliament in December 1641. Several members of the House of Commons—John Pym, Oliver Cromwell, William Strode, and Sir Arthur Haselrig—supported legislation which would have stripped the king of command of the militia. Outside of Parliament, a number of tracts appeared to justify the action. Henry Parker, sometimes described as the most radical political theorist of the early 1640s, William Prynne, the well-known gadfly in the service of the parliamentary opposition, and Stephen Marshall, the famous Puritan divine, were among two score of men who argued for transferring military authority from the king to the Parliament. Some of the principals recognized that the fundamental issue in the controversy over the Militia Bill was a change in England's government, that is, a shift in sovereignty from the king or king-in-Parliament to Parliament alone. The implications of the Militia Bill were unequivocally revolutionary. Its movement through Parliament and passage as an Ordinance[1] in the spring of 1642 had the effects of rupturing the relationship be-

---

[1]For the text of the Militia Ordinance, see Gardiner, *Constitutional Documents of the Puritan Revolution*, pp. 245-47.

tween Charles I and Parliament, polarizing the politically conscious nation as no other issue of those troubled months had done, and precipitating bloodshed. The proposition that the legislature rather than the executive should have ultimate command over the armed force of the nation was not finally settled in 1642, and it became a central element in the arguments against Oliver Cromwell's New Model Army during the Interregnum and in the protests against the standing armies of Charles II and James II. In 1689, the principle was finally written into the Bill of Rights in Article VI that forbade a professional army in peacetime without the consent of Parliament. The arguments in favor of the Militia Bill/Ordinance are, therefore, of special significance.

Certain aspects of this issue—the political narrative, the content and significance of the messages exchanged between king and Parliament in the spring of 1642, and the political and religious thought of Henry Parker—have been studied[2] and will not be reviewed here. There is a need, however, to look more closely at the many tracts[3] (in addition to Parker's) and sermons that were written to justify Parliament's actions. These little-known pamphlets give a sure reflection of the thinking about military authority in 1642. Contrary to the argument advanced by some scholars, many men besides Henry Parker were writing about parliamentary supremacy, the derivative nature of the royal prerogative, and the limits of precedential law.[4]

The considerations that motivated members of Parliament to bring in a Militia Bill on December 7, 1641, were more complex than has been suggested.[5] The usual explanation is that the army

[2]The political narrative, whose general accuracy is acknowledged by scholars, is found in Gardiner, *History of England, 1603-1642*, vol. 10, *passim*; the messages between king and Parliament in the spring of 1642 are discussed in J. W. Allen, *English Political Thought, 1603-1644* (New York, 1938), pp. 386-412, and B. H. G. Wormald, *Clarendon: Politics History and Religion, 1640-1660* (Cambridge, 1951), pp. 47-113; the most important of several studies of Henry Parker's thought are W. K. Jordan, *Men of Substance* (Chicago, 1942), and Margaret A. Judson, "Henry Parker and the Theory of Parliamentary Supremacy," *Essays in History and Political Theory* (Cambridge, Mass., 1936), pp. 138-67. They do not deal with the coincidence of Parker's views and those in the pamphlet literature.

[3]At least twenty-three tracts were written in support of Parliament's actions, at least twenty in support of the king.

[4]See Allen, *English Political Thought*, p. 424; Judson, "Henry Parker and the Theory of Parliamentary Supremacy," p. 149.

[5]For a more detailed examination, see Lois G. Schwoerer, "The Fittest Subject for a King's Quarrel," *J.B.S.* 11 (1971): 45-76.

that was raised to fight the Irish Rebellion in October, an army which the critics of the king feared would be turned against Parliament, led directly to the bill. Without doubt, this factor introduced a sense of urgency to the proceedings in the House of Commons, but it was only one of several events and concerns responsible for the Militia Bill. Of near equal importance were the rumors of plots involving the court, the provocative actions of Charles I with respect to a guard for parliament, and parliamentary tactical considerations related to the Impressment Bill. Further, a near-paranoid interest in Parliament's having its own guard and an ongoing concern (voiced earlier in the debates on the Petition of Right) to restrict the powers of the deputy-lieutenants also played a part. It may be suggested that even if the Irish Rebellion had not occurred, some kind of legislation respecting the militia would have been introduced. In the fall of 1641, the king's critics were not trying to implement a theory of parliamentary supremacy by wresting from the king the two prerogatives (of military command and appointment of ministers), still left him.[6] Indeed, there was some reluctance to claim command of the armed forces, a power which touched the very essence of royal sovereignty. It was not until January 1642, when the king attempted to arrest members of Parliament, that the opposition claimed command of the armed force. That step was motivated by fear, not political theory. But once the step was taken, it had to be justified.

The Militia Ordinance, while it was, of course, related to the earlier bill, was a direct response then, to an act of intended violence by the king. Charles's attempt to arrest the five members threatened the careers, fortunes, and lives of the parliamentary leadership and, by implication, of the entire opposition. This step hardened the determination of extremists and moderates and removed many doubts. Whatever the theoretical and constitutional implications, the armed force of the nation could not be left in the king's hands if his critics were to survive.

The idea that an ordinance[7] issued by Parliament without the king's consent could transfer ultimate command of the militia

[6]C. V. Wedgwood, *The King's War, 1641-1647* (New York, 1959), p. 21.

[7]A parliamentary ordinance was a declaration passed by both Houses and issued without the assent of the king. Such a device had been used since August 20, 1641, by the Long Parliament. Sir Simonds D'Ewes had looked into the precedents and had quite erroneously assured the House of an ordinance's great and ancient authority.

from the crown to Parliament was logically inconsistent with traditional constitutional principles. The idea that Parliament alone should command the armed force of the nation was also illegal and unconstitutional. Although both Houses were dominated by radical parliamentarians in the spring of 1642, men were uncomfortable with what they were doing. An observer commented upon how busy the members were in their effort to bring the militia "within the jurisdiction of the houses of Parliament, and yet they pretend no lessening or dishonour to the King."[8] In the debate of February 8, 1642, for example, only Henry Marten, the first and most forthright of a tiny group of republicans in the Long Parliament, was confident that the king had no power to veto bills passed by both Houses. He maintained that "the King's consent should be included in the votes of the Lords"[9] and that the assent of both houses was sufficient to make a law. Most members were unsure. As the issue moved to a conclusion, Sir Simonds D'Ewes noticed a sense of "sadness and guilt"[10] in the debate of March 2. Although the members were not moved sufficiently by Bulstrode Whitelocke's impassioned speech[11] against the ordinance on March 5 to reject the ordinance, unease about its legality continued. In April, the predominant sentiment was to abandon the ordinance altogether and accept instead an amended version of the Militia Bill which Charles presented on April 11.[12] It was argued that such a course would satisfy the whole kingdom and compose all differences. So enthusiastic was D'Ewes that he declared in the debate on April 20 that the king's bill was

---

There is no evidence that a parliamentary ordinance was ever issued during the Middle Ages without royal authority. See Gardiner, *History of England 1603–1642* 10: 4, and British Museum (hereafter cited as B.M.), D'Ewes Journal, Harleian Manuscripts, 163, f. 475. The folio numbers to the Harleian Manuscripts follow those used in the index to that manuscript.

[8]*C.S.P.D., 1641–43*, p. 260.

[9]B. M., D'Ewes Journal, Harleian Manuscripts, 162, f. 375 verso. For a study of Henry Marten, the first man to voice republican ideas in the Long Parliament, see C. M. Williams, "The Political Career of Henry Marten, with Special Reference to the Origins of Republicanism in the Long Parliament" (Ph.D. diss., Oxford University, 1954).

[10]B. M., D'Ewes Journal, Harleian Manuscripts, 163, f. 409 verso.

[11]Rushworth, *Historical Collections* 4: 525–26.

[12]Gardiner, *History of England 1603–1642* 10: 186, notes that the bill has not been preserved and that it is necessary to deduce its contents from the debate. Wormald, *Clarendon*, pp. 103–7, discusses Edward Hyde's reaction to Charles's move and the underlying intentions of the king.

the most necessary legislation "that had ever come into the House." In a rhetorical flight, he compared it to the "Paladium [sic] in Troy in which the very safety of the city consisted" and was moved to hope that all men would see the wisdom of it, "even Turks, Jews and infidels."[13] Only Henry Marten again adamantly opposed it, and his motion to reject it failed for lack of a second.[14] Instead, the House proceeded to amend the king's Militia Bill which Charles himself rejected on April 28.

The sense of ambivalence about the Militia Ordinance was also reflected in the leadership's eagerness to explain itself. Messages, resolutions, and responses to the king, many of which were contradictory, confused, and incoherent were regularly issued.[15] They were widely circulated and, as the crisis deepened, released to the public before being sent to Charles.[16] On March 14, 1642, the House of Commons appointed a committee of its most distinguished members (thirty-one in number) to prepare a declaration "to satisfy the kingdom" of the legality and necessity of its actions.[17] On March 16, a committee of the Long Robe was asked to set forth why the king was obliged by law to pass the ordinances that the two houses presented to him.[18] Although the legality of ordinances was asserted, only a man identified as "Honest Hall"[19] denied unequivocally that the king's assent was necessary to a true law. The "most powerful and active members"[20] sought to allay fears by protesting that the Militia Ordinance was defensive and that they had no intention of attacking the king. Pym, John Hampden, Denzil Holles, and Sir Philip Stapleton were joined by lawyers such as St. John in encouraging wavering members to support the Ordinance.[21] The concurrence in the House of Lords of the lord keeper (Edward lord Littleton), and his confident assertion that the Ordinance was legal also carried a good

---

[13]B. M., D'Ewes Journal, Harleian Manuscripts, 163, f. 475 verso.

[14]*Ibid.*, f. 475, f. 475 verso.

[15]Parliament's declarations are described as "ambiguous, obscure, and at times a little stupid" by Jack Hexter, *The Reign of King Pym* (Cambridge, Mass., 1961), p. 175.

[16]W. D. Macray, ed., *The History of the Rebellion and Civil Wars in England, Begun in the Year 1641 by Edward, Earl of Clarendon* (Oxford, 1888), 2: 64, 69.

[17]*C.J.* 2: 478; Sir Ralph Verney, *Verney Papers, Notes of Proceedings in the Long Parliament* [Camden Society, XXX] (London, 1845), pp. 162–64.

[18]*Reports of the Historical Manuscripts Commission* (hereafter cited as *H.M.C.*), *MSS of Duke of Buccleuch and Queensberry* 1: 292.

[19]*Ibid.*; Verney, *Verney Papers*, pp. 162, 165.

[20]Whitelocke, *Memorials* 1: 172.   [21]*Ibid.*, p. 165.

deal of weight with men who were uncertain how to vote.[22] For these reason, not because of carefully expounded arguments about a constitutional theory, the Militia Ordinance was passed and implemented

Charles I unequivocally rejected the Militia Ordinance. When asked on March 9 if he would not allow Parliament to command the militia for a time, his response was vehement: "By God, not for an hour." "You have asked that of me in this, was never asked of any King and with which I will not trust my wife and children."[23] All during the troubled spring of 1642, Charles I countered the efforts of Parliament with his own barrage of declarations and responses. Written mostly by Edward Hyde, they were aimed primarily at men outside of Parliament and had the effect of winning adherents to the king's side.[24] Charles's policy was to argue that an ordinance issued by Parliament was illegal and to maintain that he was willing to settle the militia by the legal procedure of a parliamentary bill. But the suggestion that he would agree to some kind of restriction of his command of the militia was disingenuous. Charles understood better than most of his contemporaries that inherent in the struggle for command of the militia was a fundamental constitutional change which would have stripped the monarchy of real power. Later, he described the controversy as the "Fittest Subject for a King's Quarrel" and explained that "Kingly Power is but a shadow" without command of the militia.[25] He never had any intention of giving up his authority over the armed force of the nation. In support of his position, he declared that, if the Militia Ordinance passed, he would have no credit abroad, and argued that the nation's security depended on his reputation with foreign princes. He reminded his critics that they were bound to him by the oaths of supremacy and allegiance and that, therefore, they should be "tender" of his royal rights. His right to command the militia was a "point of the greatest importance, in which God and the Law hath trusted us solely." Charles scored a telling point when he confessed that he had justified his own arbitrary government of the recent past on the grounds of necessity

---

[22]*Ibid.*, pp. 165, 171, 175–76. Littleton was known as a "profound lawyer," "well-versed in the records." He told Hyde he voted for the Militia Ordinance to disarm the Commons. Littleton joined the king in May.

[23]Rushworth, *Historical Collections* 4: 533.

[24]Wormald, *Clarendon*, pp. 65, 83–84, 100, 105, 160.

[25]*The King's Cabinet Opened* included later in Harleian Miscellany 7: 525.

and imminent danger and warned members of Parliament that they should take care not to "fall . . . into the same error upon the same suggestions." As for himself, he promised hereafter to abide by the law.[26] In view of the strength and appeal of the king's position, Parliament's supporters needed to enlarge upon what they had said to offer still more persuasive arguments. This was done by men outside Parliament—by a number of radical pamphleteers and preachers.

A real battle of pamphlets (not unlike that of 1697-1699 over King William III's army) took place in 1642. On both sides were men of talent and reputation. The most important of Parliament's proponents was the eminent political theorist of the early 1640s, Henry Parker. His *Observations upon Some of His Majestie's Late Answers and Expresses* attracted more attention than any other tract in the controversy and alone prompted a whole sequence of animadversions, answers, and rejoinders.[27] The most distinguished preachers of the decade were also involved. Famous among those for Parliament were Stephen Marshall, known as "that Geneva bull," and regarded at the time of the controversy as an "Augustine, the truly polemical Divine of our times,"[28] and John Goodwin, who was noted for his "perspicuity and acuteness." Both were Fast-Day preachers. For the king were Henry Ferne, Charles's chaplain extraordinary, whose first published work[29] was also the first book openly on the king's side, and Henry Hammond, the archdeacon of Chichester. The well-known controversialist, William Prynne, took the part on behalf of Parliament. Men personally

[26]This summary of the king's policy with respect to the militia is based on Rushworth, *Historical Collections* 4: 533-34, 540, 545-46, 548-50.

[27]Henry Parker, *Observations upon Some of His Majesties Late Answers and Expresses* (London, 1642), which followed an earlier version with slightly different title dated May 21, 1642, was printed on July 2, 1642. There was a second edition in 1642. For titles of Parker's tracts and the chronological sequence of replies and rejoinders, see William Haller, ed., *Tracts on Liberty in the Puritan Revolution, 1638-1647* (New York, 1934), 1: 24, 26, 27 and notes 14, 16; Jordan, *Men of Substance*, pp. 142-43, n. 4.

[28]Henry Hammond, *A Vindication of Christ's Reprehending St. Peter, from the Exceptions of Master Marshall* (n.p., n.d., but printed with Henry Hammond, *Of Resisting the Lawful Magistrate*) [Oxford, 1644]. M. F. Weinstein, " 'Jerusalem Embattled': Theories of Executive Power in the Early Puritan Revolution" (Ph.D. diss., University of Maryland, 1965), provides a recent discussion of Marshall's thought.

[29]Henry Ferne, *The Resolving of Conscience, upon this Question. Whether . . . Subjects May Take Arms and Resist?* (Cambridge, 1642). The tract was reprinted at London in 1642, with a second edition printed at Oxford in 1643. The article in the *Dictionary of National Biography* (hereafter cited as *D.N.B.*) asserts that this tract was the first openly on the king's side.

close to Charles came to the king's defense. John Spelman, a man respected for his learning and love of history, whose premature death cut short his intended appointment as one of Charles's secretaries of state, wrote a highly effective response to Parker.[30] The young courtier, Sir Dudley Digges, the man probably most beloved by the king, who had moved from opposition in 1628 to support of Charles, also defended the crown in print.[31] Curiously enough, there is no evidence that Edward Hyde contributed to the exchange of pamphlets. Nor did John Milton write a response to Dudley Digges, as he is sometimes said to have done.[32] Less famous men were also engaged in the literary battle. Of these, John March was the most impressive. Notwithstanding that he was a lawyer, trained at Grey's Inn, he wrote a careful defense of Parliament's actions, in which he said that an "overstrict observance of the Law may sometimes be unlawfull," and that an unreasonable law "doth not oblige men to obedience."[33] Peter Bland, about whom nothing but his name is known, brought enthusiasm, confusion, and contradiction to the exchange of tracts.[34] And finally, there were powerfully written tracts whose authors must remain completely anonymous but whose titles alone show the radicalism of their authors.[35]

The interest was widespread and persistent. As late as October 15, 1642, the militia issue was described as the "main thing now looked upon and pried into by all eyes."[36] Time and money were freely ex-

---

[30]John Spelman, *A View of a Printed Book Intituled, Observations upon His Majesties Late Answers and Expresses* (London, after September 9, 1642).

[31]Dudley Digges, *An Answer to a Printed Book, Intituled, Observations upon Some of His Majesties Late Answers and Expresses* (Oxford, 1642).

[32]See Frank A. Patterson, ed., *The Works of John Milton* (New York, 1931–1938), 18: 636, n. 6; and Don M. Wolfe, ed., *The Complete Prose Works of John Milton* (New Haven, 1959), 2: 34.

[33]John March, *An Argument or Debate in Law: Of the Great Question Concerning the Militia: As It Is Now Settled by Ordinance of Both Houses of Parliament. By Which It Is Endeavoured, To Prove the Legalitie of It, and To Make It Warrantable by the Fundamentall Laws of the Land* (London, September 30, 1642), pp. 8, 43.

[34]Peter Bland, *A Royall Position . . . or an Addition to a Book Intituled Resolved upon the Question* (London, 1642), pp. 9, 11.

[35]Two examples of anonymous tracts are: *Touching the Fundamentall Lawes . . . to Which Is Annexed, the Privilege and Power of the Parliament Touching the Militia* (London, February 24, 1643), and *The Privileges of the House of Commons in Parliament Assembled, wherein 'tis Proved their Power Is Equall with That of the House of Lords, If not Greater, Though the King Joyn with the Lords. However, It Appears that Both Houses Have a Power above the King* (London, 1642).

[36]*The Vindication of the Parliament, and their Proceedings: or: Their Military Design Proved Loyal and Legal* (London, October 15, 1642), in *Harleian Miscellany* 8: 46.

40

perīded in the effort. Peter Bland was willing to finance the reprinting of a tract to supply corrections and a missing page. He took the advice of his printer about using a new title page to assure good sales.[37] The well-connected John Spelman had his problems with printers. He explained the delay in getting his pamphlet to the public: he had to await the "conveniency of a Presse."[38] Charles I complained regularly that the "Presses Swarm" with pamphlets and printed papers and his supporters echoed him, adding that "fractious Preachers" deliver sermons dealing with "matters of the times" instead of salvation.[39] A check of the McAlpin and Thomason Catalogues for 1642 and early 1643 confirms the contemporary view that more pamphlets were written about the militia issue than any other.

The lines of the argument that most unequivocally supported the Militia Ordinance and Parliament's assumption of the command of the militia were set out by Henry Parker in *Observations*. The basic points that he made were reiterated and elaborated in many other tracts and sermons, and a few innovative ideas and fresh illustrations were added. The tracts written by lesser men were, perhaps, less elegant and coherent than Parker's, but the issues they explored— parliamentary supremacy, the derivative nature of the royal prerogative, the limits of precedential law and the connection between power and sovereignty—were the same. All of them, Parker included, if his own words are to be credited,[40] were monarchists, but the monarchy which was implicit in their thought was a very different institution from that known to England prior to the controversy. One has only to recall the arguments about other kinds of military questions in 1628 to appreciate how radical the thinking of many men had become in 1642.

The first tract to appear on the issue, *A Declaration of the Great Affaires*, came out around April 22, 1642, several weeks before Parker's *Observations*. In quaint terms, it posed the basic problem confronting everyone. "The Devil hath cast a Bone," wrote the unknown author, "and rais'd a contestation betweene the King and Parliament touching the Militia: His Majesty claimes the disposing of it to be in Him by right of Law; The Parliament saith *rebus sic*

---

[37]Bland, *A Royall Position*, p. 15

[38]Spelman, *A View of a Printed Book*, preface.

[39]Rushworth, *Historical Collections* 4: 547; Digges, *An Answer to a Printed Book*, p. 25; William Hall, *A Sermon Preached at St. Bartholomews the Lesse in London on the XXVIII Day of March 1642* (London, 1642), preface.

[40]Parker, *Observations*, p. 41–42.

stantibus and *nolenti Rege*, the Ordering of it is in them."[41] The implication was plain: The heart of the issue could not be just command of the militia, but sovereignty in the state. Parker plainly saw that, in the "intricacy"[42] of England's mixed government, one element had to be supreme and that supremacy mattered most in the area of military power and especially in a time of crisis. For Parker and others, that supreme element in the practical affairs of government was the Parliament, not the king. Their difficulty was to demonstrate this. They could not easily appeal to precedent, law, or past custom. Instead, they based their arguments on necessity, natural law, the law of reason and the "fundamental laws of the nation." They argued analogously to show the reasonableness of their position. Parker and some others predicated their position on a belief in a contract form of government and on a notion that ultimate sovereignty resides in the people and is exercised by Parliament. Many of them embellished their arguments with legalisms and legal references.

One approach to the problem was to explore the nature of royal prerogative, a subject which, one writer admitted, was "much talked of, . . . but little knowne."[43] Henry Parker denied categorically that kings receive their power from God. On the contrary, the original of royal power was "inherent in the people"; they were the "fountains and efficient cause,"[44] he wrote. At the foundings of government, the people handed over certain authority to the king, but limited him at the same time, so that from the beginning, the power of the king was "conditionate and fiduciary."[45] Thus, the king's prerogative power was, in general, derivative and restricted. Parker had argued in an earlier tract that royal prerogative was bound by law. Then he had written that royal prerogative "ought to be declared out of the written and knowne Lawes of the Kingdome . . . wee ought not to presume a Prerogative, and thence conclude it to be a Law, but we ought to cite the Law and thence prove it to be Prerogative."[46] The same point was reiterated by a lesser pamphleteer in 1642. The king's "prerogative is

[41]This anonymous tract appeared also under the title *A Question Answered, How Laws Are To Be Understood and Obedience Yielded? Necessary to the Present State of Things Touching the Militia* (London, 1642). It angered the king, who demanded that the House of Lords find out who wrote it and punish him and the publisher: *C.S.P.D., 1641-43*, p. 308; Whitelocke, *Memorials* 1: 167.

[42]Parker, *Observations*, p. 44.

[43]*A Discourse upon the Questions in Debate between the King and Parliament* (London, September 1642), p. 5.

[44]Parker, *Observations*, pp. 1, 2.   [45]*Ibid.*, p. 4; cf. p. 20.

[46]Henry Parker, *The Case of Shipmoney briefly discoursed* (London, 1640), p. 14.

but what power the Law [as framed in Parliament] gives him," declared one writer.[47]

As to the specific prerogative over the militia, Parker did not deny that it rested with the king, but he said, for reasons to be discussed, that Charles should have consented to the Ordinance and should not have used his "fiduciary power."[48] Other writers approached that question differently. For example, one writer defined royal prerogative as the power to "rule Arbitrarily"[49] in cases which had not been covered by law and granted that the king did possess prerogative power over the militia. But when the people do not trust the king, they have a right to demand that the royal prerogative be "exemplified into a law," which would define its limits. The military prerogative of the crown had not been defined by statute. The Militia Ordinance did that and should be regarded as an example of this basic right of the people. It simply extended the law into an area which formerly was not adequately covered by law. The author contended that the laws established when goverments are first organized or at some later time cannot possibly provide for every eventuality. Parliament has the right, as in the Militia Ordinance, to meet the needs of changing circumstances and to frame laws that invade the area of prerogative and, by defining that prerogative, increasingly restrict it.

John March conceded that "by Law" and custom ultimate authority over the militia traditionally rested with the king. But he asserted that if Parliament felt threatened (and when else did it really matter?), then the two houses had the power to sever the prerogative over the militia from the king. Although the King alone could not give away his military authority, Parliament could.[50] Still another spoke of Parliament's "reassuming"[51] the power of the militia which it had given to the king. A very few, sometimes inconsistently, simply denied that the king ever possessed the prerogative over the militia.[52] In all these tracts, then, royal prerogative was construed as derivative from and dependent upon Parliament. By arguing in this fashion, the

---

[47]Peter Bland, *Resolved upon the Question . . . wherein Is Likewise Proved, that . . . the Setling of the Militia As 'tis Done by the Parliament . . . Is According to . . . Law* (London, 1642), p. 12.

[48]Parker, *Observations*, pp. 12–13.

[49]*A Discourse upon the Questions*, pp. 5, 6, 9.

[50]March, *An Argument or Debate in Law*, pp. 1, 5.

[51]*Touching the Fundamentall Lawes*, p. 10 (2nd p. 10).

[52]Bland, *A Royall Position*, p. 7; *Militia Old and New, One Thousand Six Hundred and Forty Two. Read All or None: and Then Censure* (London, August 18, 1642); *The Case of the Commission of Array Stated* (n.p., October 20, 1642), p. 5.

pamphleteers could logically draw the conclusion that Parliament's assumption of the command of the militia in a time of crisis was justifiable.

On another level, it was argued that the dangers confronting the nation justified the steps Parliament had taken. Parker argued that the safety of the people (the *salus populi*) took precedence over all other considerations. "The Law of Prerogative itselfe, it is subservient to this Law," he wrote.[53] Other pamhleteers were equally unequivocal.[54] Now there is nothing intellectually sophisticated about an appeal to "danger" and "necessity." That argument was used by royalists in the 1620s and 1630s; it is a time-worn excuse for circumventing law. But in the hands of the pamphleteers, the idea served as a starting point for arguments of complexity and force. Appeal was made to the law of nature, which Parker described as the most "transcendent and overruling of all humane Lawes." It allows people without disloyalty to save themselves. Parker asked his readers to suppose a situation in which a general of an army turns his cannons on his own soldiers. In such a situation, the soldiers were, of course, released from their obligation to obey the general. The same was true of a king who attacks his people; they are free to resist.[55]

Lesser writers echoed the point about the law of nature.[56] John March stressed that in time of danger the law of reason legalized actions that otherwise would be illegal. For example, a prison break was regarded as a felony in law under normal circumstances, but not as a felony according to the law of reason if the prison is on fire. Similarly, Parliament had no legal right to command the militia, but in time of danger the law of reason made it legal for Parliament to assume control of the militia.[57] The notion that there was a law of reason that was higher than man's law was not new; it was part of the medieval tradition. But another closely related point was novel. This argument held that a distinction should be made between reason or the public good (which were equated) and the letter of the law. If the implementation of a law violated reason or the common good, then that law was void and might be resisted. An equitable interpretation

[53]Parker, *Observations*, pp. 3, 8.

[54]*The Vindication of the Parliament and their Proceedings*, in *Harleian Miscellany* 8: 63.

[55]Parker, *Observations*, pp. 4, 16; cf. p. 35.

[56]*Touching the Fundamentall Lawes*, pp. 10, 11; *A Discourse upon the Questions*, p. 15; *The Vindication of the Parliament and their Proceedings*, in *Harleian Miscellany* 8: 63.

[57]March, *An Argument or Debate in Law*, pp. 7, 43.

44

of the law gave the king the right to use military power against foreign invaders or domestic rebels but not the right to use it against Parliament or "Commonwealth." If the monarch violated the equity of the law (which need not be spelled out, no more than a general need be told not to turn his guns against his own soldiers), military authority might be taken from him.[58]

The limitations of law and precedents were underscored by Parliament's protagonists in still other ways. Admit, argued one writer, that there was no law or precedent to make the Militia Ordinance legal. It did not matter. The good of the nation could not depend upon the judgments of the past. How could any new precedents or laws be framed if Parliament always needed precedents "to steere by."[59] The consent of the members of Parliament to the ordinance was sufficient. Goodwin was bold enough to argue that while the goodness of an individual was not enough to make an act lawful it did lend a "strong presumption" of legality to the act.[60] It was commonly affirmed that Parliament could do no wrong. Thus, by the terms of this argument, Parliament's moral excellence rendered its actions legal.

The argument that necessity justified Parliament's actions was predicated on the assumption that Parliament was the proper judge of whether danger and necessity existed. For Parker, there was doubt that Parliament was the "supreame judicature, as well in matters of State as matters of Law"; it was the "great Councell of the Kingdome, as well as of the King."[61] Parliamentary resolutions had asserted that very point. Preachers and other pamphleteers reiterated it. In the judgment of the great preacher, Stephen Marshall, every state had to have within it a body to preserve it in time of danger, and for him, that body was Parliament.[62] Arguing the same point, another writer asked who other than Parliament could possibly judge whether the nation was in danger? The king was misled by evil counselors and

[58]For example, *A Declaration of the Great Affaires* (London, 1642), pp. 5, 6; *The Vindication of the Parliament and their Proceedings*, in *Harleian Miscellany* 8: 48: "The Equity of the Law, and not the Letter of the Law, is the true Law."

[59]Bland, *Resolved upon the Question*, p. 15; cf. p. 14 and To the Reader.

[60]John Goodwin, *Anti-Cavalierisme, or, Truth Pleading As Well the Necessity, As the Lawfulness of this Present War* (London, 1642), p. 13.

[61]Parker, *Observations*, p. 28. The point was emphatically repeated in Henry Parker, *A Political Catechism, or Certain Questions Concerning the Government of this Land* (London, 1643), p. 11.

[62]Stephen Marshall, *A Plea for Defensive Arms . . . and . . . the Lawfulnesse of Parliaments Taking Up Defensive Arms Is . . . Asserted* (London, 1642), pp. 24, 25, 26.

counselors themselves were beneath Parliament.[63] It was said that the two houses were the "epitome" of the nation, the "representative body."[64] As a corollary, it was also said that the nation was bound to accept Parliament's judgment, whatever the judgment was.[65] The idea reflected what Parker had written, namely, that "there can be nothing said against the Arbitrary supremacy of Parliaments."[66]

None of the tracts seriously considered that the House of Commons was patently not representative. Only one insignificant tract admitted the fact.[67] Parker and others simply asserted the contrary. No pamphleteer recommended a new election to assure a representative character.[68] Further, the idea that Parliament might declare that danger existed for its own selfish purposes was dismissed. Proponents simply denied, in the face of overwhelming evidence to the contrary, that Parliament would ever act in an arbitrary fashion.[69] They used the argument that D'Ewes had made in December 1641—that there was a difference between submitting to vast military authority which was answerable to Parliament and submitting to the king under compulsion.

Another argument justifying Parliament's action was, in effect, a rebuttal to Charles's contention that members were bound by the oaths of supremacy and allegiance to support him. On the contrary, it was said, members were bound by their oaths of allegiance and supremacy to take over command of the militia. On March 15, the House of Commons voted that the Militia Ordinance was not in "any way against the oath of allegiance."[70] Prynne argued that the oaths members took were dependent upon the king's coronation oath, and since the king had violated his oath, members were released from theirs.[71] March developed a more complicated argument, insisting that

---

[63]*A Discourse upon the Questions*, pp. 9, 15.

[64]*Touching the Fundamental Lawes*, p. 11; Marshall, *A Plea for Defensive Arms*, p. 24.

[65]March, *An Argument or Debate in Law*, pp. 14, 16. Also, *The Vindication of the Parliament and their Proceedings*, in *Harleian Miscellany* 8: 50.

[66]Parker, *Observations*, p. 36.

[67]*Truth and Peace Honestly Pleaded* (n.p., November 1642), referred to in Allen, *English Political Thought 1603–1644*, p. 441.

[68]M. A. Thomson, *A Constitutional History of England* (London, 1938), 4: 11.

[69]For example, March, *An Argument or Debate in Law*, p. 15; William Prynne, *Vox Populi* (London, 1642), p. 3. The *Journals* for both Houses show that Parliament swiftly and ruthlessly repressed opposition to the Militia Ordinance. For example, *L.J.* 4: 652, 653; 5: 6, 7; *C.J.* 2: 471, 472, 473, 492, 503, 507, 510, 513. The most important episode occurred at Maidstone in Kent.

[70]Clarendon, *History of the Rebellion* 1: 592–93.   [71]Prynne, *Vox Populi*, p. 5.

oaths obliged members to protect and defend the king, and if Parliament had not taken command of the militia, the king and nation would have been destroyed. Thus, the oaths bound them to do as they had done "under sinne of perjurie."[72] Besides, March went on, the oath of supremacy did not mean that the privileges of the king should be preferred to those of the common weal, which in fact, come first.[73] The argument was a curious and indefensible interpretation of the meaning of the oaths; and it was blasted by the king's friends.[74] That it was made must indicate that contemporaries were concerned about the conflict between the oaths they had taken and their actions.

Another line of argument used was that if one agrees that the militia is absolutely the king's, then there is no point in having laws or striving for liberty, for the king had the power to destroy everything.[75] This argument reflected the realization that a military force would be more powerful than law and that the control of the militia meant sovereignty in the state. One pamphleteer put the proposition this way: If the militia belonged to the king alone, then Englishmen might as well "burn the Statutes" which had been made and "save a labour of making more."[76] Laws could make no difference in a contest with muskets. The king's command of the militia meant that he possessed the "power to mow the fertill meadowes of Britain as often in a Summer as he pleaseth."[77] Such a power, proponents of Parliament argued, had to be severed from the King and given to Parliament who would act in the interests of the common good.[78]

Although in the debate in the House of Commons few argued directly that Parliament alone possessed legislative powers, many pamphleteers advanced this idea. Some tracts categorically stated that the king's confirmation of legislation was accidental rather than essential.[79] It was simply asserted that the vote of the king was included in the vote of the Lords. March stressed that Parliament was one body composed of the King, Lords, and Commons. Although absent in person, the king was not absent in law: the king was head of the body, and to admit his absence in law was equivalent to acknowledging the

---

[72]March, *An Argument or Debate in Law*, p. 27.   [73]*Ibid.*, p. 28.

[74]For example, *Certain Materiall Considerations* (London, 1642), p. 11.

[75]*Touching the Fundamentall Lawes*, pp. 11-12. Cf. Peter Bland, *Resolved upon the Question*, p. 13; March, *An Argument or Debate in Law*, p. 26.

[76]*Touching the Fundamentall Lawes*, p. 12.

[77]*A Discourse upon the Questions*, p. 4.

[78]March, *An Argument or Debate in Law*, pp. 29, 41, 43.

[79]For example, *The Instructions of God's Word* (London, 1642); and William Prynne, *The Aphorismes of the Kingdom* (London, 1642).

death of Parliament, which was patently untrue.[80] Moreover, if the absence of the king were acknowledged, that absence was illegal and, therefore, could not invalidate a law passed by the House of Commons.[81] Another pamphleteer argued that since Parliament may legislate without dispute in unimportant matters, such as the paving of roads, it may with much better justification legislate in a question of such supreme importance as the militia.[82] Others argued, in language as opaque as that used in the declarations of Parliament, that "fundamentall law . . . coucht" in Nature and written in "her Magna Charta" required obedience to a parliamentary Ordinance, even though the king had not assented to it.[83] Further, the ancient institutional character of Parliament as the highest court of law in the land was offered, as it had been in Parliament's statements, to justify the idea that Parliament may declare what the law of the land is and may not be overruled by the king. The argument was that the power of lower courts was conferred by the king's patents, and their decisions could not be overruled by the crown. Accordingly, the actions of the Parliament, the highest court of all, could not be countermanded by the king.

Implied in all that was written by pamphleteers and preachers was the notion that men have the right to resist the king. Prynne[84] stressed that the Biblical injunction, "Touch not mine annointed," referred to the people, not to kings and that it was lawful for subjects to take up arms against a monarch who invades their rights. Marshall also asserted the right of subjects to disobey their monarch. Much of what was said was consistent with the general medieval assumption that a tyrant may be resisted. But the matter was cast in quite specific terms by an anonymous pamphleteer who declared that if the king's commands were against the order of both houses of Parliament, then those commands should be disobeyed. He went on to describe Parliament as the "soul" of the king and to conclude from this, in a tortured argument, that obeying Parliament was equivalent to obeying the king, even if thereby an order of the king were disobeyed.[85]

---

[80]March, *An Argument or Debate in Law*, p. 15. The same point was made by William Prynne, *The Opening of the Great Seal of England* (London, 1643), p. 32.

[81]March, *An Argument or Debate in Law*, p. 17.

[82]*A Discourse upon the Questions*, p. 15.

[83]*The Observator Defended in a Modest Reply* (London, 1642), p. 3.

[84]William Prynne, *A Vindication of Psalme 105.15 . . . Proving . . . that It Is More Unlawfull for Kings To Plunder and Make War upon their Subjects . . . Then for Subjects To Take up Armes against Kings* (London, 1642).

[85]*Vindication of the Parliament and their Proceedings*, in *Harleian Miscellany* 8: 49, 59.

In justifying Parliament's command of the militia, these pamphlet-eers were advocating a radical change in England's government, just as the king's friends charged.[86] None of them in 1642 explicitly advocated republicanism. Many, including Parker, protested their devotion to the monarchy. The credibility of this position was helped by their insistence upon separating the person of the king and the institution of monarchy.[87] Thus, they could attack the king's ministers and his policies without destroying the kingship itself. When the militia issue was first brought before the Parliament, the aim was for a change of policy, not a change of constitution. But the effect of what was said and done in Parliament and in the press was to strip the crown of its most important prerogative, to elevate Parliament above the king, and to lodge sovereignty in it. The monarchy that was left possessed only the shadow of authority. It was the king and his friends who refurbished the argument of mixed and balanced government that had been commonly used in the past.[88] By contrast, such an idea was seldom mentioned by Parliament's friends. Nor did they deal with the need to restrain the power of Parliament if liberty and property were to be preserved. They did not even seem aware of it. The militia issue, more than any other, propelled men along a path of radicalism.

Once the question of military power was opened in Parliament it proved impossible to resolve it without war. On neither side was there anyone with enough wisdom and courage and intellectual strength to heal the breach. No compromise was logically possible when the question of sovereignty and military power was at issue. To have two supremacies, insisted an eloquent if little-known contestant, is ridiculous.[89] Charles I knew this, and that is why he found the militia controversy such a fit subject for a king's quarrel. Henry Parker understood the implications too, as did a larger number of pamphlet-eers and preachers in 1642 than has been recognized. Englishmen's

[86]Ferne, *The Resolving of Conscience*, pp. 30, 45, 46, was especially emphatic. Also Spelman, *A View of a Printed Book*, pp. 20, 41.

[87]For example, Bland, *Resolved upon the Question*, pp. 5–7; *The Militia of the King and Kingdome*, p. 39.

[88]See Corinne Weston, "Beginnings of the Classical Theory of the English Constitution," *Proceedings of the American Philosophical Society* 100 (1956): 133–44, and her book, *English Constitutional Theory and the House of Lords, 1556–1832* (London, 1965), especially pp. 23–43.

[89]Richard Burney, *An Answer: or, Necessary Animadversions, upon Some Late Impostumate Observations Invective against His Sacred Majesty* (London, 1642), pp. 14–15.

CHAPTER IV

THE NEW MODEL ARMY
CRITICIZED:
1647–1660

The legacy of the Civil Wars and the Commonwealth and Protectorate was a "rooted aversion to standing armies and an abiding dread of military rule."[1] The parliamentary gentry grew to dislike the army Oliver Cromwell created in 1645 even more than the army Charles I had raised in the 1620s. They feared the protector's military prerogative just as they had the king's power to command the militia. The New Model Army began as an instrument to win the Civil War and became an instrument to secure a revolutionary government whose base of popular support grew increasingly narrow. It was kept standing for fifteen years. Thus, for the first time in its history, England directly experienced the effects of a large peacetime military establishment.

Hostility toward the professional soldiers was expressed by men of all political persuasion—royalists,[2] Presbyterians, republicans, Levellers, and Fifth Monarchists. But men on the left, especially republicans, developed the strongest indictment in both parliamentary debates and the press. Animosity toward the New Model Army was a constant theme from 1647, but it peaked at specific times in reaction to forcible interventions of the army in politics and in response to constitutional proposals offered for settling the government.

[1]Firth, *Cromwell's Army*, p. 381.
[2]For obvious reasons, royalists detested the New Model Army, but they composed no elaborate statements about their dislike.

The new element that hardened the diffuse antimilitarism already existing was the New Model Army. In composition, size, self-image, and political role the New Model Army was unique in English military history. The effect of the Self-Denying Ordinance by which the army was established was to create a nonaristocratic officer corps, including men from the middle and lower middle classes. Promotion from the ranks on the basis of ability was a radical and innovative policy which had never been practiced before and was not to be followed after the Restoration.[3] The social origins of the officers was one of the reasons for the apprehension over the army.

There were more men in arms than ever before: about 44,000 soldiers in 1647, about 34,000 in 1652 and about 10,000 in September 1658.[4] The cost of the army from 1649 to 1660 has been calculated at from £1,200,000 to about £2,000,000 per year. It is clear that in size and cost the peacetime army was bigger and more expensive than any England had ever known.

Officers and men of the New Model Army tended to be imbued with a sense of mission, filled with the "godly spirit," and infected by radical religious and political opinions. This religious and political self-consciousness owed much to Oliver Cromwell and to the chaplains and preachers who were with the army, especially John Saltmarsh, William Dell, William Sedgwick, and Hugh Peter.[5] These men preached heady notions and helped to promote a unique esprit de corps. For example, one of the earliest army tracts, *A Declaration, or, Representation of the Army*, dated June 14, 1647, declared that the army was no "meere mercinary Army, hired to serve any Arbitrary power of a Stat[e]"; but had been created by Parliament to defend its "owne and the peoples just rights and liberties."[6] An interest in politics and political activism was also encouraged by the Levellers, who, as early as 1645, began to penetrate the New Model Army. The Levellers were among the most radical spokesmen for civil rights that surfaced

[3]Firth, *Cromwell's Army*, pp. 41, 49, 53.

[4]*Ibid.*, pp. 34–35, 184; cf. John T. Rutt, ed., *The Diary of Thomas Burton, Esq., Member in the Parliaments of Oliver and Richard Cromwell from 1656 to 1659* (London, 1828), 1: lxxxvin, for size in 1654.

[5]Robert S. Paul, *The Lord Protector, Religion and Politics in the Life of Oliver Cromwell* (London, 1955), pp. 67–68; Leo Solt, *Saints in Arms* (London, 1959), for a succinct study of the chaplains in the New Model Army. See especially pp. 6–16. For the role of Hugh Peter, see Raymond Stearns, *The Strenuous Puritan, Hugh Peter, 1598–1660* (Urbana, 1954).

[6]*A Declaration, or, Representation of the Army* (June 14, 1647), in William Haller and Godfrey Davies, eds., *The Leveller Tracts, 1647–1653* (New York, 1944), p. 55. Henry Ireton was probably the author. See p. 51.

during the Interregnum. Their major leaders, John Lilburne, William Walwyn, and Richard Overton, while differing in detail and degree of radicalism, subscribed to the same general principles.[7] The Levellers' ideas and leaders helped to translate the soldiers' concern for religious liberty and constitutional and political change into a specific program. This spirit and radicalism in the army were further cause for conservatives to fear the soldiers.

Such attitudes were translated into action. In 1647 the Army refused to disband at Parliament's order. Its political activity, thereafter, is well known. By acts of raw force (Pride's Purge in December 1648, the execution of the king in January 1649, the dissolution of the Rump in April 1653, the invitation to the Barebones Parliament to disband in December 1653, the part played in the system of major-generals in 1655, and the setting up and pulling down of governments in 1659–60), the army revealed itself to be an illegal instrument of power. Paradoxically, Cromwell was probably sincere in his efforts to find a legitimate place in the government for the army. But the political tyranny implicit in the army terrified most men. It was feared first as a force that imposed a despotic government. By the end of the 1650s, it was also feared as an instrument of political corruption.

In 1647 and 1648, the arguments against the army were expressed within the context of the effort of the Presbyterian majority in the House of Commons to disband the New Model Army and the New Model Army's refusal to obey. In these very tense circumstances, arguments against the army were articulated by two groups: the Levellers, who after a very short time had become disenchanted with the army, and Presbyterian gentry in and out of Parliament. The Levellers, in their three *Agreements of the People* of 1647, 1648, and 1649, argued for limiting the military requirements the government could impose on the individual. Parliament (which in Leveller thought would exercise sovereignty in the name of the people) was to be restricted in specific ways to protect the rights of the people. Parliament was to be denied the power of impressment on the grounds that

[7]There are two biographies of John Lilburne, M. A. Gibb, *John Lilburne: A Christian Democrat* (London, 1947), and Pauline Gregg, *Free-Born John: A Biography of John Lilburne* (London, 1961), but biographies of the other leaders are still needed. For Leveller ideology, see Theodore C. Pease, *The Leveller Movement: A Study in the History and Political Theory of the English Great Civil War* (London, 1916); Joseph Frank, *The Levellers, A History of the Writings of . . . John Lilburne, Richard Overton, William Walwyn* (Cambridge, Mass., 1955). For qualification of the democratic elements in Leveller thinking, see C. B. Macpherson, *The Political Theory of Possessive Individualism* (Oxford, 1962), pp. 107–59.

"every man's conscience . . . [should be] satisfied in the justnesse of that cause wherein he hazards his life."[8] Such a notion had no practical influence in the seventeenth century, but the Levellers' sensitivity to the individual's conscience in the fighting of a war should be noticed. They were the first to include in a constitutional proposal the right of the "conscientious objector."

The Levellers also insisted that military authority be subservient to civilian control, namely, under Parliament. The *Agreement of the People* of 1647 declared that a soldier who resisted the orders of the Representative (the name used for Parliament), except orders in violation of the *Agreement*, should lose the benefits of English laws and "die without mercy." In the *Agreement* of 1649, an elaborate procedure was set out for placing the control of military personnel not just in the Parliament but in the hands of the people themselves. No army was to be raised except by the Representative. The Representative was to appoint only the commander-in-chief and general staff, while all other officers were to be *elected* by citizens in counties and cities where the troops were raised.[9]

The Levellers also objected to the use of martial law in peacetime by the army. Two tracts[10] printed in the fall of 1647 argued this point. Appeal was made to the Petition of Right. It was said that the army had not the remotest right to exercise martial law and that its actions were the "height of arbitrarie tyrannie, injustice and oppression."[11] Another point only mentioned by the Levellers, but to become a central consideration in the debates on the "Other House" in 1659 and in the standing army tradition after the Restoration, was that military officers would corrupt a civil government and should be barred (along with members of the Council of State and anyone else receiving public money), from election to Parliament.[12] Finally, an interest in reforming

[8]John Lilburne, *Foundations of Freedom: Or an Agreement of the People* (London, December 10, 1648), p. 11. Don W. Wolfe, *Leveller Manifestoes of the Puritan Revolution* (New York, 1944) p. 291, regards the date on the tract as an error.

[9]John Lilburne, *An Agreement of the Free People of England*, in Haller and Davies, *The Leveller Tracts 1647-1653*, p. 327. William Walyn, Thomas Prince, and Richard Overton also signed the tract.

[10]One was *A Defence for the Honest Nownsubstantive Soldiers of the Army, against the Proceedings of the General Officers To Punish Them by Martiall Law.* For date and place of publication, see Wolfe, *Leveller Manifestoes*, pp. 65, 243. The other was [John Lilburne], *Englands Freedome, Souldiers Right.* For Lilburne's authorship, see Wolfe, *Leveller Manifestoes*, pp. 65, 242. The tract is printed on pp. 248-58.

[11][Lilburne], *Englands Freedome, Souldiers Rights*, p. 2.

[12]Lilburne, *Foundations of Freedom*, p. 10; Lilburne, *An Agreement of the Free People of England*, in Haller and Davies, *The Leveller Tracts 1647-1653*, p. 321.

the militia and in changing the command structure along the lines that critics of the king had freely discussed in 1628 and 1641-42 was perceptible in Leveller thinking. For example, *A Declaration, or, Representation* condemned the large powers wielded by deputy-lieutenants and recommended regulation of their authority and removal of their nonessential powers.

Gentry in and out of Parliament who, on other issues, would have liked to see the Levellers "levelled to the very ground"[13] shared their objections to a standing military power, their conviction that the militia should be in the hands of Parliament, and their interest in regularizing the military power of the government. The tract, *The Peaceable Militia*, which appeared in August 1648 expressed criticism of the army from the right. The anonymous author contended it was more important to "restrain and guard the Power (whatsoever it is, and in whomsoever it resides) which is exercisable over the Subjects of England," than it was to dispute whether king or Parliament should hold ultimate authority over the militia.[14] The most important restraint on the military powers of England's government was that "upon no pretence whatsoever" should a standing army be maintained in the nation. The burden of heavy taxes was only one objection to a permanent force. The use of martial law to discipline an army was also deplored as a violation of the "Law of this land," particularly of the Petition of Right. Declaring that he will not even mention the "many inconveniences" of an army and the "antipathy" between soldiers and civilians, the pamphleteer stressed that a standing army should be avoided because it inevitably imposed an arbitrary government.[15]

Citing ancient statutes and the Petition of Right, the author sought to show that the military authority of the government was restricted. For example, no man may be pressed into an army except in time of invasion, be obliged to serve outside his county except in the case of actual invasion, be required to quarter soldiers against his will, or be subject to martial law in time of peace. All this was true, the pamphleteer argued, whether the power of the military was in the hands of the king or Parliament.[16] All things considered, the author concluded that it was better to entrust the power of the militia to the king than to

---

[13]See William Prynne, *The Levellers Levelled to the Very Ground* (London, 1647), whose title provides the phrase.

[14]*The Peaceable Militia*, pp. 1, 2. I cannot agree with Western, *The English Militia in the Eighteenth Century*, p. 3, that this tract contains "all" the arguments against standing armies that would be repeated thereafter.

[15]*The Peaceable Militia*, pp. 2-4. [16]*Ibid.*, pp. 5-6.

Parliament, for it was easier to shake off tyranny in a prince than in a legislative body.[17]

The Peaceable Militia was significant in the evolution of the anti-military attitude. It was the first pamphlet to pull together the current arguments against a standing army. It urged a conservative solution of the question of command of the militia (i.e., leaving it in the hands of the king with Parliament exercising the right of taxation) but, at the same time, showed a deep concern for protecting the individual in terms of the military obligations that the government could impose on him. The author favored many of the same restrictions (for example, no impressment in peacetime, no billeting, and limits on what the lieutenancy could require of a man) that had been argued for in 1628, in the early years of the Civil War, and in Leveller tracts.

Antiarmy sentiments were also heard from other quarters. Bitter tracts, written probably by the indefatigable William Prynne, hurled imprecations against the army and called for its disbandment.[18] In London, tension between the army and the residents was very deep.[19] From the counties, came petitions which urged that the army be disbanded because the burden of billeting and taxes was insupportable.[20] In Parliament, interest grew throughout 1648 in an Ordinance to reform the militia and appoint lieutenancies on whom Parliament could rely. There is even a hint that the new militia might serve the Parliament as a guard.[21] The major goal of a militia law was to create a local, nonprofessional force lodged in the hands of Presbyterians that could serve as a counterweight to the professional army. This was an idea not hitherto advanced; thereafter, it was to be implicit in Presbyterian thinking about military matters.

The Militia Ordinance was meticulously drawn. It was developed in the spring of 1648 by a committee chaired by members of the "middle group," John Bulkeley and John Boys, and piloted from August to December 2, when it was passed, through committee hearings and the

---

[17]*Ibid.*, p. 12.

[18]For example, William Prynne, *VIII Queries upon the Late Declaration of and Letters from, the Army* (London, 1647); *A Declaration of the Officers and Armies, Illegall, Injurious, Proceedings and Practises against the XI Impeached Members . . . Tending to the Utter Subversion of Free Parliament* (London, 1647); *A True and Ful Relation of the Officers and Armies Forcible Seising of Divers Eminent Members of the Common House, Decemb. 6 & 7, 1648* (London, 1648). The list may be extended: *The Petition of Right of the Free-Men of the Kingdom of England* (London, 1648) and *The Machivilian Cromwellist and Hypocritical New Statist* (London, 1648).

[19]Samuel R. Gardiner, *History of the Great Civil War* (London, 1884), 4: 115, 121, 125.

[20]David Underdown, *Pride's Purge* (Oxford, 1971), pp. 94–95, 100.   [21]*C.J.* 6: 69.

debates in the whole House by a young conservative Presbyterian, Robert Harley.[22] J. R. Western regards it as the "true parent of all subsequent militia legislation."[23] He argues that in it were prefigured the terms of the Militia Bill of 1659 and the bills that settled the militia at the time of the Restoration, all of which were essentially directed against a professional army. In specifying military obligations and in setting out the powers of the lieutenancy, the Ordinance reflected a parliamentary interest and concern that reached back to 1628.

The terms of the Militia Ordinance made plain the aims of the parliamentary Presbyterians. First, ultimate authority over the militia was placed in the hands of Parliament. Second, the command structure of the militia was devised in such a way as to place the militia in the hands of the aristocracy. The militia commissions for all the counties were appointed. For the first and last time, property qualifications for members of the militia commissions were set out in statutory form. Third, the powers which the lieutenancy could exercise were carefully specified. For example, the lieutenancy had the authority to lead the militia out of the county, but only if ordered to do so by Parliament "and not otherwise." It was empowered to assess subjects, but only according to a specified rate.[24]

If the Militia Ordinance of 1648 had been implemented, the resulting force would have gone a long way toward returning the local government to the substantial gentry and providing Parliament with a counterweight to the professional army. The legislation of 1648 was the first occurrence of a law framed to create a local militia that would protect Parliament from a professional army; it would not be the last. Recourse to the militia became a predictable response that resurfaced many times during the Interregnum and in the years after the Restoration.

On December 6, 1648, four days after the Militia Ordinance was passed, the House of Commons was "purged" of its Presbyterian members by Colonel Pride. The leaders of the resulting "Rump" believed that the Militia Ordinance had been an attempt to undermine the army and to create a militia as a bulwark against it. All three men who had served as chairmen of the committee that drafted the Ordinance were

[22]For identification of these men, see Underdown, *Pride's Purge*, chart, pp. 369, 375; *C.J.* 5: 663-65, 668, 671; 6: 1, 26, 33. Also David Underdown, "The Parliamentary Diary of John Boys, 1647-48," *Bulletin Institute of Historical Research* 39 (November 1966): 141-64 (hereafter cited as *B.I.H.R.*).

[23]Western, *The English Militia in the Eighteenth Century*, p. 6; cf. p. 10.

[24]C. H. Firth and C. S. Rait, eds., *Acts and Ordinances of the Interregnum: 1642-1660* (London, 1911), 1: 1247-51.

secluded. Indeed, Bulkeley and Harley may be grouped among the men whom the Rump regarded as the "hard core of the Army's enemies," for both were arrested, Bulkeley at the time of the "purge" and Harley some days later.[25] Within a fortnight, the Militia Ordinance was repealed. It was ordered that the repeal be printed and circulated to the counties and that a committee be appointed to draw up a new ordinance for settling the militia.[26]

Pride's Purge, the trial and execution of Charles I, the abolition of the House of Lords, and the establishment of the first republic in England put an end, for the moment, to the ideas which had been articulated in *The Peaceable Militia* and were inherent in the Militia Ordinance of December 2, 1648. Disenchantment with the army and with Cromwell, however, deepened during the Commonwealth years. A series of events (the expulsion of the Rump by Cromwell with the assistance of his musketeers on April 20, 1653, the removal of the members of the Nominated Parliament by the army with Cromwell's tacit approval eight months later on December 12, the elevation of Cromwell to the position of lord protector on December 16, and the establishment of the Protectorate on the basis of the Instrument of Government) provoked negative comment, and specific warnings of the dangers of military government were raised.[27] Until the fall of 1654, criticism of the army and the military power of the government was fragmentary and was part of a larger political struggle between the Army and the Parliament, or the Cromwellians and the republicans, some of whom were military officers. When opportunity presented itself in the meeting of the first Parliament of the Protectorate called for September 1654, those stronger antimilitary sentiments were expressed in both press and parliamentary debate.

The first Parliament of the Protectorate was elected in keeping with the provisions set out in the Instrument of Government.[28] Partly because of the electoral changes, men who could be expected to oppose a professional, permanent army in the hands of the executive were returned. Republicans such as Haselrig, Thomas Scot, and Robert

[25]Underdown, *Pride's Purge*, p. 210; cf. pp. 147, 179, 211, 212.   [26]*C.J.* 6: 97, 98.

[27]See, for example, Colonel John Streater, *A Glympse of that Jewel Judicial, Just, Preserving Libertie* (London, 1653).   For John Streeter, see Austin Woolrych, "The Good Old Cause and Fall of the Protectorate," *Cambridge Historical Journal* 12 (1957): 134 (hereafter cited as *C.H.J.*).

[28]The Instrument of Government is reprinted in Gardiner, *The Constitutional Documents of the Puritan Revolution, 1625-1660*, pp. 405-17. George D. Heath, "The Making of the Instrument of Government," *J.B.S.* 6 (May 1967): 15-34 is a recent study.

Wallop were elected, as were Presbyterians such as John Bulkeley, Colonel John Birch, and Sir George Booth.[29] The first order of business was to consider the government of the Protectorate. In the course of scrutinizing the articles of the Instrument of Government in Grand Committee,[30] members took issue with Article IV which dealt with military power. It provided that "the Lord Protector, the Parliament sitting, shall dispose and order the militia and forces, both by sea and land, for the peace and good of the three nations, by consent of Parliament, and that the Lord Protector, with the advice and consent of the major part of the council, shall dispose and order the militia for the ends aforesaid in the intervals of Parliament."[31] By Cromwell's speech to the House on September 12, members were made to understand that the protector regarded this provision as the most important of the "fundamentals" of government, an Article that was not to be changed.[32] Cromwell reinforced his views that day by using soldiers to block the entrance to the House of Commons until members subscribed to the Recognition, an oath of loyalty to the lord protector, and a promise not to change the government as settled in One Person and a Parliament.[33] This episode must have stiffened the resolve of critics of the protectorate to limit the military power which the executive could exercise under the terms of the Instrument of Government. It was observed by the Venetian secretary that the "real sentiment" in Parliament was to prevent the protector from having absolute command of the army in the intervals of Parliament. Members were encouraged in this view by the existence of the same sentiments among some army officers and by the appearance in October of tracts arguing the point.[34]

In a debate on November 17, critics of the Protectorate defined standing army as "such forces, as upon extraordinary emergencies, and to supply the other [i.e., the militia] . . . [should] be raised by *authority of Parliament,* and to be maintained at the *public charge."* The militia was described as the "intrinsic force of the nation," said

[29]The list of members elected to this Parliament is in *Old Parliamentary History* 20: 296–308 (hereafter cited as *O.P.H.*).

[30]*Ibid.,* p. 348. In October and November, members' attention was riveted on the Instrument of Government. Throughout November, mornings and afternoons were given to it (*ibid.,* pp. 375, 377, Cobbett, *Parliamentary History* 3: 1459.

[31]Gardiner, *Constitutional Documents,* p. 406.

[32]*O.P.H.* 20: 364–65, 370.

[33]*Ibid.,* pp. 369, 371.

[34]*Calendar of State Papers and Manuscripts Relating to English Affairs Existing in the Archives and Collections of Venice, 1653–1654,* p. 277 (hereafter cited as *C.S.P.V.*).

to include not only the trained bands and the commissions of array, but also the "general tenures of the nation."[35] These definitions repay reflection. Plainly, the speaker was trying to establish that standing forces should be limited to an emergency (a contradiction in the meaning of the word "standing") and that they were to be raised and paid by Parliament. Thus, the "standing force" was not answerable to the executive. It was not to be kept in time of peace. Critics of the Protectorate were impatient that Cromwell's friends "would not understand any difference between"[36] the militia and a "standing force." Parliamentary control of the military, whether militia or regular army, was the goal. An anonymous speaker declared that the protector should have rights in the military only as a "trust derived from . . . [Parliament]," a trust which had been "reposed in . . . [Parliament] for the good of the nation."[37] Another member said that "standing forces were never meant to be in a single person, otherwise than by the consent of Parliament."[38]

Such sentiments were reflected in two votes in January 1655. On January 17, Article IV was rejected by eighty-nine to fifty votes.[39] And on January 19, a proviso was added that the militia ought not to be raised or used but by the consent of Parliament.[40] But, none of this had any practical effect, because Parliament was peremptorily dissolved on January 22 without passing one act. The debate, however, with its strong emphasis on parliamentary supremacy and authority over the armed force was significant, as part of the line of ideological development that preceded the debates on settling the government in 1659.

Outside of Parliament during these same months, similar convictions about military authority were expressed by radicals in the press and in the army in Ireland and Scotland.[41] The Venetian observer noticed in early November that many seditious pamphlets were circulating in London.[42] Most important was *The Humble Petition of Several Colonels of the Army*, dated October 18, 1654.[43] It was signed by

[35]Rutt, *The Diary of Thomas Burton* 1: lxxix. Emphasis supplied. Samuel R. Gardiner noted that the term "standing force" was not used in the Instrument of Government. See *History of the Commonwealth and Protectorate* (London, 1903), 2: 335-36 and n. 1. The equation of the militia and feudal array should be noticed.

[36]Rutt, *The Diary of Thomas Burton* 1: lxxx.   [37]*Ibid.*, p. lxxxii.

[38]*Ibid.*, p. lxxxiii.   [39]*Ibid.*, p. cxxxi.   [40]*Ibid.*, p. cxxxii.

[41]J. G. A. Pocock, "James Harrington and the Good Old Cause: A Study of the Ideological Context of His Writings," *J.B.S.* 10 (November 1970): 32.

[42]*C.S.P.V., 1653-1654*, p. 277.

[43]B.M. 669, f. 19, 21; see also *C.S.P.D., 1653-1654*, p. 303, for a slightly different and misdated version.

three army colonels, Matthew Alured, John Okey and Thomas Saunders, who were known as republicans and Baptists and, as such, adherents to radical political and religious principles. Many other officers, it was noted on the Petition, would have signed, if Cromwell had not thrown Alured into jail. The three signers of the broadside had met in London with the former Leveller, John Wildman, and had given him the task of writing the petition.[44] The appearance of the *Petition* disturbed Cromwell, who feared that disaffected men in the Army and Parliament might unite against him.[45]

The *Petition* connected the distrust of the army to a more general ideological framework. Recalling the language of the *Declaration of the Army* of June 14, 1647, it began by declaring that the army had engaged in the struggle against the king, not as a mercenary army, but as the instrument to secure the rights and liberties of the nation. The point at issue had been Charles's opposition to parliamentary command of the militia. The Army had fought for frequent, freely elected Parliaments entrusted with supreme authority in all civil and military matters. This was the "good cause," that would be lost if the power of the militia was placed in the hands of a single person and his council for two-and-one-half of every three years. Such an arrangement would give the protector more power than the king. The *Petition* reflected the traditional conviction that men of substance would have no reason to support a tyranny and concluded with the plea that Parliament consider the rights of the nation and settle the government according to the law of God and the principles set out in the Leveller proposal, *An Agreement of the People.*

Social, moral, and economic arguments for opposing military power were often mentioned but seldom stressed in parliamentary debates and pamphlets. However, Prynne's tract, *Pendennis and All Other Standing Forts Dismantled, or Eight Military Aphorisms*, whose preface was dated December 6, 1654,[46] emphasized those points and well illustrates the nature of such arguments. The purpose of *Pendennis* was to show that all garrisons and forts and their comple-

---

[44]Maurice Ashley, *John Wildman* (London, 1947), p. 86, locates the first meeting at the home of a London merchant and includes among the participants Colonel Francis Hacker, who reported all to John Thurloe, Cromwell's secretary of state. Ashley asserts that Wildman wrote the petition, which seems reasonable, given the references to previous Leveller documents in whose composition Wildman certainly had a hand.

[45]*C.S.P.V., 1653-1654*, pp. 277, 281.

[46]William Prynne, *Pendennis and All Other Standing Forts Dismantled: Or Eight Military Aphorismes* (London, 1657), to the reader (1654).

ment of soldiers were, in both war and peace, useless, hurtful, and unnecessary.[47] First, the cost was enormous. The army, Prynne declared, "undoes an undone people" who "like Issachars" lies under the heavy burden, "even with broken backes and bleeding hearts."[48] The money would be much more effectively spent on projects to advance trade and manufactures, to improve the land, to put poor people to work, and to provide relief for the maimed. Second, the nation is robbed of the productive labor of the soldiers who contribute nothing to the economic health of the nation but impoverish the people to support themselves.[49] Third, Prynne deplored the moral habits of a standing army in peacetime. His description of the immoralities, inanities, and boredom of a peacetime garrison is timeless and amusing. What do the soldiers do all day? These lusty men spend their time eating, drinking, whoring, sleeping, and standing watch at night but only to gaze about and call to one another, "Who goes there?"[50] They make off with wives and daughters and leave "not a few great Bellies and Bastards on the inhabitants and the countries's charge."[51] Prynne's advice was to dismantle the garrisons and dismiss the mercenaries and return the defense of the nation to the nobility and gentry whose birthright and privilege it had always been. The feudal array and the militia were more effective, cheaper, and less inconvenient than any mercenary army.[52] And further, since England was an island, the navy was the real fortress on which the country should rely.[53]

The system of major-generals and the so-called "new militia," which was set up in 1655, provoked another outburst of antimilitary sentiment in 1656 and early 1657. Eleven regular army officers were appointed, each as a major-general, over the eleven districts into which England was divided. Instructed to suppress rebellion and crime, the major-generals were empowered to assess and collect a decimation tax (a tax on real and personal property of former royalists), to sequester men who refused to pay, to license trade, and to encourage godliness and uprightness.[54] They were given command over the new militia, which was created to serve as an auxiliary to the

---

[47]*Ibid.*, Prynne reluctantly excepted garrisons in the three largest cities.

[48]*Ibid.*, pp. 1, 3–6, 7, 15, 25, 26. Issachars, an ancient Biblical tribe, was engulfed by the Assyrians in 734 B.C.

[49]*Ibid.*, p. 7.　　[50]*Ibid.*, and pp. 29–30.　　[51]*Ibid.*, p. 8.　　[52]*Ibid.*, p. 20.

[53]*Ibid.*, pp. 3, 4.

[54]D. W. Rannie, "Cromwell's Major-Generals," *E.H.R.* 10 (1896): 482–97, 500, 505, for an account of the activities of the major-generals. *C.S.P.D., 1655*, p. 296, for an account of their instructions.

professional army. Predominantly a cavalry force composed of volunteers who were paid £8 a year, the new militia cost an estimated £80,000 a year, to be raised by the decimation tax. A travesty of the traditional militia force, it could be led out of the local county upon order of the major-general.[55]

Modern scholarship has concluded that the rule of the major-generals and the new militia was, generally speaking, efficient rather than tyrannical. Contemporaries felt differently; the major-generals were disliked by almost everyone as petty tyrants. The royalist, Edward Hyde, recalled that the major-generals "carried themselves like so many bassas with their bands of janizaries."[56] An anonymous farmer complained that he felt no security in his property from "these swordsmen," and Ludlow accused them of interfering with law and banishing anyone who did not obey their order.[57] In essence, the system of major-generals and the new militia represented, as the deputy-lieutenants had under Charles I, the intrusive, interfering power of the central government.[58] When the elections for the Parliament of 1656 were being held, it was predicted that men "will down with the major-generals, the decimators, and the new Militia."[59]

The Parliament assembled on September 17, but it was not until December 25 that Major-General Disbrowe brought in a bill to continue the decimation tax on royalists for the maintenance of the militia.[60] The most significant argument against the bill was expressed on January 7, 1657, by Sir John Trevor, M.P. for Arundel. Trevor was alarmed because the "new militia [was] raised with a tendency to divide this Commonwealth into provinces . . . in plain terms, to cantonize the nation." The encroachment of the central government terrified him. The effect of the major-generals and the militia was to "prostitute our laws and civil peace to a power that never was set up in any nation without dangerous consequences." He reminded the House of the reign of Charles VII in France, from which he dated the beginning of that nation's "slaveries," and equated that experience with the system of major-generals and the "new militia."[61] The significance is plain: country gentlemen did not want to be supervised or

---

[55]Ivan Roots, "Swordsmen and Decimators—Cromwell's Major-Generals," *The English Civil War and After, 1642-1658*, ed. R. H. Parry (Berkeley, 1970), p. 82, for costs, p. 80 and n. 11, for arguments favoring the militia.

[56]Clarendon, *History of the Rebellion* 4: 17; cf. 41.

[57]C. H. Firth, ed., *The Memoirs of Edmund Ludlow: Lt.-General of the Horse in the Army of the Commonwealth of England, 1625-1672* (Oxford, 1894), 2: 3.

[58]Roots, "Swordsmen and Decimators," p. 87.   [59]*C.S.P.D., 1656-57*, p. 87.

[60]Rutt, *The Diary of Thomas Burton* 1: 230.   [61]*Ibid.*, p. 315.

superseded by agents of the central government. In large part, the dislike of the major-generals reflected the gentry's anger that their social and political status and role in the country had been undermined. The Venetian observer perceived this to be the case when he wrote that Parliament had refused the tax bill not out of love for the royalists but "to protect and maintain its own privileges."[62] This attitude, noticed earlier in the reaction to the deputy-lieutenants' exercise of authority under Charles I, was an important ingredient in the evolving complex antiarmy attitude.

When subsequent debates about the military were held during the Interregnum, as in 1659, the major-generals and the new militia were recalled with more bitterness even than the professional soldiers in the New Model Army. In another respect, the system was significant. The new militia reflected a new concept of the nature and role of the militia, for such a force was not unlike a standing army. It was composed of paid volunteers who were always on call, under a professional general, liable to serve anywhere in the country, and answerable ultimately to the executive authority. Although the system was dismantled by the failure of the tax bill to pass in 1657, the concept remained and was carried over to the Restoration period when it influenced men close to Charles II.[63]

While criticism of the system of major-generals was gathering momentum in and out of Parliament, James Harrington's *The Commonwealth of Oceana* appeared. Harrington had trouble getting his book printed in the fall of 1656 at least partly because friends of Cromwell regarded it as a blatant attack on the system of major-generals.[64] But the *Oceana* by the depth and coherence of its analysis transcended the immediate problem posed by the major-generals.[65] The *Oceana* offered a theory about military affairs that marked its author as the first genuine theoretician on the subject in England. Harrington's thought included classical political theory and history (Plato, Aristotle, Livy, and Polybius), the works of Machiavelli, Hobbes's *Leviathan*, the Bible, and the new scientific interests of the seventeenth century. Harrington referred to Selden, Bacon, and Raleigh. Further his work had affinities with Leveller thinking. Of

---

[62]*C.S.P.V., 1657–1659*, p. 13.

[63]Western, *The English Militia in the Eighteenth Century*, pp. 7–8.

[64]John Toland, "The Life of James Harrington," *The Oceana and Other Works of James Harrington, Esq., with an Exact Account of His Life*, ed. John Toland (London, 1727), p. xviii (hereafter cited as Toland, *Works of Harrington*).

[65]See J. G. A. Pocock, "James Harrington and the Good Old Cause," especially 30–39, for a theory about the inception of the *Oceana* and its connection with other tracts.

these sources, Machiavelli and the classical examples he used were the most important for Harrington's notions about military organization.[66]

Fundamental to Harrington's views of military power were the changes in economic and social relationships that he discerned. He argued that the balance of property determined both the form of government and the form of military organization[67] and that both were related. Harrington believed that a shift in the ownership of land had occurred in England, and the effect was to destroy the power of the English nobility, and with it, the power of the monarchy. He argued that a kingship has to rest on one of two pillars, either a nobility with its military system of retainers or a standing army.[68] The former had been decisively undermined at the end of the fifteenth century, when land had flowed from the hands of the nobility into the hands of the yeomanry, "whereof consisted the main body of the Militia, hereby incredibly advanc'd."[69] Therefore, political institutions (the monarchy) and military organization (presently the New Model Army, a standing army) must naturally change to reflect the shift in land ownership to the people.[70] "Wherever the Balance of a Government lys," he declared, "there naturally is the Militia of the same."[71] In his view, England was ready to adopt as a system of government, a republic, and a military organization, a citizen militia, like those of ancient Israel, Macedemon, or the Republic of Rome. As for the other possible support to a kingship, a, standing army, Harrington found the idea of it intolerable. Only when a government is first established, he felt, should paid soldiers be allowed. In any other circumstance, a professional standing army was "pernicious,"[72] always "fatal" to popular government. Drawing upon Greek mythology, Harrington, in a curious analogy, likened a "mercenary Army, with a standing Generall" to the "fatall Sister that Spins."[73] He understood all too well from the

[66]Raab, *The English Face of Machiavelli*, pp. 185–217 *passim*, for comments about Harrington's thought, sources, and relationship to Machiavelli.

[67]*Oceana*, pp. 42, 70; *The Art of Lawgiving*, p. 388, and *Political Aphorisms*, p. 521, in Toland, *Work of Harrington*. For comment on Harrington's view of the relationship between economic relationships and political power, see J. G. A. Pocock, *The Ancient Constitution and the Feudal Law: A Study of English Historical Thought in the Seventeenth Century* (Cambridge, 1957), especially pp. 128–30.

[68]*Oceana*, pp. 53, 70; *The Prerogative of Popular Government*, p. 267, in Toland, *Works of Harrington.*

[69]*The Art of Lawgiving*, in Toland, *Works of Harrington*, p. 389.   [70]*Ibid.*, p. 432.

[71]*Ibid.*, p. 388.

[72]*The Prerogative of Popular Government*, in Toland, *Works of Harrington*, p. 279.

[73]*Oceana*, in Toland, *Works of Harrington*, p. 188. It is not clear what Harrington meant by this. Like Milton, he may have confused the three Fates with the Furies.

example of Cromwell's New Model Army, which was financed by public funds and maintained as part of the apparatus of government, the practical implications of a standing army.[74]

In part, Harrington wrote to offer a carefully spelled out alternative to the existing military and political systems. Obligations of good citizenship, he was said to have affirmed, prompted him to write the *Oceana*;[75] surely the hope that he might persuade his countrymen to adopt the political and military systems he advocated led him to publish fourteen other tracts in 1659. The military alternative advocated by Harrington was to place the nation's defences in the hands of a citizen militia composed of propertied men, who continued in their own trades, but were educated in military virtue and science and remained in continual readiness.[76] He developed a detailed scheme. Military obligation was to be proportionate to the wealth of the citizen. All citizens were expected to serve, servants were not allowed to. Their lack of property and their dependent relationship unsuited them for military and political responsibilities.[77] To form the citizenry into troops and to provide for their training and leadership, Harrington worked out a complicated method of lots and elections—the seventeenth-century version of universal military training.

To justify his system of defense, Harrington advanced several considerations. To those who felt it was ridiculous to see a nation exercising its citizens in military discipline, Harrington offered the example of "the glorious Commonwealth of Rome." It was "the Sword in the hands of her Citizens" that made her great.[78] To others who felt that his "universal military training" was too dear a price to pay, he responded with a warning: "there is no other [system] that dos not hazard all." Under any other method, "you are some time or other a Prey to your Enemys, or to your Mercenarys."[79] His proposed army would banish idleness and luxury and, by keeping the nation in a state of preparedness, also prevent war.[80] Further, it was

---

S. B. Liljegren, ed., *James Harrington's Oceana* (Heidelberg, 1924), p. 355, does not explicate the matter.

[74]I disagree with J. G. A. Pocock, "Machiavelli, Harrington and English Political Ideologies in the 18th Century," *William and Mary Quarterly* 22 (1965): 560-61 (hereafter cited as *W.M.Q.*), who argues that Harrington understood a standing army only as praetorians or janissaries.

[75]Toland, *Works of Harrington*, p. xix.

[76]*The Art of Lawgiving*, in Toland, *Work of Harrington*, p. 452.

[77]*Oceana*, pp. 173-75; *The Art of Lawgiving*, p. 453, in Toland, *Works of Harrington*.

[78]*Oceana*, in Toland, *Works of Harrington*, p. 100.

[79]*The Art of Lawgiving*, in Toland, *Works of Harrington*, p. 454.   [80]*Ibid*.

less costly. Harrington may have been unsophisticated about state finance,[81] as what mid-seventeenth-century Englishman was not?, but he knew as well as any contemporary that to maintain a standing army was a very expensive undertaking. He believed that land, not a system of taxes, was the only viable means of supporting a military instrument. An army such as he proposed could not be an economic burden. A budget [82] for the military which he worked out in *The Oceana* demonstrated this.

Harrington's theories about military organization and obligation were of great importance in the development of the antistanding army attitude during the Interregnum. Cast in theoretical terms though they were, his views were offered as a practical alternative to the existing military structure. Everything he wrote about armies was indirectly a condemnation of the Cromwellian military system. Just as he proposed a different political organization, a Republic or Commonwealth, so he urged a different kind of army. Both the political and the military structures reflected the fundamental economic and social changes he discerned in English society. In the debates in Parliament, his friends argued against the military in terms that were permeated with Harringtonian principles. But to no avail. Neither his recommendations for a government nor for an army were accepted. Harrington's thought, moreover, continued to play a central part in the evolution of the antistanding army ideology. In the 1670s and 1680s his friend Henry Neville, and others, were to resurrect and change it, adapting it to the questions posed by standing armies then. And at the climax of the standing army issue in 1697-99, Harrington's ideas were again called upon to frame the arguments against professional soldiers.

With the death of Oliver Cromwell in September 1658, the accession of his son Richard, and the calling of a Parliament for January 1659, there was another burst of interest in the possibility of changing the government.[83] From the spring of 1659 through the spring of 1660, as men jockeyed for political advantage and sought to persuade other men to support them, they again articulated their misgivings about military power. What was said in Parliament and written was

[81]Cf. Pocock, "Machiavelli, Harrington and English Political Ideologies," p. 560, for a different reading of Harrington's views.

[82]*Oceana*, in Toland, *Works of Harrington*, pp. 224-25.

[83]For these months, see Godfrey Davies, "The Army and the Downfall of Richard Cromwell," *Huntington Library Bulletin*, no. 7 (1935), pp. 131-67; Godfrey Davies, *The Restoration of Charles II* (Huntington, California, 1955); Woolrych, "The Good Old Cause," pp. 133-61.

largely reiterative, but the emphasis in the argument was emphatic. The focus was on parliamentary control of the armed forces, whether professional or militia, and upon keeping army officers out of the government because they would corrupt it.

Among the tracts written by men on the right were *England's Confusion*, which was attributed to Arthur Annesley; *A Short, Legal, Medicinal, Useful, Safe, Easy Prescription, To Recover Our Kingdom, Church, Nation, from Their Present, Dangerous, Distractive, Destructive Confusion*, by Prynne; and *The Re-Publicans and Others Spurious Good Old Cause*, also by Prynne. The latter is of special interest because of Prynne's remark that the army would destroy the mixed and balanced government "which hath made this Nation for many years both famous and happy."[84] It is noteworthy that Prynne made this point in 1659, because the idea was to become central in the antistanding argument as it was articulated later in the century.

From the left came at least fourteen tracts by Harrington including *The Art of Lawgiving* and *Political Aphorisms*, which were designed to advertise and promote the principles of *Oceana*. Parliamentary republicans wrote many tracts whose purpose was to create an alliance with some junior officers and men in the Army, as opposed to the Army grandees, to win them back to the "good old cause," and to use them to establish a true republic.[85] Millenarian tracts also pleaded for a return to the good old cause, which included parliamentary command of the military. Readers were reminded that one of two main reasons for the Civil War was the issue of the king's control of the militia.[86] Among the tracts influenced by Leveller thinking were *Lilburns Ghost* and *The Leveller*. The latter argued that the people themselves should be "masters of their own Arms, and . . . commanded in the use of them by a part of themselves (that is their Parliaments) whose interest in the same with theirs."[87] A number of scurrilous tracts and popular verses of uncertain origins also appeared and defamed and besmirched the army. *The Red-Coats Catechisme* serves as an example.[88]

[84]William Prynne, *The Re-Publicans and Others Spurious Good Old Cause* (London, 1659), p. 15.

[85]Woolrych, "The Good Old Cause," especially pp. 137–42.

[86]*The Cause of God, and of these Nations Sought out and Drawn Forth from the Rubbish of the Lusts and Interests of Men, and Lifted up into Sight* (London, 1659), p. 5; John Canne, *A Two-Fold Shaking of the Earth* (London, 1659), pp. 108–9.

[87]*The Leveller: Or the Principles & Maxims Concerning Government and Religion, Which Are Asserted by Those That Are Commonly Called, Levellers* (London, 1659), p. 9, Ashley, *John Wildman*, p. 136, identifies Wildman as the author.

[88]Examples of antiarmy ballads are noted by Davies, *The Restoration*, pp. 159–60.

Richard's first Parliament met from the end of January to the end of April in 1659. A number of dedicated republicans were returned, among them Haselrig, Scot, Ludlow, and Weaver, and proponents of Harringtonian principles Henry Neville and Captain Adam Baynes.[89] The majority in this Parliament, however, were probably royalists and Presbyterians,[90] among whom Sir Richard Temple spoke out energetically against the army and all of whom disliked it. Thurloe felt that there was no way to predict how the Parliament would vote on any of the issues except the question of the military. On that, almost all members were opposed.[91]

The debates on how to order the government provided an opportunity to recommend changes in the military. If a genuine reformation in the government was to be achieved, then the position of the military had to be altered. The question of settling the command of the military "comprehends the whole matter,"[92] asserted one speaker, for where military power was lodged, there was sovereignty. One line of argument was that Parliament should have the command of the army and of the militia. Haselrig reminded the House that he had brought in the Militia Bill in December 1641 and declared that it had been decided in subsequent months that the command of the militia was in the House and that the king had no veto power over the actions of the House.[93] Other republicans, Thomas Scot, Sir Henry Vane (who cannot at this time be identified surely with either the parliamentary republicans or the Harringtonians)[94] and others spoke to the same point.[95] The major exponent of Harrington's philosophy, Henry Neville, argued that the gentry no longer depended upon the lords, but have all the lands themselves and accordingly the power of the militia should be held by them. The militia, Neville felt, should be "settled first" and in a way that was consistent with the shift in power in England.[96]

A second major theme in the arguments about the military was that army officers should be barred from the "Other House." The point

[89]Godfrey Davies, "The Elections to Richard Cromwell's Parliament," *E.H.R.* 63 (1948): 488-501.

[90]*Ibid.*, p. 499.

[91]Ivan Roots, *The Great Rebellion, 1642-1660* (London, 1966), p. 235.

[92]Rutt, *The Diary of Thomas Burton* 4: 473.   [93]*Ibid.*, 3: 35; cf. 317.

[94]Barbara B. Taft, "The Seventeenth-Century English Republicans" (unpublished manuscript), p. 264.

[95]Rutt, *The Diary of Thomas Burton* 3: 313, 316; 4: 472; cf. William Schilling, ed., "The Parliamentary Diary of Sir John Gell: 5 February-21 March 1659" (M.A. thesis, Vanderbilt University, 1961), pp. 55-57, 121.

[96]Rutt, *The Diary of Thomas Burton* 3: 132-35; Schilling, "The Diary of Sir John Gell," p. 39.

was that their position in the army created a conflict of interest which made it impossible for them to vote the interests of the nation. The argument that there should not be "placemen" in the government, that anyone holding a paying office should be barred, was not new; it had been included in the tracts written by the Levellers in 1647–48. Many men of diverse political connections spoke to this question, none more emphatically than John Stephens.[97] He began by declaring that he wanted a government "by law, and not by the sword," and he called upon the House to remember the experience all had had of the "mischief of the sword." For his part, Stephens testified that he had found the "little fingers of Major-Generals . . . heavier than the loins of the greatest tyrant kings that went before."[98] Stephens was joined in his attack by others, among them Sir Richard Temple who called for a hereditary house and flatly asserted that military officers are simply not "suteable" members of a legislature.[99]

In the Long Parliament that was restored by the Army in the spring of 1659, an effort was made to place the militia in the hands of men the Parliament could trust so that it could act as a counterpoise to the army. In May, the army was fearful that the militia that was being formed would be turned against it.[100] In July, bills for settling the militia of London and of England and Wales were passed.[101] A royalist assessed the effect of such legislation, saying that if rigorously applied it would be the "ruyne of the present standing army" and make the nation "slaves" to Parliament.[102] The revived Long Parliament was soon dissolved by the officers, in part at least because of the militia legislation that had been passed.[103]

In February 1660, when the secluded members were brought back once more, the same kind of action was taken to make the militia

[97]The speaker was John Stephens, recruiter for Tewkesbury in the Long Parliament, M.P. for Gloucestershire 1658-59, and not James Stephens (Rutt, *The Diary of Thomas Burton* 3: 158). I am indebted to P. H. Hardacre for this identification.

[98]Rutt, *The Diary of Thomas Burton* 4: 11.

[99](Temple): Schilling, "The Diary of Sir John Gell," p. 174, and Rutt, *The Diary of Thomas Burton* 4: 40; Hobart: Schilling, "The Diary of Sir John Gell," p. 137, and Rutt, *The Diary of Thomas Burton* 3: 543; (White): Schilling, "The Diary of Sir John Gell," pp. 154, 173-74, and Rutt, *The Diary of Thomas Burton* 3: 590, 4: 39; (Archer): Rutt, *The Diary of Thomas Burton* 4: 10.

[100]George F. Warner, ed., *The Nicholas Papers: The Correspondence of Edward Nicholas, Secretary of State*, vol. 4, 1657-60 (London, [Printed for the Camden Society, third series] 1920), p. 146.

[101]Firth and Rait, *Acts and Ordinances* 2: 1320-42.

[102]Warner, *The Nicholas Papers* 4: 176.

[103]Davies, *The Restoration of Charles II*, pp. 114-15; Western, *The English Militia in the Eighteenth Century*, p. 6.

independent of the army and composed of "persons of the best quality and fortunes."[104] On March 12, a Militia Bill, which was said to have been much debated, was passed.[105] With the passage of this bill, the agents of the king were confident of a restoration.[106] Their assurance must have been deepened when in mid-April twenty thousand militia men assembled in Hyde Park, cheered Charles, and drank his health on their knees.[107] Despite the protests of the Army against the Militia Bill, General George Monck approved it.[108] By the bill, the ancient authority of the gentry in the militia was reasserted before the Restoration.

In the evolution of the antistanding army attitude, the Interregnum holds a central place. The New Model Army and the system of major-generals, with its accompanying new militia, gave the country practical experience with the problems of the professional soldier that deepened and widened the general prejudice that had already existed among Englishmen in the early seventeenth century. The memory of that experience and the knowledge of the theories and comments advanced contributed to the ongoing development of the antimilitary attitude.[109] Although the antistanding army ideology was not so fully and elegantly articulated as it would be at the end of the century, many basic themes were stated: that Parliament and not the executive should command the military force, whether army or militia; that the military authority of the state over the individual should be limited; that army officers should be barred from the legislature because of the conflict of interest inherent in their position; and that the militia might serve as the counterpoise to the army, representing the interest of the local and parliamentary gentry.

Men of all political persuasions came to distrust military power. The persistent disapprobation of the army was of central importance in the restoration of the Stuart monarchy. Basically, the Restoration of Charles II was a repudiation of government by the sword and a test of how deeply Englishmen had come to dislike and distrust a professional military instrument.

[104]Edward Hyde (first earl of Clarendon), *State Papers Collected by Edward Hyde, Earl of Clarendon, 1661* (Oxford, 1767-86), 3: 705.

[105]Warner, *The Nicholas Papers* 4: 205. Firth and Rait, *Acts and Ordinances* 12: 1425-55.

[106]*Thurloe State Papers* 7: 841-42, 867.

[107]Hyde, *State Papers* 3: 734-35.

[108]C. H. Firth, *Memoirs of Edmund Ludlow*, pp. 248-49.

[109]For a different view, see Pocock, "Machiavelli, Harrington and English Political Ideologies," p. 562.

CHAPTER V

THE MILITARY SETTLEMENT
AT THE RESTORATION:
1660–1667

From 1660 to 1673, the intensity and extent of interest in standing armies and the militia diminished. The Cromwellian Army was disbanded, but the Disbanding Act of September 13, 1660 specifically allowed the king to raise as many soldiers as he wished, so long as he paid them, and Charles II's establishment of royal guards in a public ceremony early in 1661 passed without public objection. The settlement of the militia was postponed by the Convention Parliament, which sat from April to December 1660, but the first Militia Act, passed by the Cavalier Parliament in July 1661, stated unequivocally that the command of the militia was by the king alone. Feudal tenures were abolished with only isolated opposition. The old fear of professional soldiers flared briefly, however, in 1667 when an army was raised for the Dutch War. It was used then with acute political acumen as a propaganda weapon to destroy a political enemy, the earl of Clarendon. In the articles of treason, the charge that he recommended a standing army was placed first.

The diminution of interest in antimilitary principles is explained by several factors. The expectation, which was promptly satisfied, that the former New Model Army would be disbanded removed that provocation. During the Convention Parliament and early years of the Cavalier Parliament, attention was focused on other issues associated with restoring the Stuart monarchy—first, religion, and then land, finance, and indemnity. The discovery of innumerable plots against the government and frequent domestic uprisings (most notably Venner's Rebellion in January 1661 and the Northern or Derwentdale Plot of October 1663) justified for certain men, who might otherwise have been uncompromising opponents, the establishment of the royal Guards and the settlement of the command of the militia in the king. The total disarray of republican and other radical and libertarian groups removed from Parliament the spokesmen who, during the Interregnum, had led the attack on the Army and had argued for parliamentary command of the militia. Republicans such as Arthur Haselrig and Thomas Scot, and Harringtonians such as Henry Neville, were neither in the Convention nor in any of the sessions of the Cavalier Parliament. Their presence, oratorical and tactical skill, and attentiveness would surely have made a difference, if not in the nature of the military settlement, then at least in the debates about it.

The membership and leadership of the Convention Parliament and of the early sessions of the Cavalier Parliament offer another explanation. Recent studies have analyzed the steady "disintegration of puritan power" in the spring of 1660.[1] Presbyterians who had sought just prior to the Restoration to impose limitations on the monarchy, along the lines of the Newport Treaty (which included parliamentary command of the militia), were neither persistent nor unified in pressing for limitations.[2] Their failure to shape the House of Lords as they wished, their consequent inability to control it once it was reconvened, and their posts in government awarded by Charles eroded, by early May 1660, their interest in attempting to impose general conditions.[3] With respect to the military settlement, there was no genuine leadership or organization. Whatever role as leader of the Presbyterians in the Convention Parliament Philip lord Wharton[4] might

---

[1]See Douglas R. Lacey, *Dissent and Parliamentary Politics in England 1661-1689* (New Brunswick, 1969), especially chapter 1. J. R. Jones, "Political Groups and Tactics in the Convention of 1660," *Historical Journal* 6 (1963): 159-77, argues that the Parliamentarians were less cohesive and alert than the royalists. See R. S. Bosher, *The Making of the Restoration Settlement 1649-1662* (London, 1951), for a discussion of the ineptness of the Presbyterians in the religious settlement.

[2]The most influential were Lords Manchester, Northumberland, and Wharton. See Lacey, *Dissent and Parliamentary Politics*, p. 7 and n. 17; G. F. Trevallyn Jones, *Saw-Pit Wharton* (Sydney, 1967), pp. 154, 156.

[3]Lacey, *Dissent and Parliamentary Politics*, pp. 8-9; Jones, *Saw-Pit Wharton*, pp. 160, 161, 164, 165. Between April 27 and May 2, the House of Lords tried and failed to win parliamentary command of the militia.

[4]See Jones, *Saw-Pit Wharton*, and G. F. Trevallyn Jones, "The Composition and Leadership of the Presbyterian Party in the Convention," *E.H.R.* 79 (1964): 307-54, for the thesis that Wharton was the leader of the Presbyterians in the Convention Parliament.

73

have played, he was indecisive and half-hearted as a member of the Committee on the Militia in the House of Lords, and there is no evidence that he expressed concern over the terms of the Disbanding Act, as they were being discussed during August or when the Act was passed in September.

As for the House of Commons, where Parliamentarian interest might have been expected to predominate, there was a similar lack of unity, leadership, and commitment to the ideals of the past two decades. Once the restored House of Commons of the Long Parliament was dissolved, the opportunity to impose limitations on the monarchy was lost. Members were not united in the spring of 1660 on the constitutional limitations to be imposed, and by mid-May, all efforts to impose limitations were abandoned.[5] It has been asserted that General George Monck sabotaged any attempts to impose restrictions on the king. Monck's strong opposition to a motion to appoint a committee to determine which of the terms of the Newport Treaty should be demanded of Charles II was "echoed with . . . a shout over the house" that marked the end of interest in limiting the monarchy.[6] Although there were men in the House of Commons (among them Arthur Annesley,[7] Richard Knightley, William Pierrepont, John Stephens, and William Prynne) who earlier had opposed the New Model Army and supported parliamentary control of the militia, none of them assumed leadership in settling military questions at the Restoration. Fear of domestic uprisings, the contagious enthusiasm for monarchy, and perhaps, as a contemporary later charged, the neglect of the public good in favor of private interest,[8] help explain their disinterest.

There was remarkable unanimity among the Convention Parliament, the Army itself, and the king and his advisers about the necessity of disbanding the Cromwellian Army. In the Convention Parliament, there was probably more agreement on this than on any other question.[9] Such agreement was predictable in an assembly of coun-

---

[5]Lacey, *Dissent and Parliamentary Politics*, pp. 5–6, 10.

[6]Davies, *The Restoration*, p. 346. The motion had been made by Matthew Hale.

[7]Arthur Annesley was president of the Council of State and sat in the Convention Parliament for Carmarthen borough. He was not elevated to the peerage until April 20, 1661, when he was created first earl of Anglesey. A Presbyterian, he conformed publicly. See Lacey, *Dissent and Parliamentary Politics*, pp. 459–63.

[8]Henry Neville, *Plato Redivivus* (1681) in *Two Republican Tracts*, ed. Caroline Robbins (Cambridge, 1969), pp. 196–98. Neville uses Sir William Pierrepont as the example of a wise man who did nothing for the public service after the Restoration.

[9]Mary W. Helms, "The Convention Parliament of 1660" (Ph.D. diss., Bryn Mawr, 1963), pp. 232, 359.

try gentlemen and lawyers who traditionally distrusted the professional army, resented the cost, and feared for their political liberties and position.[10] But there was no one to elevate the matter to the level of a constitutional principle, or to examine closely the wording of the Disbanding Act of September 13, or to comment negatively on the clause that allowed the king to raise as many soldiers as he wished so long as he paid them.

The disbanding turned, of course, on raising money to pay off the soldiers. As early as May 5, London had lent Parliament £50,000,[11] and on May 16, Arthur Annesley, the president of the interim Council of State, proposed that the House go into Grand Committee to consider how to pay the Army and Navy.[12] Over the summer, members were unable to develop a satisfactory plan for disbanding the Army, and on August 25, it was resolved to seek General Monck's advice.[13] Five days later, the general's plan was presented. In the debate that ensued, Sir William Morrice (Monck's kinsman, a newly appointed secretary of state, a Presbyterian, and a colonel) led the attack on the Army in an eloquent statement that showed that antiarmy sentiments and the memory of Cromwell's rule were very much alive. Using a series of rhetorical comparisons, he pointed out that gunpowder was made of the same stuff that caused earthquakes and that so long as soldiers were on hand, "there would be a perpetual trembling in the nation." Warming to his theme, he compared keeping an army to keeping the skins of a sheep and a wolf, which if the two "lie together, the former would lose its wool." He elaborated by declaring that if a sheep and wolf are put into grates next to one another, "the sheep would pine and die at the sight" of the wolf. In like manner, Sir William declared the nation could not "appear like itself whilst the sword was over them."[14] Having exhausted this flight of rhetoric, he moved that the army be paid and disbanded. It was ordered that the report be referred to the Committee for the Army, which was enlarged and instructed to bring in a bill for disbanding the Army by the next day.[15]

Over the next several weeks, the method of disbanding was worked out. It was perceived by the Lords that the estimates of yields

---

[10]Of 587 members, 300 were gentlemen and 127 lawyers (*ibid.*, table 7, p. 151).

[11]*H.M.C., Fifth Report*, part 1, appendix, p. 181.   [12]*C.J.* 8: 32.   [13]*Ibid.*, p. 135.

[14]*Ibid.*, pp. 142-43; Cobbett, *Parliamentary History* 4: 115. His eloquence had already been noticed: See Hyde, *State Papers* 3: 737. For his fondness for analogies from animal life, see Cobbett, *Parliamentary History* 4: 144.

[15]*C.J.* 8: 143. Colonel John Birch was chairman.

from proposed assessments were too high, and it was suspected that such estimates had been purposely calculated to keep the king dependent upon Parliament.[16] During this time, the court asked that three regiments (those of the duke of York, the duke of Gloucester, and General Monck) be exempted from the disbanding by lot, and held until the end, a request which was granted. The bill was signed into law on September 13.

There is no record of public or private comment on the Disbanding Act. Clause one of the Act clearly stated that the process of disbanding should proceed "until the whole [army] be disbanded."[17] Clause four contained the loophole. After declaring that all garrisons were to be reduced to their condition as of 1637 and the soldiers discharged, the clause continued: "except such of them or any other his Majestye shall think fitt otherwise to dispose and provide for at his owne charge." The implication of the phrase is plain: the king has the right to keep as many soliders as he wants so long as he pays for them. This was, of course, the ancient prerogative of the crown. The number of soldiers the king might have (a point vigorously debated the previous decade) and the limitations on the king's authority over them were not mentioned. It should be noted that this clause provided at least some statutory basis for the establishment by Charles II in February 1661 of special Guards which were paid by him and absolutely under his command. Subsequent acts, too, gave indirect statutory sanction to the existence of Guards raised and paid for by the king: for example, the Act of 1662 to prevent frauds in the customs and the Act of 1670 to suppress conventicles.[18] In 1666, Parliament granted £30,000 especially for the use of the Guards, thereby giving additional legal support to their existence.[19] In 1660, then, the principle that Parliament should have control of the armed forces of the nation, a proposition which was so vigorously advocated during the Interregnum, was lost without public outcry.[20]

---

[16]Maxwell Schoenfeld, *The Restored House of Lords* (The Hague, 1968), pp. 177–78.

[17]*Statutes of the Realm* V, 238: 12 Car. II, 15; *C.J.* 8: 71. The procedure was as follows: the names of the regiments and garrisons were written on pieces of paper which were folded and put into a glass and then drawn out from time to time by members of the Privy Council. So far as can be discovered, this was the first time that such a procedure was used for a military purpose.

[18]Thomson, *A Constitutional History* 4: 155; *Statutes of the Realm* V. 250, 650.

[19]David Ogg, *History of England in the Reign of Charles II* (Oxford, 1955), 2: 444.

[20]*C.S.P.D., 1660*, pp. 206, 266, 267, and *C.S.P.V., 1659–61*, p. 179, refer to uprisings or rumors of plots on August 6 and 30 and September 13 which help explain the acquiescence.

Throughout the fall, the disbanding of the Army proceeded, beset by the problems of collecting taxes for paying the soldiers.[21] On November 23, the House heard the discouraging news that the disbanding was "at a Stand for the present" because of the financial difficulties,[22] and at the end of December, another assessment was needed to get together sufficient funds.[23] But despite setbacks and difficulties, the process of disbandment, with the exception of General Monck's regiment, which was scheduled to be dismissed on January 4, 1661, was completed by the end of December.[24] For the moment, at least, the goal of every Parliament since 1647 was realized.

The realization of this goal was in large measure a consequence of the willingness of the Cromwellian Army to disband. Although there was some resistance to disbanding, the majority of the army was acquiescent in the fall of 1660. This agreeableness reflected the antimilitarism inherent in many of the men of this unique army as well as their sense of demoralization. Monck's dismissal of dissentient men and officers in the spring also had an effect, as did the disaffection of the men because of arrears and the pay system.[25] Most of all, the expectation, which was fulfilled, of a kind of "G.I. Bill of Rights" encouraged the troops to disband. The Army had been wooed by the king in the Declaration of Breda to expect payment of their arrears,[26] and not only their arrears but an additional week's pay were granted. Provision was also made for the maimed and disabled.[27] Other legisla-

---

[21]*C.S.P.V., 1659-61*, pp. 202, 204, 214, 218, 220, 223; Edward Hyde (first earl of Clarendon), *The Continuation of His Life* (Oxford, 1759), pp. 10, 71; *C.S.P.D., 1660*, pp. 276, 305, 308; H.M.C., *Fifth Report*, part 1, appendix, pp. 157-58, 174. Problems plagued the effort: in December, £30,000 for disbanding troops in Scotland was lost at sea.

[22]*C.J.* 8: 190.

[23]Helms, "The Convention Parliament of 1660," p. 260.

[24]*Parliamentary Intelligence December 24–December 31, 1660*, bound as number 53 in a volume in the British Museum entitled *Dr. Burney's Tracts* 1: 842-43; see also *The Kingdome's Intelligencer, December 31–January 7, 1661*, number 1, in *Dr. Burney's Tracts* 2: 14. The process of disbandment as reported by the government may be followed in the weekly editions of these two papers and Mercurius Publicus, all bound together.

[25]Godfrey Davies, "The Army and the Restoration of 1660," *Journal of the Society for Army Historical Research* 32 (1954): 26-29.

[26]The last paragraph in the Declaration of Breda promised the king's consent to any act or acts of Parliament "for the full satisfaction of all arrears due to the officers and soldiers of the army under the command of General Monck." Cf. H.M.C., *Fifth Report*, part 1, appendix, p. 154, where it is remarked that the best way to quiet the army was to pay it.

[27]An Order of the House of Commons for the care of Maimed Soldiers was printed on December 17, 1660.

tion allowed all soldiers to practice a trade or open a shop without satisfying apprenticeship requirements. This provision was based on a precedent from the Cromwellian period and was a strong inducement to accept the disbandment.[28]

Charles II and the court were also in favor of disbanding the Cromwellian force. Ludlow remarked that the disbanding of the Army was certainly not due to the king's aversion to a standing army, "for the whole course of his life demonstrates the contrary." It was rather that Charles thought that the soldiers, given their background, were "dangerous companions" and that he would be safer without them.[29] Clarendon agreed, recalling that the king was well aware of the "ill constitution of the Army, the Distemper and Murmuring that was in it."[30] Further, Charles's pressing need to economize recommended dissolving the New Model Army.[31]

Charles handled the Army astutely. From the spring of 1660 to the total disbandment, Charles dissembled his apprehension and developed a public face toward the army calculated to blunt its animosity and win its allegiance. For example, The Declaration of Breda of April 14, 1660 promised not only the full payment of arrears but also suggested that the Army would be received into the service of the king upon the same good pay and conditions that the soldiers presently enjoyed. It is just possible that this phrase reflected a momentary flirtation on Charles's part with the idea of keeping the old army as Count Schomberg had recommended to him in 1659,[32] but it is much more likely that it was propaganda to assuage the hostility of the soldiers. On May 21, he promised Monck, in an exaggerated statement of good faith, to make good whatever had been promised the army.[33] And on May 26, the king in a message to Monck to be communicated to the officers asserted that he could "never be without a just esteeme of such a great and well-disciplined army."[34] And finally, to show his entire trust in the Army, he, soon after the Restoration, took as his own a regiment, formerly commanded by Colonel Upton

[28]*C.S.P.D., 1653-54*, p. 264. *C.S.P.V., 1659-61*, p. 202. Also, Ogg, *England in the Reign of Charles II* 1: 156.

[29]Firth, *Memoirs of Edmund Ludlow* 2: 326.

[30]Hyde, *Continuation of His Life*, p. 10.

[31]*Ibid.*, pp. 10, 71. Also *C.S.P.D., 1660-61* 1: 206, 207; *C.J.* 8: 174; *L.J.* 11: 173-76; Henry B. Wheatley, ed., *The Diary of Samuel Pepys* (London, 1893), 1: 90; H.M.C., *Fifth Report*, part 1, appendix, pp. 146, 154, 167.

[32]Bishop Gilbert Burnet, *History of My Own Time*, ed. O. Airy (Oxford, 1802), 1: 302-3.

[33]Hyde, *State Papers* 2: 745-46.

[34]Warner, *The Nicholas Papers* 4: 209.

Crook, and called it the "Royal Regiment."[35] Charles also wooed General Monck by according him courtesies and honors, greeting him first when he stepped ashore on May 30, calling him father, elevating him to a dukedom, and appointing him commander-in-chief of all the land forces in England, the army, and the militia.[36]

Charles's concern to placate and disband the Cromwellian army should not suggest a lack of interest in a strong military force to protect his government against domestic insurrection and foreign threat. Unquestionably, he wanted a body of troops loyal to him and independent of Parliament (such as he had seen on the Continent). Of equal importance, he wanted the question of the command of the militia settled in his favor. Like James II and William III after him, Charles II took a greater personal interest in his guards, arsenals, and the militia than he did in any other issue. This interest was the corollary of his settled determination never to go on his travels again. He was known to feel that his father's troubles would not have occurred had he had a strong force at his disposal.[37]

At about the same time the Disbanding Bill was introduced in the House and six months before Venner's Rebellion in January 1661, which is always cited as the episode that led immediately to the creation of the royal Guards, Charles was laying plans to raise some troops beyond the ceremonial Guards, which had been reestablished upon his return.[38] An undated and unsigned proposal for a military establishment costing £118,528 and including foot, horse, and general officers was drafted probably in late July or early August.[39] On September 1, it was rumored that, although the old army was disbanding, "they will have a new army maintained of 6 or 8,000 men for some certaine time."[40] Around the same time, Charles frankly told the Spanish Ambassador that he wanted to organize an army from his

[35] Walton, *History of the British Standing Army, 1660–1700*, p. 7. See *Mercurius Publicus, June 28 to July 5 1660*, number 27 in *Dr. Burney's Tracts* 1: 431.

[36] Duke of Albemarle's commission, dated August 3, 1660, may be found in Walton, *A History of the British Standing Army*, appendix 1, pp. 779–83. *C.S.P.V.* 32: 153. In reporting the honors Monck had received, the Venetian Ambassador commented that there was no doubt the king would be militarily strong.

[37] John Dalrymple, *Memoirs of Great Britain and Ireland from the Dissolution of the Last Parliament of Charles II until the Sea-Battle off La Hogue* (Edinburgh, 1771), 2: 39: Colbert to Louis XIV, November 13, 1669, reporting a remark by Charles II.

[38] H.M.C., *LeFleming Mss.*, p. 24.

[39] Public Record Office, S/P. 29/29/45 (hereafter cited as P.R.O.), with a manuscript note by Lt. Col. F. W. Hamilton that the draft dates from late July or early August 1660 and not from 1661, the date given in the printed *Calendar*.

[40] H.M.C., *Fifth Report*, part 1, appendix, p. 168; cf. Laurence Echard, *History of England* (London, 1720), p. 776.

own resources—in other words "without the consent of Parliament."[41] In November, Colonel John Russell was given a commission to raise a regiment of 1,200 foot guards.[42] The next month, the king's guards were posted at "all the corners of London and the palace" to secure the government against a plot by various sectaries and Fifth Monarchists which had been discovered.[43] At the end of December, the Venetian Ambassador reported that he thought a special force of guards would be created, composed of soldiers presently in Flanders, who would form a "regiment of brave, devoted veterans to guard the King's person."[44]

Against the background of these preliminaries, the Court's response to Venner's Uprising, which occurred on January 4, 1661, was predictable. Insignificant as this Millenarian rebellion appears in retrospect,[45] it was fought with a frenzy which alarmed both citizens and the court. "His Majesties Lifeguard" and General Monck's regiment helped to put down the insurrectionists. Monck's officers were reported to have seized this incident as an opportunity to argue that the regiment not be disbanded. Monck agreed. Some soldiers in the old army blamed him for the disbanding, and for reasons of personal security, Monck wanted to keep his regiment embodied.[46]

In the absence of the king, who was at Portsmouth, the council met early on the day following the episode, and upon the proposal of the duke of York, it was agreed to suspend the disbanding of General Monck's Regiment of Foot, which, according to the order of Parliament, was to have been disbanded. Further, the council decided to write to the king seeking his approval of what they had done and

---

[41]Leopold Von Ranke, *History of England Principally in the Seventeenth Century* (Oxford, 1875), 3: 336-37.

[42]F. W. Hamilton, *History of the Royal Grenadier Guards* (London, 1874), 1: 43; cf. *C.S.P.D., 1660-61*, p. 489, for estimates in January 1661.

[43]*C.S.P.V., 1659-61*, p. 229.

[44]*Ibid.*, p. 231. Such a scheme may have been modeled after Denmark, where a royal despotism had been installed in 1660. See Caroline Robbins, *The Eighteenth Century Commonwealthman* (Cambridge, Mass., 1959), p. 26. Two drafts of the Confirmation of Hereditary Right of the Danish King are among the State Papers. One is in Clarendon's hand. Both are dated October 8, 1660. See P.R.O., *State Papers*, Foreign, Denmark, S/P. 103/3.

[45]The estimates of those involved vary: Hyde, *Continuation of His Life*, p. 73; Wheatley, *The Diary of Samuel Pepys* 1: 319, 321, 322-23; *C.S.P.D., 1660*, pp. 470, 471; Burnet, *History of My Own Time* 1: 278-79. The latest study of Millenarianism is B. S. Capp, *The Fifth Monarchy Men* (London, 1972).

[46]*Mercurius Publicus, January 3-January 10, 1661*, number 1 in *Dr. Burney's Tracts* 2: 15-16, for account of the participation of the guards and Monck's regiment. Also Hamilton, *History of the Royal Grenadier Guards* 1: 67.

urging him to raise more men to secure his government.[47] Charles II agreed and "immediately" ordered the raising of a new regiment of guards of twelve companies and a new regiment of horse of eight troops and gave out commissions to raise regiments of horse in the future.[48] These guards were to be added to the regiment (presumably Colonel Russell's) "new raised" by the king.[49] This response gratified the duke of York, who took occasion to criticize the earl of Southampton and the lord chancellor for not earlier advising the king to strengthen himself.[50]

By January 26, estimates of the cost and numbers of the king's Guards had been settled, and the establishment may be said to date from then.[51] Formal, public recognition of this was given on February 14. In a symbolical ceremony on Tower Hill, in which Prynne took part, General Monck's regiments of foot and horse were dismissed and reembodied as the Lord General's Regiment of Foot Guards and the Lord General's Troop of Guards, otherwise known respectively as the Coldstream Guards and, until 1670, as the Third Troop of Life Guards.[52]

The public establishment of the Guards in February 1661 passed without recorded objection, except from the earl of Southampton, who argued in private with Clarendon that the experience of the Cromwellian interlude had taught the country the effects of a military government and that inevitably the soldiers would become unmanageable and the king willing to use them for his own ends. The earl declared that he could not stand by and "see the ruin of his country begun" and that he would not be bribed into silence. But Clarendon allayed his fears, promising to divert the king from creating any more guards than necessary, and Southampton finally agreed that if the project went no further, he could bear it, but he pointed out it would not be easy to

---

[47]Hyde, *Continuation of His Life*, p. 73; James Macpherson, ed., *Original Papers, Containing the Secret History of Great Britain, from the Restoration, to the Accession of the House of Hannover* [sic] *to which are Prefixed Extracts from the Life of James II As Written by Himself* (London, 1775), 1: 18; J. S. Clarke, *Life of James II* (London, 1816), 1: 390.

[48] Clarke, *Life of James II*, p. 390.

[49]Thomas Gumble, *Life of General Monck* (London, 1671), p. 402.

[50]Clarke, *Life of James II*, p. 390.

[51]*C.S.P.D., 1660–61*, p. 489. The intermediate steps may be followed in: Wheatley, *The Diary of Samuel Pepys* 1: 323, 324; *C.S.P.D., 1660–61*, pp. 471, 477; H.M.C., *De L'Isle and Dudley MSS* (1626–1698), 6: 508.

[52]Walton, *History of the British Standing Army*, pp. 1 and 1–8 *passim*, for a detailed statement on the king's Guards and the priority accorded them; *Mercurius Publicus, February 14–21, 1661*, number 7 in *Dr. Burney's Tracts* 2: 137–39 for the ceremony.

"fix numbers."[53] Clarendon recalled that the restored government was so shaky and so threatened that "no Man at that time thought [the Guards] to be more than was necessary."[54]

The Guards, like the New Model Army before them, were different from any other force the nation had had before. They were considerably more numerous than any of the ceremonial guards previous kings had had, numbering in 1661, according to "An Abstract of His Majesty's Guards," 3,200 men and 374 officers.[55] Moreover, they were created by a legitimate king in peacetime without any recourse to Parliament. The Venetian Ambassador thought they were "noteworthy" because they were "entirely dependent" upon the king.[56] In view of the wide efforts immediately preceding the Restoration to make the military force dependent upon Parliament, this fact was extraordinary. Equally noteworthy was the partisan quality of the king's Guards. The court was bombarded with requests for a post in the Guards by men who recommended themselves on the basis of their past loyal service to Charles I.[57] The earliest army list dating from the spring of 1661 showed that many of the officers were former royalist field officers.[58] As early as July 1661, it was also noted that many of the Guards were Catholic.[59] So long as Charles held the affection and trust of his subjects, these facts were accepted. But as events and policies poisoned the relationship between the king and Parliament, the Guards became the object of increasing suspicion and objection.

With respect to the militia, the king achieved, at least on the surface, another victory over Parliamentarian interests, namely unequivocal confirmation of his sole command of the militia. The Convention of 1660 failed to settle the militia, but in three bills passed by the Cavalier Parliament in 1661, 1662, and 1663, the command of the militia was declared to be in the hands of the crown and the details of the operation of the militia were spelled out. The principle of parliamentary command was thereby lost, although day-to-day control of

[53]Burnet, *History of My Own Time* 1: 280.

[54]Hyde, *Continuation of His Life*, p. 73. Cf. *C.S.P.V., 1659–61*, p. 247; Anchitell Grey, *Debates of the House of Commons from the Year 1667 to the Year 1694* (London, 1763), 2: 393: In a debate on February 7, 1673–74, Sir Thomas Meres remarked that he did not recall any "exception" made to the guards in the early 1660s.

[55]B.M., Additional Manuscripts, 28, 82 (hereafter cited as Add. Mss). Reproduced in Walton, *History of the British Standing Army*, p. 843.

[56]*C.S.P.V., 1661–64*, p. 84. ·

[57]*C.S.P.D., 1660*, pp. 11, 19, 25, 32, 33, 189, 341, 360, 443–45, 482, 488, 494, 570.

[58]Hamilton, *History of the Grenadiers* 1: 47–49; *C.S.P.V., 1659–61*, p. 255; Cf. *C.S.P.D., 1665–66*, p. 477.

[59]*C.S.P.V., 1661–64*, p. 18.

the operation of the militia by the county gentry was not. In the early years of the Restoration, the militia continued to be regarded, as it had been before, as the special military instrument of the gentry and as a counterpoise to any forces the king had. Further, in several debates on the settlement of the militia, some of the themes of the antiarmy ideology were raised by isolated voices. Though the antimilitary tradition was muted, it nonetheless continued.

Although the settling of the militia was listed first among the main issues confronting the Convention Parliament in May 1660, members devoted relatively little attention to it.[60] During the summer the initiative was seized by the king and court. What Charles and his advisers hoped to achieve was a militia force similar in character to the "new militia" that Cromwell had projected in 1655,[61] a force independent of the county gentry, well trained enough to serve as an auxiliary to any other force at hand, and a kind of police to thwart domestic insurrection. Such a militia would, of course, have many of the characteristics of a standing army.

Among the first steps the court took was to appoint lord-lieutenants sympathetic to the king.[62] It may be that, thereby, the king was attempting to reaffirm his prerogative power over the militia.[63] In addition, the court tried to supervise closely the operation of the militia. In July, Secretary Nicholas sent detailed instructions to the lord-lieutenants about managing the militia, requiring them to choose "well-affected" officers, to keep volunteers and the militia separate, and to send in accounts of their proceedings to the council.[64] So successful were their efforts that periodically over the next three months Nicholas expressed his satisfaction with the way the militia was shaping up.[65] Unquestionably, the militia did serve the interests of the crown and the nation by acting as a deterrent to sectaries and dissentient members of the Army during the disbanding throughout the fall.[66]

During this time, no recorded attempt was made by Parliamentarians to settle the militia question by parliamentary Act. But on November 6, Richard Knightley, remembered for his opposition to

---

[60]*C.S.P.D., 1660–61*, p. 608.

[61]Western, *The English Militia in the Eighteenth Century*, p. 8.

[62]H.M.C., *Fifth Report*, part 1, appendix, p. 153.

[63]*Ibid.*, p. 194. Also Western, *The English Militia in the Eighteenth Century*, p. 10.

[64]*C.S.P.D., 1660–61*, p. 150. See p. 466 for indication of objections in the House to the raising of volunteers.

[65]*Ibid.*, pp. 185, 277, 305, 354.

[66]*C.S.P.V., 1659–61*, pp. 204, 207; *C.S.P.D., 1660–61*, p. 354.

the Army in Richard's Parliament, moved to bring in a Militia Bill. Opposing the motion was a Royalist spokesman, Sir Henry Cholmely, who asserted that the militia was already in the king's hands, that the question had "set them together by the Ears" before, and that it should be left alone.[67] The motion passed, however, and the committee that was appointed was chaired by Knightley and included men who, like him, were known for their antimilitary convictions: Prynne, Pierrepont, Annesley, and Secretary Morrice. The poet, Andrew Marvell, who later excoriated the army as well as the government in verse, also sat on this committee.[68]

The debate on the bill which was brought in a fortnight later, on November 16, illustrates the lack of cohesiveness among Parliamentarians. The draft of the bill has been lost, but it contained some kind of provision for martial law, presumably to be exercised by the lord-lieutenants. In a response reminiscent of earlier objections to martial law, members of the committee, especially Pierrepont, adamantly opposed this section. Royalists supported the provision. Members agreed finally to the recommendation of Sir Heneage Finch, the solicitor-general, who was regarded as the "official representative of the court,"[69] that a second reading was in order so that the terms might be better understood. Prynne announced that he had in his possession a letter purporting to detail examples of the tyrannical behavior of some of the lord-lieutenants, but his motion to have it read was defeated 181-to-105.[70]

At the second reading of the Militia Bill on November 22, objections were even more emphatically stated.[71] To all this Sir Heneage Finch, again, responded, answering the points that had been raised

[67]*C.J.* 8: 175. *The Parliamentary or Constitutional History of England from the Earliest Times to the Dissolution of the Convention Parliament* (London, 1751-61), 23: 2 (hereafter cited as *Parliamentary History.)*

[68]*C.J.* 8: 175. Marvell commented approvingly on the militia in a letter of November 17, 1660 to Hull. See H. M. Margoliouth, ed., *The Poems and Letters of Andrew Marvell* (Oxford, 1952), 2: 2.

[69]*D.N.B.* article on Sir Heneage Finch.

[70]*Parliamentary History* 23: 15; *C.J.* 8: 184-85.

[71]The most articulate opponent was John Stephens, the same man who spoke against professional soldiers in Richard's Parliament. As already noted, it is certain that the speaker in Richard's Parliament was John Stephens, elected from Gloucestershire, not James Stephens, elected from Gloucester City. John Stephens was returned to the Convention Parliament from Bristol; James, so far as may be determined, was not elected to the Convention. An Edward Stephens sat for Gloucestershire in the Convention. See *Parliamentary History* 21: 250, 251; 22: 215, 218 and *Return of Every Member . . . in Each Parliament* (London, 1878), part 1, pp. 504, 508. I am indebted to P. H. Hardacre for untangling the several men with the same surname.

"very excellently, and with some sharpness." His motion to commit was accepted.[72] Two days later, a contemporary observed that the bill for the militia "goeth on shortly," for, he said, significantly, "the Pr[esbyterian?] finds himself outwitted and that it will strengthen the King's power instead of lessening it." He predicted, however, that the bill would pass.[73] The Militia Bill was not brought up again before dissolution on December 29, 1660. Although complaints associated with the settling of the militia were raised at various times, particularly about arbitrary actions of the lord-lieutenants, nothing came of the protests.[74] The delay in framing a militia bill played into the hands of Royalists, who were eager to postpone a decision on the militia until a new Parliament when, hopefully, they could be assured of a majority of members sympathetic to their own point of view.[75]

The government continued to move purposefully. When Clarendon spoke at the prorogation of the Convention Parliament, he referred to the king's disappointment that the militia question had not been settled and to his wish that all might know by a declaration of Parliament that Parliament and king were in agreement on the militia.[76] Until then, the king would, with the Privy Council, issue commissions of lieutenancy in the counties so that the militia might function as a deterrent to disorders. Further instructions for lord-lieutenants regarding the militia were prepared.[77]

It was in the Cavalier Parliament on July 30, 1661 that a Militia Bill was passed. The Act fixed the command of the militia on the king, and the terms were unequivocal: "the sole supreme government, command and disposition of the militia" as well as, so the Act ran, "of all forces by sea and land, . . . is, and by the laws of England ever was, the undoubted right" of the crown. And, lest there be any doubt about the role of Parliament, the Act specifically stated that "both or either of the Houses of Parliament cannot, nor ought to, pretend to the same [authority]."[78] The Act made plain that Parliament had no right to

---

[72]*Parliamentary History* 23: 22-24.

[73]H.M.C., *Fifth Report*, part 1, appendix, p. 196.

[74]*Parliamentary History* 23: 51-52; Cobbett, *Parliamentary History* 4: 161.

[75]Helms, The Convention Parliament of 1660, p. 268.

[76]Cobbett, *Parliamentary History* 4: 171-72.

[77]*C.S.P.D., 1660-61*, p. 459. The Court's continued efforts, to about 1667, to strengthen control over the militia may be followed in the *C.S.P.D.* and in Western, *The English Militia in the Eighteenth Century*, pp. 10-29. One interesting detail not mentioned by Western is that Charles ordered the militia money raised by the lieutenancies of North and South Wales to be deposited in Ludlow Castle and used to pay the garrison there (P.R.O., SP 44/20/f. 54).

[78]13 Car. II, Stat. I, cap. 6: *Statutes of the Realm* 5: 308-9.

raise soldiers or levy a war against the crown, and any such action or authority must be repressed. Further, to protect the crown, the Act specified that all officers and soldiers were to take the oaths of allegiance and supremacy. This was the first time that statutory definition had been given the king's military authority. The willingness of the Cavalier Parliament to do this should be contrasted with the unwillingness of MP's in 1628 even to mention the royal prerogative in the Petition of Right.

No account of the debates on the Militia Bill of 1661 has survived. There may have been objections. But, writing in 1675 with special reference to the oath in the bill, the "Person of Quality" asserted that no one in 1661 dared "freely to debate the matter," and that "the humor of the Age" was so strong in favor of royal prerogative that it swept "Wise and good Men down before it."[79] Still later the Tory apologist, Roger North, insisted that the Militia Act was simply "declaratory" of ancient common law and was nothing new. He doubted that anyone at the time thought the militia was not in the hands of the king (!), but he explained that the reason for spelling out the authority of the crown in the law was to make it impossible for malcontents to claim, on the basis of precedents from 1641 and 1642, the command of the militia themselves.[80] The fact that the bill was so frequently before the House and was referred to as the "greatest business . . . upon their hands," suggests a contest.[81] On the other hand, evidence has survived to show that the Presbyterians took steps to change other legislation, and it seems reasonable to think that, had they been vigorous and persistent with respect to the militia, some contemporary comment on that would have survived too.[82] Dislike of this first Militia Bill was expressed later. For example, in 1679 Roger Morrice declared that the Cavalier Parliament had "violated the fundamental laws of the Kingdom and had assisted arbitrary power and infringed law . . . by declaring the militia to be in the power of the King solely which never parliament before had done."[83]

[79]*A Letter from a Person of Quality to His Friend in the Country* (London, 1675), p. 2. Cf. John Humfrey, *Advice before It Be Too Late: Or, a Breviate for the Convention, Humbly Represented to the Lords and Commons of England* (London, 1689), felt the Militia bills were an example of "gross flattery."

[80]Roger North, *Examen, or an Enquiry into the Credit and Veracity of a Pretended Complete History* (London, 1740), pp. 428-29.

[81]*C.J.* 8: 254-303; the slow progress was commented upon: Andrew Browning, *Thomas Osborne, Earl of Danby and Duke of Leeds—1632-1712* (Glasgow, 1944-1951), 2: 9; H.M.C., *Fifth Report*, part 1, appendix, p. 160.

[82]Lacey, *Dissent and Parliamentary Politics*, pp. 33-35.

[83]*Ibid.*, p. 34. See also p. 278, n. 26, referring to similar comment by Morrice.

The "Person of Quality" said flatly that the Militia Bill set up a "standing army by a Law, and swears Us into a Military Government."[84]

Two more bills, one in 1662 and another in 1663, tidied up the details of the operation of the militia.[85] Both bills incurred objections that revealed the continued existence of antimilitaristic sentiments. The second Militia Bill was piloted through the House of Commons during the spring of 1662 by Heneage Finch.[86] Presbyterians attempted to win special provisions for the London militia. John Fowke, an alderman of the city, and long-term opponent of the crown, served as their spokesman. So intemperate did he become in protesting the House's proceedings that he was severely scolded kneeling at the Bar of the House and only missed being sent to the Tower.[87] Although the proviso was defeated, a second attempt was made the same day to get it passed. That the friends of the king were annoyed and perhaps alarmed by this example of Presbyterian energy is suggested by the fact that within a month's time the election of one of the tellers (Sir James Langham) in favor of Fowke's amendment to the Militia Bill was voided in an action which was an exception to the House's standing rules.[88]

On March 7, 1662, Sir John Holland spoke opposing the Militia Bill and proposing a substitute. The speeches revealed the point of view of a country gentleman actively involved in the Norfolk Militia. Holland strenuously objected to the bill on the grounds that the provisions were inadequate and that the rates for supplying the militia were equated with too high an income level. He predicted that the consequence would be a 50% reduction in the size of the militia. He was referring to the fact that the proposed bill specified that all subjects with an annual income of £500 were to supply a horse, whereas previously all having an income of £300 were required to supply a horse. Such an arrangement, Holland maintained, would reduce the militia to the point that it could not adequately protect the king and the nation. A weakened militia, he feared, would strengthen

---

[84]*A Letter from a Person of Quality*, p. 2.

[85]*Statutes of the Realm* 5: 358-64, 443-46.

[86]*C.J.* 8: 324 (appointment of a committee to bring in the bill) and 343-84 *passim*.

[87]*Ibid.*, p. 386; Lacey, *Dissent and Parliamentary Politics*, p. 37. The incident was recalled on May 3, 1678. See Grey, *Debates* 5: 317. For Fowkes's earlier record of opposition to the crown, see Valerie Pearl, *London and the Outbreak of the Puritan Revolution* (Oxford, 1961), pp. 316-20. She does not mention this episode at the Restoration.

[88]Lacey, *Dissent and Parliamentary Politics*, p. 38.

the notion of some men who "do conceive that neither King nor Kingdom can be safe but by a standing army." His purpose was to prevent such designs, he said, and persuade people who favored a standing army that "both king and kingdom may be safe under the defence and protection of a militia raised out of the persons of interest in the nation."[89]

Holland rose again on May 7 to protest a proviso[90] sent down by the House of Lords which would have allowed their Lordships and gentlemen of wealth to discharge their obligations to the militia by paying £10. For Holland, the principle at stake was the same; he wanted to assure that military responsibility should be borne by the men of property of the county and not placed upon others who were paid, and who had neither social standing nor real interest in local affairs. The example of Cromwell's new militia was in the forefront of his mind as he attacked the proposal. "I cannot forget," Holland said, "that in the late usurping time that the ancient Militia raised out of the freeholders and persons of interest of this nation was laid by and a troop of eight pound men raised in every county who were to be in readiness at all times and upon all occasion to be executors of the Tyrant's will."[91] The proviso lost.

In the House of Lords, debate on the second Militia Bill raised a constitutional issue. The question was whether the word "lawfully" should be inserted before the word "Commissioned" in the clause that required the lord-lieutenants and other militia officers to swear that it was unlawful to take up arms against the king or "those that are Commissioned by him." Arguing for the insertion was the earl of Southampton, and against it was Anglesey. The point was a minor one[92] but that it was raised suggests the lingering concern of some men to restrict specifically the crown's military power. The proposal was lost, which further testifies to the strength of the crown's interests in the early years of the Cavalier Parliament.

[89]Caroline Robbins, ed., "Five Speeches, 1661-1663, by Sir John Holland, M.P.," *B.I.H.R.* 28 (1955): 197-98.

[90]*C.J.* 8: 423 refers to the proviso from the House of Lords as "One, for Ten Pounds, to be paid in lieu of an Horse." The proviso itself has been lost. Schoenfeld, *The Restored House of Lords*, does not deal specifically with this proviso, but see pp. 144-45 for comments about the efforts of the Lords to keep the right of assessing themselves.

[91]Robbins, "Five Speeches, 1661-1663, by Sir John Holland," pp. 199-200. For Cromwell's new militia, see chapter 4.

[92]Schoenfeld, *The Restored House of Lords*, pp. 215-16. The Venetian Resident regarded the second Militia Bill as a "very essential point of extreme consequence" (*C.S.P.V., 1661-64*, p. 146).

With the passage of the third Militia Bill in 1663,[93] the operation of the militia was fixed by statutes which continued in force for the next one hundred years. Although the command of the militia was stated to be in the hands of the king, in truth the militia bills had created a force whose operation was in the hands of the lieutenancies of the several counties. In practice, the king's power was effectively restricted.[94] Three statutes, two very detailed, spelled out the operation of the militia and restricted the prerogative power of the king. Despite the interest of the king and court, and their specific efforts in the early years of the Restoration to make the militia an efficient instrument of the central government, the county militia never became a military instrument on which the government could surely depend. Using the terms of the acts, the county lieutenants saw to that. In working out the details of the legislation, the country gentry bested the court. Charles and Clarendon must have recognized this, and it may be speculated that an embarrassed sense of defeat is the reason that the chancellor is silent in the *Continuation of His Life* on the militia legislation.[95]

The final feature of the Restoration military settlement was the abolition of all tenures by knights' service to the king or any one else, which in effect confirmed ordinances[96] passed during the Interregnum and the de facto abolition which existed. This bill[97] acknowledged what had for years been true: that the old feudal array was moribund and that the Court of Wards and Liveries,[98] which was also abolished, was an anachronism. That the bill was the first to be

[93]On April 3, 1663, Sir Thomas Meres reported that the committee appointed to consider the militia bills had taken much care and heard many objections and therefore was bringing in still another bill, which was passed in July. See *C.J.* 8: 464, 469, 480-95, 516, 518, 524. A "Mr. Milward" often chaired the Committee of the Whole to consider the bill. He must have been the Robert Milward returned on April 5, 1661, from Stafford Boro., Stafford, probably the "cousin" referred to by the diarist, John Milward (*Return of Every Member* 1: 528; Caroline Robbins, ed., *The Diary of John Milward September 1666 to May 1668* [Cambridge, 1938], p. 243).

[94]Thomson, *A Constitutional History* 4: 154; Western, *The English Militia in the Eighteenth Century*, pp. 16-25; Thomson, *The Twysden Lieutenancy Papers, 1583-1668*, introduction, pp. 17-19.

[95]There is only one mention of the militia legislation and that concerns the Parliament's reaffirmation that the command of the militia rests with the crown. See Hyde, *Continuation of His Life*, p. 137.

[96]Ordinances of February 24, 1646, and November 27, 1656; see C. H. Firth and C. S. Rait, *Acts and Ordinances* 1: 833; 2: 1043.

[97]*Statutes of the Realm*, 5: 259-66. 12 Car. 2: 24.

[98]See H. E. Bell, *The History and Records of the Court of Wards & Liveries* (Cambridge, 1953).

ordered suggests the near unanimity of opinion about it,[99] but one writer, Fabian Philipps, in three tracts published in 1660, 1661, and 1664, raised persistent objections to the act, which are interesting because of the antiarmy sentiments expressed to justify his views. Central in Philipps's thought was an elitist idea, inherent in the antiarmy ideology and in the legally prescribed organization of the militia, that the defense of the nation should rest in the hands of men of substance.[100] Philipps argued that the abolition of tenures would destroy virtue and lead inevitably, as during the reign of Cromwell, to the creation of a standing army.[101] To pay soldiers, he warned, would cost ten-to-twenty times what it would to depend upon the old feudal array.[102] No contemporary comment on Philipps's pamphlets has been discovered, but in the next decade, an anachronistic longing for the feudal array was expressed along with the thought that the militia might be regarded as the heir to knights' service.

The Second Dutch War (1665-67) provided the circumstance for the most significant outburst of antimilitary sentiment during the 1660s. The war was begun in 1665 for commercial reasons at the enthusiastic urging of Parliament and a war group at court.[103] Compared to the First Dutch War (1652-54), which had brought some naval glory and much economic advantage, the Second Dutch War was a severe disappointment. Underfinanced in comparison to the Dutch Navy, the English Navy seldom distinguished itself. By the winter of 1666, the burden of taxation seemed intolerable. Added to this financial distress were the Great Plague, which ravaged London and some of the provinces in 1665, and the Great Fire, which leveled London in 1666. In the spring of 1667, peace negotiations were begun, which encouraged Charles to reduce expenses by a program

[99]Davies, *The Restoration*, p. 347. However, Arthur Annesley, for one example, opposed the abolition of the Court of Wards.

[100]Fabian Phillips, *Teneda non Tollenda: Or the Necessity of Preserving Tenures in Capite and by Knight Service* (London, November 1660), pp. 24, 91, 94, 112; also Fabian Phillips, *Ligeancia Lugens: Or Loyaltie Lamenting the Many Great Mischiefs and Inconveniences which Will Fatally and Inevitably Follow the Taking Away of the Royal Pourveyances, and Tenures in Capite and by Knight Service* (London, 1661), pp. 3, 5, 27.

[101]Phillips, *Ligeancia Lugens*, pp. 6, 28, 42-44, 47; Phillips, *Tenenda non Tollenda*, pp. 110-11, 247.

[102]Fabian Phillips, *The Mistaken Recompence: Or The Great Damage and Very Many Mischiefs and Inconveniences which Will Inevitably Happen to the King and His People* (London, 1664), The Epistle, p. b [6].

[103]A brief account is in David Ogg, *England in the Reign of Charles II* (Oxford, 1962), 1: 283-321; and J. R. Jones, *Britain and Europe in the Seventeenth Century* (New York, 1967), pp. 50-66, on the Anglo-Dutch wars in general.

of naval retrenchment.[104] Thus denuded, the nation was ill prepared for the audacious attack in June by the Dutch Navy on the naval arsenal at Chatham.[105] A number of English ships were either destroyed or seized. For the English, it was a humiliating episode. Divine vengeance, the machinations of Frenchmen, Dutchmen, or even more likely Papists, and mismanagement in high places were all blamed[106] for the fire and the national disgrace at Chatham.

The outrage was translated into a verbal attack on the troops which Charles had promptly raised as a result of the Chatham episode.[107] The intensity of the criticism of the government and the depth of the antimilitary sentiment were revealed immediately. When the House met on July 25, it refused to adjourn for four days at the king's order (because of the thin attendance) until a resolution was passed that all troops raised for the war should be disbanded as soon as peace was concluded.[108] Old Cavaliers rather than Parliamentarians led the attack.[109] Sir Thomas Tomkins,[110] a strong Royalist but a great enemy of Clarendon's, introduced the motion in an extreme form, calling for the immediate disbandment of the troops. He was supported by "five other old Cavaliers,"[111] and joined by Parliamentarians who, in the next decade, would regularly attack the king's soldiers. William Garroway qualified the motion, saying that Tomkins meant as soon as peace was concluded. Sir Thomas Littleton argued darkly that there were some men about the king who wanted him to keep up a standing army in time of peace, that the resolution must be passed that day for the Parliament might find itself prorogued. The motion was unanimously carried.

What is one to make of this attack on the army? The element of genuine fear should not be discounted.[112] Nor should the element of

[104]See E. S. de Beer, ed., *The Diary of John Evelyn* (London. 1955), 3: 489 and n. 2.

[105]See P. G. Rogers, *The Dutch in the Medway* (London, 1970).

[106]*C.S.P.D., 1667*, pp. 188–89.

[107]Charles Dalton, ed., *English Army Lists and Commission Registers, 1661–1714* (London, 1960), 1: 65–68.

[108]Robbins, *The Diary of John Milward*, pp. 83–84; *C.J.* 8: 692; Cobbett, *Parliamentary History* 4: 363.

[109]Bodleian Library (Oxford University), Carte Manuscripts 35, ff. 649–50.

[110]Clarendon described Tomkins as a man who was used by others in the House to initiate proceedings: Edward Hyde (first earl of Clarendon), *The History of the Rebellion and Civil Wars in England . . . : also His Life Written by Himself* (Oxford, 1843), p. 1238. Pepys remarked that Tomkins made "many mad motions" in the House: Wheatley, *The Diary of Samuel Pepys* 3: 155.

[111]Bodleian Library, Carte Manuscripts 35, ff. 649–50.

[112]Wheatley, *The Diary of Samuel Pepys* 7: 39, 45, 50.

disdain and dislike of the military be ignored.[113] But the resolution was, more probably, a symbolic gesture against the most visible and potentially most dangerous instrument of a government whose policies and practices members of the House increasingly distrusted and disliked. Without suggesting the existence of a full-blown "country party" in July 1667, one may still suggest that the attack on the army reflected "country" politics and mentality.[114] There was no more effective way to convey to Charles their distrust and disapprobation than to petition him to disband soldiers he had raised in an emergency. There was symbolism in the attack in 1667, just as there had been in the controversy over the militia in 1641-42 and would be again in later decades of the seventeenth century.

On July 29, Charles met Parliament in the afternoon, it having been arranged that the speaker should not come to the House of Commons in the morning in order to avoid any further action which would embarrass the court.[115] The king responded directly to the resolution of July 25. To the modern reader, it seems a disarming speech, but contemporaries were said to have found it not "pleasing . . . at all."[116] Charles asked what "one thing he had done since his coming into England to persuade any sober person that he did intend to govern by a Standing Army." He observed that he was "more an Englishman than so." He recalled that last year he had raised some troops which had been disbanded as soon as the season permitted. He remarked that surely he had waited long enough this year—he hadn't issued any commissions at all until after the enemy had done its damage. He defended the new soldiers by saying that they themselves would be glad to disband. Assuring members that the disbandment would take place, Charles prorogued Parliament until October 1667.

When Parliament reconvened, its fury, despite the steady disbandment of the troops raised in June,[117] was still unspent. Disbanding of the king's Guards, it was reported, was the goal of some critics of

[113]See for example, Charles Daves, ed., *Samuel Butler 1612-1680, Characters* (Cleveland and London, 1970), pp. 313-14: "A Soldier."

[114]The term "Country Party" was first used in the fall session in 1667: see Clayton Roberts, *The Growth of Responsible Government in Stuart England* (Cambridge, 1966), p. 166.

[115]Wheatley, *The Diary of Samuel Pepys* 7: 45; cf. Bodleian Library, Carte Manuscripts, 35, ff. 649-50.

[116]Wheatley, *The Diary of Samuel Pepys* 7: 44; Cobbett, *Parliamentary History* 4: 364; see Robbins, *The Diary of John Milward*, p. 84, for the speech.

[117]See *C.S.P.D., 1667*, pp. 363-4, 390, 393, 396, 399, 426, 434, 471, 472, 475, 477, 505, 527, for progress of the disbanding.

the government.[118] The main goal, however, was to get rid of Edward Hyde, now earl of Clarendon, the lord chancellor, whose policies, administration, and personality had cost him the confidence of Charles and the king's other chief advisors, and who was the target of a group of men in Parliament who sought to advance their own interests by his downfall.[119] The first article against Clarendon on his impeachment was the charge that he advised the king to govern by a standing army. Placing that charge first suggests that Clarendon's enemies believed that it would carry great weight, enough to support an accusation of high treason.[120] A paper entitled "Authorities To Prove the First Article Treason" was drafted by someone prominently involved in the impeachment proceedings.[121] The debate in Parliament on Article I was prolonged.[122] But respect for law finally muted hysteria, and Article one was defeated by a vote of 172-to-103.[123]

This was the first time, but not the last, that the prejudice against standing armies was used as a smear tactic to destroy a political enemy. Clarendon described the charge as "the most unpopular and ungracious Reproach that any Man could lie under."[124] He denied unequivocally that he favored military rule and pointed to the fact that the soldiers had always regarded him as their enemy.[125] A prominent Presbyterian confirmed this, declaring that Clarendon had opposed the rule of the army in England.[126] The duke of York reported that Charles had admitted to him that Clarendon had never advised ruling by an army.[127] It was said that James had shamed his brother into denying publicly that there was any substance to the standing army charge.[128]

[118]Clarke, *Life of James II* 1: 426 refers to a conversation the earl of Northumberland had with both Charles and the duke of York.

[119]For an account of Clarendon's impeachment, see Roberts, *The Growth of Responsible Government in Stuart England*, pp. 155-73.

[120]*Ibid.*, p. 166. A draft of the Heads of Particulars against the earl of Clarendon dated October 26, 1667, listed the standing army charge as the seventh article, not the first. See Bodleian Library, Carte Manuscripts, 35, ff. 800-1.

[121]See B.M., Stowe Manuscripts 425, ff. 86-98, referred to by Roberts, *The Growth of Responsible Government in Stuart England*, p. 166, n. 1. Fourteenth-century authorities are listed but no conclusions are drawn.

[122]One lasted "eight hours." Hyde, *Continuation of His Life*, p. 449.

[123]Grey, *Debates* 1: 32.

[124]Hyde, *Continuation of His Life*, p. 449.

[125]*Ibid.*, pp. 449, 481.

[126]Richard Baxter, *Reliquiae Baxterianae* (1696), part 3, p. 20, quoted in Roberts, *The Growth of Responsible Government in Stuart England*, p. 158.

[127]Macpherson, ed., *Original Papers . . . Life of James II* 1: 39.

[128]Dennis T. Witcombe, *Charles II and the Cavalier House of Commons 1663-1674* (Manchester, England), p. 68.

Though the early years of the Restoration were relatively quiet with respect to the standing army controversy, the period was important in the evolution of the standing army issue. Legislation in 1660 gave some legal basis to professional soldiers serving the crown so long as the king paid them, and laws in 1661–63 settled the constitutional position of the militia under royal command. These laws provided the framework within which the issue was debated in subsequent years. In the 1660s, nothing new was added to the reasons why standing armies should be feared and no major tracts were written. What was new was the deliberate exploitation of the prejudice against standing armies for partisan political advantage.

The memory of Cromwell's military government played a part in the antimilitarism expressed. Some men saw a close affinity between Charles's goals for the militia and Cromwell's new militia of 1656 and offered criticism in those terms. Tracts written by Fabian Philipps specifically referred to the Cromwellian experience, as did some men in debates on the disbanding of the army. But at no time were the arguments against the military expressed in the detail or with the theoretical and constitutional sophistication that they had been during the Interregnum.

CHAPTER VI

PRINCIPLE AND PROPAGANDA
IN THE 1670s

The cry "No Standing Armies" reappeared in the 1670s. Reflecting a distrust of Charles II's foreign and domestic policies along with a genuine fear of soldiers, the criticism of the troops began in the spring of 1673, became increasingly insistent in 1674, threaded through parliamentary debates in 1675 and 1677, and reached the point of parliamentary hysteria in 1678 and 1679. These attacks were a measure of the estrangement between Charles II and his supporters, who were more firmly organized as the Tory Party during this decade, and a growing number of men in Parliament, who by 1673 formed an identifiable "Country Party" and became by 1678 the "first Whigs." The standing army issue was part of the ammunition used by the "country interest" and reflected the distrust of the court felt by men who did not hold office. The question was exploited as a propaganda weapon and a parliamentary tactic to undermine confidence in the court, smear royal ministers, and discredit foreign and domestic policies. At the same time, opposition to standing armies reflected a Whig philosophy of government which advocated a restricted monarchy and a powerful Parliament—that is, a "tempered" version of republicanism and parliamentarianism. Spokesmen for the opposition assumed the leadership in condemning the king's armed forces, but they were joined by men who on other matters supported the court.

There was little theoretical speculation about the army in the press during this decade, but the issue did appear in a handful of tracts, among them *A Letter from a Person of Quality* and *A Letter from a Parliament Man to His Friend*, printed in the fall of 1675, Andrew Marvell's *An Account of the Growth of Popery and Arbitrary Government* (1677), and Henry Neville's *Plato Redivivus* (1681). The real battle over the question of standing armies was fought primarily in parliamentary debates.

There were thirty-seven members of the House of Commons, of 513, who led the opposition in the 1670s to Charles II's armed forces and argued for a remodeled, nonprofessional militia as the land defense of the nation. The most prominent spokesmen were Colonel John Birch, Sir Thomas Clarges, Sir Thomas Lee, Sir Henry Powle, and William Sacheverell. Other notable speakers were Sir William Coventry,[1] William Garroway, Sir Thomas Littleton,[2] Lord William Russell, and Sir William Williams.[3] A small minority, they resisted Charles II's enlarged army and the policies associated with it for the entire decade and often managed to carry resolutions against the army by unanimous vote. Their success can be attributed in part to their great oratorical ability and persuasiveness. Powle and Littleton were said to manage the House with the "greatest dexterity." A contemporary thought Birch was the "best speaker to carry a popular assembly before him that he had ever known," while Sir William Coventry was regarded as a "wise and witty gentleman," the "best speaker in the House."[4] These men were also widely read,[5] skilled in the law, hardworking, and well prepared to take charge of parliamentary matters. They introduced motions about the army and the militia, served on committees, reported from committees to the House, initiated debates, carried addresses to the House of Lords, and exploited opportunities to keep the standing army issue before the Parliament and to connect it, sometimes tenuously, with some other issue that was being discussed.

[1]The brother of Sir Henry Coventry, Charles's secretary of state.

[2]The second baronet and the father of the Sir Thomas Littleton who supported King William's project for a large army in 1697–99.

[3]In the parliamentary sessions during the decade there were at least forty significant debates on standing armies. Powle made 27 major speeches against standing armies, Birch 19, Lee 18, Sacheverell 16, and Clarges 15. Sir John Hotham, Sir Edward Vaughan, and John Mallet should also be mentioned along with the Presbyterians Hugh Boscawen and John Swynfen as important spokesmen. (William Russell received the courtesy title of Lord Russell in 1678.)   [4]See *D.N.B.* articles.

[5]For one example, William Garroway was described as a "walking library." See unpublished draft biography of Garroway at the History of Parliament Trust.

All had lived as young adults through the Interregnum period.[6] The memory of that experience was direct and personal and must have been a factor in their apprehension over Charles's army. Cromwell's army, however, was seldom mentioned in the debates. This may have reflected the feeling that such knowledge was too commonplace to warrant mention and that it was not an effective tactic to remind members of a recent experience through which almost all of them had lived. Further, these spokesmen delighted in classical and historical allusions, which came readily from their reading, and examples were adduced from the ancient world and England's medieval past. Or, they turned to the contemporary scene, especially to events in France, to buttress their arguments against professional soldiers. Even more to the point, a reference to Cromwell's army could have been regarded as a violation of the act of Indemnity, which was supposed to have forgiven everything (except the execution of the king) that had happened during the Civil Wars and Interregnum. When Tories brought up those troubled years, they were called to order. Finally, a reference to Cromwell's army would have been politically rude and unwise in an assembly containing men who were themselves former Cromwellians or connected with old Cromwellians. But opponents of the army surely believed that the same kind of dangers that flowed from Cromwell's army would flow from Charles's military forces. Both armies had to be paid, housed, and disciplined, and both were feared as instruments of tyranny and corruption in the hands of the executive.[7]

Some of the men had taken part in earlier attacks on standing armies. Birch had argued in 1660 for disbanding the Cromwellian forces and had chaired the committee for disbanding the army. Hugh Boscawen had served on that committee, while Sir Thomas Meres reported from the committee that brought in the Militia Bill of 1663. Sir Thomas Littleton and William Garroway had participated in the debate in July 1667 in which the army raised for the Second Dutch War was attacked. Thus, there were some men who had been wary of Charles's army from its very inception and were easily alarmed when it was enlarged in the 1670s.

[6]Most of the leading opponents of the army were in their forties. For example, in 1675 Birch was 59, Coventry 47, Powle 45, Lee 40, Sacheverell 37, and Williams 41.

[7]For a different view, see Pocock, "Machiavelli, Harrington and English Political Ideologies," pp. 562-63.

Some of these spokesmen served as deputy-lieutenants or officers in their county militia force.[8] The local militia which their class controlled was an acceptable military force, while a standing army threatened not only law, liberty, and Parliament but also their social status and power in the county. Their plea to depend upon the militia was made in an assembly filled with men who also served in the militia. In the fall session of 1678, it has been calculated that 337 of the members were either deputy-lieutenants or militia officers.[9] These facts help to explain why votes on the issue could often be unanimous.

The names of the major opponents of the standing army read like a roster of the leadership of the "Country Party," or as it was called by the end of the 1670s, the Whig Party. When Shaftesbury evaluated the membership of the newly elected House of Commons in the spring of 1679, all the major spokesmen against the army, except Sir William Coventry, were marked OW—meaning Old (experienced) and Worthy (men on whom he could count).[10] This identification of the opposition to standing armies with the leadership of the Country Party refutes the suggestion sometimes made that the antiarmy attitude was especially characteristic of the Tory party and Tory assumptions. It is true that in the eighteenth century, antiarmy prejudice migrated to the Tory party, but as has been shown, its origins were heavily indebted to republican and libertarian traditions. In the 1670s, it was the "country"-Whig interest which exploited the fear for both partisan and ideological reasons. In their hands, the fear was shaped into a propaganda weapon and used as a parliamentary tactic to discredit the king, his ministers, and his policies.

Criticism of a standing army in the parliamentary sessions of 1673 and 1674 was precipitated by the Third Dutch War (1672-74), the several domestic policies associated with it, and the presence in England of newly raised levies. Fought in alliance with Catholic France against Protestant Holland, the war became increasingly unpopular with "country" members who suspected the court of in-

---

[8]For example, Birch, Garroway, Hotham, Lee, Meres, Swynfin, Vaughan, and Williams.

[9]John C. R. Childs made this calculation, at my request, using the unpublished materials in the files at the History of Parliament Trust and his own notes. He counted 241 deputy-lieutenants and 96 militia officers.

[10]J. R. Jones, "Shaftesbury's Worthy Men," *B.I.H.R.* 30 (1957): 232-41.

clining toward Catholicism and absolutism. The government's domestic policies, notably, the Stop at the Exchequer in January 1672,[11] which in effect financed the war without recourse to Parliament and in the process ruined many bankers, and the Declaration of Indulgence in March, which granted toleration to dissenters and Catholics and opened the whole question of the king's suspending and dispensing power, could be perceived as evidence of that inclination. Distrust of Charles II's political and religious intentions was reflected in the distrust of the soldiers he raised[12] for the war.

The king's handling of troops who were left in England because of the naval prowess[13] of the Dutch provided specific grounds for anxiety and criticism. To feed and house the soldiers Charles II employed the traditional expedient of quartering the men in inns and public houses and, as necessary, in private houses. This he publicly ordered in 1672. Lacking barracks, Charles, as all other kings before him, had no alternative. The reaction to the policy was traditionally hostile, although there was no widespread popular outrage as there had been, for example, in 1628.[14] Some members of Parliament, however, complained bitterly about billeting and used it as evidence of a design to impose an absolute government in England.

To strengthen procedures for disciplining the soldiers, Charles issued a code of "Orders and Articles of War" in 1672.[15] The code set out regulations for courts-martial, authorized the use of the death penalty, and imposed on all soldiers oaths of allegiance to the king and of obedience to military officers. Although these military orders were printed in the summer of 1673, they were never used for soldiers

[11]William A. Shaw, *Calendar of Treasury Books, 1669–72*, especially pp. xxxvii–lxvii; Ogg, *England in the Reign of Charles II* 2: 448–49.

[12]A modern study of the methods Charles used to raise the army, the specific numbers added to the guards or formed into other regiments, and the numbers in the troops, companies, and regiments is needed. The difficulties posed by such a task are outlined in Dalton, *English Army Lists* 1: introduction. For examples of the steps Charles took, see *C.S.P.D., 1671–1672*, pp. 33, 152, 154, 174, 299, 344, 557. W. D. Christie, ed., *Letters Addressed from London to Sir Joseph Williamson* (London [Camden Society], 1874), 1: 116, indicates that fourteen thousand men were raised by the summer of 1672.

[13]See Ogg, *England in the Reign of Charles II* 1: 358–61, 364; Jones, *Britain and Europe in the Seventeenth Century*, pp. 62–63.

[14]Hampshire seems to have experienced the most acute difficulties, but it is not clear why. Further study of the local situation there and the general question of billeting in the decade is needed. For example of protest see *C.S.P.D., 1673*, p. 136.

[15]Thomson, *A Constitutional History* 4: 156, points out that the code was based on an earlier code issued by Parliament during the Civil War.

on English soil.[16] The reason was that officers feared that Parliament might "call them to question for it."[17] Members of Parliament were reported to be disturbed over the oath of allegiance and obedience, and to disapprove of the use of martial law and the death penalty.[18]

Next, Charles issued on December 4, 1672, a "Proclamation for prevention of disorders from the newly raised soldiers quartered till they are required."[19] The proclamation was illegal because the procedure it outlined by-passed the normal common law process,[20] not because it imposed martial law. It was objected to by Parliamentarians, however, on the grounds that it introduced martial law and was used as proof of a royal design to impose absolutism. There is no evidence to show the popular reaction to the proclamation. In view of the war and the lack of system in providing discipline for the army, it would seem that parliamentary criticism of this proclamation was in part politically inspired.

Such considerations as these, rather than episodes in which the soldiers were turned against subjects or against Parliament, provoked rumors in the fall and spring of 1672–73 that the troops were "designed to control law and property."[21] Both Charles and his lord chancellor, Shaftesbury, took the rumors seriously enough to mention them in their speeches opening Parliament on February 5, 1673. Both boldly announced that, the rumors notwithstanding, more regiments had been raised. From the beginning of the session, members of the House of Commons lost no opportunity to stress the danger of a standing army. Spokesmen in the debate on the repeal of the Declaration of Indulgence tenuously linked the Declaration and a standing army.[22] In the debate on grievances, the army was central. The proclamation of December 4 some said introduced martial law. The evils of quartering were recited. Others complained that soldiers

---

[16]John C. R. Childs called my attention to the fact that the military orders were not implemented and supplied the references in notes 17 and 18.

[17]Christie, *Letters . . . to . . . Williamson* 1: 158.

[18]*Ibid.*, pp. 116–17; E. M. Thompson, ed., *Letters addressed to Christopher, 1st Viscount Hatton, 1601–1704* (London [Camden Society], 1878), 1: 111.

[19]Robert Steele, ed., *Tudor and Stuart Proclamations 1485–1714* (Oxford, 1910), 1: 3576; *C.S.P.D., 1672–1673*, pp. 243–44.

[20]Thomson, *A Constitutional History* 4: 157.

[21]Cobbett, *Parliamentary History* 4: 503, 506. Also *C.S.P.V., 1673–1675*, pp. 2, 9–10, 23; and C. H. Josten, ed., *Elias Ashmole (1617–1692). His Autobiographical and Historical Notes, His Correspondence and Other Contemporary Sources Relating to His Life and Work* (Oxford, 1966), 4: 1310, 1311; Burnet, *History of My Own Time* 2: 1–4.

[22]Grey, *Debates* 2: 17.

had been sent from Scotland. Lee stressed the adverse economic consequences of an army which siphoned off manpower, thereby reducing the number of available workers and raising the wages of servants.[23] Despite the efforts of supporters of the king, Sir John Duncombe and the secretary of state, Henry Coventry, to defend the policies of the court, the Proclamation of December 1672 was listed as a grievance. The diarist, Sir Edward Dering, declared that the critics of the king exaggerated the danger of the proclamation and suggested that they attacked it as a way of discrediting the king.[24]

In response to the Commons's Address on Grievances, Charles promised that before they met again he would take care that no man should have any reason to complain.[25] Dissatisfied by this reply, on March 28 some members urged that the Address on Grievances and the king's reply be printed. The motion is pertinent for two reasons: first, it suggested a recognition of the political capital to be won from the criticism of the army. Proponents argued that printing of the address would help "end many disputes in the country about quartering of soldiers."[26] Second, the vote on the motion was exactly even, 105 to 105, which suggests that the king's friends possessed greater strength than the account of the debate might indicate. The motion was defeated by the speaker's vote, and the king adjourned Parliament that same day to October 20, 1673.[27]

Over the summer of 1673, the attitude towards Charles's army stiffened as a result of the continued presence in England of soldiers that had been raised to fight in the Third Dutch War. Evidence shows that the English government intended to send the soldiers to the continent.[28] The preparations, which included a general muster of the army at Blackheath in the spring and summer of 1673, however, played an important part in firming public opinion against the soldiers. It is not difficult to understand why a large number[29] of poorly

---

[23]*Ibid.*, pp. 131–32.

[24]B. D. Henning, ed., *The Parliamentary Diary of Edward Dering* (New Haven, 1940), pp. 142, 144.

[25]Grey, *Debates* 2: 163; *C.J.* 9: 276.   [26]Grey, *Debates* 2: 175–77, for the debate.

[27]*Ibid.*, p. 177; *C.J.* 9: 281. The Licensing Act put legal obstacles in the way of printing the address but is not enough alone to explain the vote: Ogg, *History of England in the Reign of Charles II* 1: 370.

[28]*C.S.P.D.*, *1673*, for example, pp. 30, 33, 35, 37, 43–44, 122, 128, 129, 197, 260, 261, 287, 293. Sir Arthur Bryant, ed., *The Letters, Speeches and Declarations of King Charles II* (New York, 1968), p. 265.

[29]Estimates of the number of soldiers at Blackheath vary. Twelve thousand infantry were expected. *C.S.P.D.*, *1673*, p. 353, preface, p. xiii and references cited there; *C.S.P.D.*, *1672–1673*, p. 420; Christie, *Letters . . . to . . . Williamson* 1: 116.

disciplined troops at Blackheath, only five miles or so southeast of London, should have been frightening. Although it was freely speculated that the army would be turned against English subjects, the camp became a kind of tourist attraction.[30] In fact, the general muster was held as planned, and on July 14, the army decamped. Although the soldiers had not been at Blackheath a long time, their presence had undermined confidence in Charles's intentions. From Blackheath, the army, now under the command of Count de Schomberg,[31] the recently appointed captain-general of all the land forces, was sent to Yarmouth to await an opportunity to be transported to the continent. The opportunity never came. On August 11, the battle of Texel revealed the failure of the combined English and French fleets to establish command of the seas and "marked the end of attempts to land troops" on the continent.[32] Three weeks later the government ordered the camp at Yarmouth dismantled, the numbers of men in the regiments reduced, and the soldiers sent into winter quarters. There is no evidence of wanton destructiveness by the troops.

When Parliament met on October 20, 1673, however, the army was criticized in more vehement terms than those used before.[33] The debate on the king's request for supplies was filled with "many digressions" about grievances, especially the standing army. Sir John Hotham implied that the army had no respect for Parliament. The number of Catholics among the troops was objected to, and critics charged that musters were omitted so that Papists might be concealed. Members were warned that they and the Peers might be subject to pressing, so flagrantly had statutes against pressing been violated. Yet it was acknowledged that the king had the right to raise an army so long as he paid it. In this session, that right was not challenged; it was agreed that the most effective tactic to force a change in policy was to withhold supply, and further supply was refused until the assessment granted the previous session had ex-

---

[30]Christie, *Letters . . . to . . . Williamson* 1: 84; *C.S.P.V., 1673–1675*, p. 79; de Beer, *The Diary of John Evelyn* 4: 13, 15; *C.S.P.D., 1673*, pp. 356, 425, where it is reported that commemorative brass sculptures were cast.

[31]The appointment of Schomberg, who had served in the French army, was deeply resented by xenophobic members of the House of Commons. Schomberg's parentage was thoroughly confused, deliberately or otherwise, by the king's critics. His mother was English, his father German.

[32]Ogg, *History of England in the Reign of Charles II* 1: 376.

[33]A kind of hysteria at the opening of the session is suggested by the story that a fire ball had been planted under the speaker's chair. Thompson, *Letters Addressed to . . . Hatton* 1: 118.

pired and the nation secured against the dangers from popery and popish counsels.[34]

When the debate on grievances took place three days later, the major issue again was the army.[35] There is evidence that the opposition planned this debate to exploit the antistanding army sentiment which so many members felt. For example, Colonel Birch introduced a bill for the naturalization of foreigners, which he argued would help combat the problem of underpopulation in England. At this, Sir Thomas Meres said that he too wanted to increase the number of employable people, not by bringing in foreigners, but by avoiding policies such as maintaining a standing army that made the people at hand "useless and unprofitable by bringing them up in lewd and disorderly courses."[36] He went on to urge that the army, which he termed "a legion," presumably to bring to mind the Roman legions that overran the ancient government, should be voted a grievance.[37] The unlikely connection between naturalization of foreigners to deal with the problem of underpopulation and the danger of a standing army suggests prior preparation and recognition of the propaganda implicit in the antistanding army sentiment. Further support of this point is that the arguments against the army were reiterated by so many speakers in extreme terms.[38] Fear of what the soldiers might do in the future was freely projected. The present suffering of the country was lamented in extravagant terms. Critics urged that the nation depend upon the navy and militia which, it was confidently asserted, "will defend us and never conquer us." This was the first time in the 1670s, it should be noted, that the militia was mentioned as a counterweight to the army.[39]

Still further, the term, "standing army," with all the pejorative overtones it carried from fifteen years or more of negative use, was deliberately sprinkled throughout the debate. At the end of the debates a resolution was passed which read, "that *the* Standing Army is a grievance."[40] At the insistence of William Sacheverell, the article "the" was substituted for "a" in that resolution. Dering pointed out, it

---

[34]*C.J.* 9: 285; Henning, *Diary of Edward Dering*, p. 158. For the debate, Grey, *Debates* 2: 197-214.

[35]See Henning, *Diary of Edward Dering*, p. 159, where other grievances are noted. Grey's account mentions only the criticism of the army.

[36]*Ibid.*, pp. 159-60.   [37]Grey, *Debates* 2: 216.

[38]A contemporary reported that the complaints against the army were so extreme and military men so maligned that "any person who regarded his honour" would refuse to serve in the army. See Christie, *Letters . . . to . . . Williamson* 2:59.

[39]For the debate see Grey, *Debates* 2: 216, 218-21.   [40]*C.J.* 9: 286; italics supplied.

is "easy to observe some difference in those words."[41] A fortnight later, another contemporary remarked upon the resolution, noticing that Parliament "call[s]" the forces a standing army.[42]

This wordplay was not lost upon the defenders of the court. Secretary Coventry led the rebuttal, demanding that the House define the terms "what is an Army" and what "a Standing Army" and inquiring with some sarcasm why the regiments should be called a "legion," a word which referred to a Roman band of two thousand men. Arguing that the troops could not reasonably be called a standing army, he pointed out that the army was raised for a purpose, the war with the Dutch. Regiments raised for a war, he maintained, could not rightly be described as a "standing army." Further, he asserted that for a thing to be a grievance, it had to be against law. No one, he went on, could "deny but raising of soldiers was in the king's power when he thought fit." As for the charge about martial law, Coventry acidly observed that the speaker who raised objections did not know what he was talking about.[43]

The outcome of the debate on grievances was an address to the king to tell him "in what manner" the army was a grievance. Drafted by Powle, Meres, Birch, and others, the address enraged Charles and was partly responsible for his decision to prorogue Parliament on December 4.[44]

Political observers predicted that when Parliament reconvened, members would have moderated their views.[45] They were wrong. On January 7, 1674, Charles opened a very full Parliament,[46] and both he and Heneage Finch, now his lord-keeper, attempted to placate fears and secure supply. Finch reviewed all that had been done to remove the fear of an army, asserting that the army had been drastically reduced and unruly soldiers "rigorously" punished.[47]

The disclaimers and explanations failed to mollify Parliament. The leaders of the "Country Party" exploited the antistanding army senti-

---

[41]Henning, *Diary of Edward Dering*, p. 161.

[42]Christie, *Letters . . . to . . . Williamson* 2: 71.

[43]Grey, *Debates* 2: 216; Henning, *Diary of Edward Dering*, p. 160. Among other men who supported the court in much the same terms were Sir Robert Howard, Sir Robert Carr, and Sir Richard Temple. Grey, *Debates* 2: 218, 220, 221-22. For comment on the court's defense, see Osmund Airy, ed., *Essex Papers*, (London [Printed for the Camden Society], 1890), 1: 132; Christie, *Letters . . . to . . . Williamson* 2: 65, 131.

[44]Grey, *Debates* 2: 222; *C.J.*, 9: 286; cf. *L.J.* 12: 593, where the text of the king's speech proroguing Parliament is somewhat different but the sense is the same.

[45]Christie, *Letters . . . to . . . Williamson* 2: 67, 68, 69-71, 75, 76, 79, 82, 83, 93, 94, 95, 101.

[46]*Ibid.*, p. 108; cf. Airy, *Essex Papers* 1: 161.   [47]*C.J.* 9: 286-87.

ment to identify the king and his ministers with Catholicism, French influence, and arbitrary power. Upon hearing of the dangers the country faced from Catholic plots, members asked Charles to order the militia of London, Westminster, and Middlesex be made ready at an hour's warning and the militias of other areas at a day's warning.[48] The one man who had the temerity to say the king's Guards were sufficient to protect the Parliament and court was "shouted down."[49] Not satisfied with calling upon the militia, some members argued that the way to redress grievances was to remove the king's "evil councillors."[50] The next week three of the king's chief ministers, John Maitland, duke of Lauderdale, the lord high commissioner of Scotland; George Villiers, duke of Buckingham, a member of the Privy Council without major office, whose influence was receding; and Henry Bennet, earl of Arlington, secretary of state for foreign affairs, Southern province, were interrogated by the House. For each case the antiarmy sentiment was prominent in the interrogation. The central reason for the attack on Lauderdale was the conviction that he had designed the Scottish Militia Act of 1669 to put twenty-two thousand Scottish militia at Charles's disposal to march anywhere he pleased, including England.[51] The fact that the Militia Act of 1669 was based upon an earlier act passed before Lauderdale became commissioner in Scotland and contained nothing new about the king's prerogative power to send the Scottish militia to any part of his kingdom, and the fact that the militia in Scotland was never mustered, did not diminish the force of the charge. The suspicion that Lauderdale had urged Charles to rely upon the Scottish militia to support his policies prevailed, and the address for Lauderdale's removal was carried unanimously.[52]

The duke of Buckingham was accused of appointing popish officers to his own regiments, of pressing men in Yorkshire, and of advising that a "Frenchman," i.e., Schomberg (in vain did Secretary Coventry try to straighten out members on Schomberg's parentage) be appointed general of the army. Buckingham was asked who had advised bringing the army to London to overawe the Parliament, a

---

[48]*Ibid.*, p. 292; *L.J.* 12: 601, 604-5; see K. H. D. Haley, *The First Earl of Shaftesbury* (Oxford, 1968), pp. 355-56.

[49]Haley, *Shaftesbury*, p. 356; *C.S.P.V., 1673-1675*, pp. 199-201.

[50]Grey, *Debates* 2: 233.

[51]*Ibid.*, pp. 237-40, 242; Cobbett, *Parliamentary History* 4: 626-30.

[52]Roberts, *The Growth of Responsible Government in Stuart England*, pp. 189-90 and 190, n. 1; William C. Mackenzie, *The Life and Times of John Maitland, Duke of Lauderdale, 1616-1692* (London, 1923), pp. 301, 302.

question which patently assumed as fact that the army had been brought to London for that purpose. His defense was to incriminate Arlington, a tactic which failed to move members, and an address to remove Buckingham was passed 142 to 124.[53]

Arlington was next, and the question of his connection with the standing army was of major importance, too. He was charged with advising the king to govern by an army. To this, Arlington replied in terms that must have helped soften the animosity towards him: "I wholly abominate it, and am not so vain as to think this great nation can be awed by 20,000 men." He denied that the matter was ever discussed in council meetings and asserted that he was "content to be guilty of all I am accused of, if this one thing be proved." He was asked by whose advice the army was raised and Papists appointed to commands. He replied that the army was raised because of the war and Papists were commissioned because they were believed to be skillful. To the question of who advised that the army overawe the Parliament, he responded that he could say "nothing" to that.[54] The charge of favoring a standing army, on which Arlington said he was willing to stand or fall, could not be proved against him, and for several reasons, it was resolved not to ask the king for his removal.[55]

The wrath of the Parliament against standing armies was not exhausted by these steps. On February 7, in a Committee of the Whole, Sir John Hotham opened debate with the assertion that the army was the root of all the grievances of the nation and urged his colleagues to demand that all the forces be disbanded.[56] A "very Long debate"[57] ensued because the question of the royal Guards was raised for the first time since 1663. There was clear agreement on declaring the newly raised regiments a grievance but no unanimity on whether the Guards should be disbanded as well. A small number of members argued for including the Guards. It was declared that the militia could serve as the king's Guards by turns. Another speaker urged that the Guards be defined, saying that if the guards of the French king were the model, then a force of sixteen thousand men might be intended.[58] But men who were known to be adamantly opposed to the

[53]Grey, *Debates* 2: 245, 259-60, 262-63; 385, 399; *C.J.* 9: 293.

[54]*C.S.P.D., 1673-1675*, pp. 103-6; Grey, *Debates* 2: 275-88.

[55]Grey, *Debates* 2: 303-17, 318-29; *C.J.* 9: 296; cf. Folger Manuscripts, Newdigate Newsletters, L.C. 4, where the majority in favor of Arlington is given as thirty-six.

[56]Grey, *Debates* 2: 390-91; Christie, *Letters . . . to . . . Williamson* 2: 144.

[57]Folger Manuscripts, Newdigate Newsletters, L.C. 13.

[58]For these comments, Grey, *Debates* 2: 392, 395, 397, 398.

idea of a standing army retreated before the proposition of removing the Guards as well, and they were not included in the Address on Grievances which begged the king to disband all troops that had been raised since January 1, 1663.[59] But the sharp criticism of the Guards, who had been generally accepted, testified to the decay of faith in the king. The debate about the Guards, however, never addressed the central question, the king's right to raise them without the approval of Parliament. Radical though some members were, they were not prepared in 1674 to examine the issue in terms that touched the king's military prerogative.

Despite Charles's gracious response to the Address on Grievances and his promise to reduce the forces to less than their size in 1663, some members remained disgruntled.[60] In the House of Lords, Shaftesbury was preparing a proposal to disband the duke of York's regiment.[61] To the surpise, dismay, and fear of members,[62] however, the king prorogued Parliament on February 24. He would not recall it until April 1675. Although Charles kept Lauderdale as his commissioner in Scotland and ignored the criticism of his Guards, he reduced the newly raised regiments and fixed the military establishment at just under six thousand men.[63] However small compared to continental armies, this establishment was nearly twice the size of troops in 1663. It was large enough to provoke continued resentment and fear. The king's critics had learned during these sessions how that resentment and fear could be exploited to discredit the king, his ministers, and his policies.

The year 1675 was of special importance in the history of the standing army issue.[64] Although there was only a small military establishment, fear of Charles's armed forces pervaded the debates in the spring and fall sessions of Parliament. Two circumstances nourished this anxiety: one was that Charles II had allowed an English contingent of soldiers to serve abroad in the pay of Louis XIV, and the second was the continued presence of the duke of Lauderdale in Scotland and

---

[59]*C.J.* 9: 305; Grey, *Debates* 2: 399.

[60]*C.J.* 9: 307; Folger Manuscripts, Newdigate Newsletters, L.C. 12, 14, 16, 19; Christie, *Letters . . . to . . . Williamson* 2: 150.

[61]Macpherson, *Original Papers, Containing the Secret History of Great Britain* 1: 72.

[62]Airy, *Essex Papers* 1: 179–80; Christie, *Letters . . . to . . . Williamson* 2: 154–55.

[63]*C.S.P.D., 1673–1675*, p. 494; Airy, *Essex Papers* 1: 177; Folger Manuscripts, Newdigate Newsletters, February 26, 1674, L.C. 22.

[64]But not, I think, because it marked the "birth" of the antistanding army ideology. For that view, see Pocock, "Machiavelli, Harrington and English Political Ideologies," p. 560.

the persistent apprehension that the Scottish militia would be used against England. This genuine fear of armies was exploited by the first earl of Shaftesbury and his friends in both Houses throughout the year as a parliamentary tactic to help gain certain partisan political ends. The issue of standing armies helped to bind together the Country Party in opposition to the new strength of the court and the Tory party, which had been built up through the financial wizardry and the patronage of Thomas Osborne, earl of Danby.[65]

Anxiety over the implications of English soldiers serving in the French army was very real. Just a week after Parliament opened, the first of a series of addresses demanding the recall of such soldiers was presented on April 21 to Charles II.[66] The petition was based on the argument that Louis XIV's aim was to dominate the Western world, which, if achieved, would have disastrous effects on England economically, diplomatically, and politically. It was intolerable for ten thousand Englishmen to be kept abroad to threaten English liberties and to aid the French menace.[67] Although the right of Parliament to participate in foreign or military policy was not specifically claimed, more than one member suggested that the House was competent to advise the crown in foreign and military affairs and that its advice should be heeded.[68] It is plain that the petition, by implying a restriction on the king's right to determine where soldiers could serve, invaded the royal prerogative.

A struggle between king and Parliament over the petition followed. On the grounds that his honor would be tarnished and peace endangered, Charles refused on May 8 to recall what he termed the "inconsiderable" number of English soldiers who had been in the French service since before the Treaty of Westminster. He did, however, agree to issue a proclamation to "forbid and hinder" any more men from going over.[69] Parliament was not satisfied, and during May, several lengthy and emotional debates ensued.[70] The opposition persisted in urging Charles to issue a "further and fuller Proclamation." Not until the prorogation on June 9 did these efforts end.

---

[65]The growth of the Tory Party and the work of Thomas Osborne, created earl of Danby in June 1674, may be followed in Feiling, *History of the Tory Party*, especially chapter 6, and Browning, *Thomas Osborne* 1: 109, 118–19, 132, 146–50, 166–77. For the tighter organization of the Country Party and firmer leadership of Shaftesbury, see Haley, *Shaftesbury*, pp. 366–71.

[66]*C.J.* 9: 321.

[67]Grey, *Debates* 3: 3–8. Ten thousand was the number of men given by the opposition. Spokesmen for the court never admitted so many soldiers were abroad.

[68]*Ibid.*, pp. 4, 5, 6, 7.　[69]*C.J.* 9: 333; Grey, *Debates* 3: 115–16.

[70]Grey, *Debates* 3: 128–29, 133, 136, 139.

Equally alarming to members of Parliament were the alleged threat posed by the Scottish militia and the fact that the duke of Lauderdale remained lord high commissioner in Scotland. On April 23, the House of Commons implored Charles to remove the duke of Lauderdale for the reasons they had cited previously. Members complained that Lauderdale had said in council that the king's edicts had the force of law and charged that he was "principally" responsible for the Scottish Militia Acts which made England "liable to be invaded." Dr. Gilbert Burnet, Lauderdale's former chaplain, was called in to answer questions, and he confirmed the duke's arbitrary notions.[71] On May 7, the king rejected the House's petition to remove his minister, but the opposition persisted until the end of the session in the attempt to get rid of Lauderdale.[72]

In the meantime in the House of Lords, Shaftesbury and his friends were using the menace of standing armies in speeches and tracts to oppose the Anglican Test.[73] Introduced on April 15 in the House of Lords, the Anglican Test was designed by Danby to strengthen the position of the court party by limiting office power to Anglicans. The bill required an oath of nonresistance, like that imposed by the Militia Act of 1662, of all members of Parliament and all officeholders. For seventeen days, Shaftesbury and the duke of Buckingham, along with Presbyterian lords and moderate Anglicans, opposed the Anglican Test. Their basic contention was that the proposed oath would make the government absolute. It was said that a standing army would be the inevitable consequence, for the oath itself would foment jealousies which, according to plan, would be used as an excuse to "encrease and keep up a standing army."[74] A standing army had long been planned. In a limited monarchy, such as England's, neither "merce-

---

[71]*C.J.* 9: 316, 323; Grey, *Debates* 3: 18-19, 52-53. *The Collection of Autograph Letters by Alfred Morrison* (London, 1897); *The Bulstrode Papers 1667-1675* 1: 286, 287, for Burnet's testimony before the Committee and the House. Spokesmen for the court were unable to persuade the House that there was nothing injurious to England in the Scottish Militia Act.

[72]A third address against Lauderdale passed 136 to 116; *C.J.* 9: 348; *The Bulstrode Papers* 1: 291, 293, 297.

[73]The Anglican Test is conveniently found in Ogg, *England in the Reign of Charles II* 2: 532. See Haley, *Shaftesbury*, chapter 18.

[74]*A Letter from a Person of Quality to His Friend in the Country* (London, 1675), p. 2. The best source for these debates is this famous tract. The original proof sheet with corrections may be seen in B.M., Add. Mss., 4224, ff. 228-42. It is of interest that a manuscript entitled "Reasons against the Bill for the Test by the Earl of Shaftesbury (1675)" is in the Shaftesbury Papers: P.R.O., PRO 30/24/5/294/2. Although the authorship is uncertain, the tract was written by someone close to Shaftesbury. See Haley, *Shaftesbury*, pp. 390-93.

nary nor standing Guards" were ever allowed the king. But by requiring an oath not to take up arms against the king or "those that are commissioned" by him, the Anglican Test would have the effect of bringing in "Arbitrary Government . . . and a standing Army."[75]

Further, these Lords asserted that guards and standing forces were unlawful except in time of war or rebellion. It was said that "all the guards and standing forces in England cannot be secured by any Commission from being a direct Riot, and unlawful Assembly, unless in time of open War and Rebellion."[76] Although it was not elaborated, the point was plain: in peacetime the king cannot by his authority alone make guards or standing forces legal. For the first time in public discourse, the king's right to raise soldiers so long as he paid for them, which had been tacitly allowed in the Restoration settlement of the military, was disputed. For this reason alone, the debate on the Anglican Test in the spring of 1675 is of great significance in the evolution of the antistanding army ideology.

Finally, opponents of the Test charged that the court had tried to undermine the House of Lords and upset the frame of government. Some men, therefore, must intend a "Military Government," for "the power of the peerage and a standing army are like two buckets, the proportion that one goes down, the other exactly goes up."[77] In a powerful defense of the role of the nobility and of the medieval "Gothic" form of government, the opposition declared that the histories of all northern monarchies, including England's, show that the nobility has always been the bulwark against arbitrary government and centralized military power.

The opposition Lords failed to defeat the Anglican Test, but they succeeded by their lengthy and eloquent speeches in embarrassing the court and delaying its business. Their charge that a professional, permanent army would be the inevitable consequence of an oath of nonresistance required of all members of Parliament and officeholders was a polemical conclusion, not a logically necessary one. It discredited the king, no matter the caveats which were introduced. To charge that some men close to the court intended to rule by a standing army was to play upon the deep-seated fear of country gentlemen. The insistence upon the idea that the aristocracy was a bulwark against military absolutism reflected the continuing viability of one of Harrington's themes. At the same time, the medieval past was revital-

[75]*A Letter from a Person of Quality*, pp. 16-18.   [76]*Ibid.*, p. 19.
[77]*Ibid.*, p. 33.

ized and the "Gothic" form of government idealized. Without worry-ing about the inherent inconsistencies between this emphasis and Harrington's view of the medieval period, the opposition freely joined the one to the other to serve their own ideological and polem-ical purposes. Finally, the opposition Lords challenged what had been tacitly acknowledged since the Restoration, namely, that the king had the right to raise whatever forces he pleased so long as he paid them.

The expectation that the Anglican Test would be opposed with even greater vigor in the House of Commons was one consideration among others, such as the *Shirley* v. *Fagg* law case to be discussed below, which led an exasperated Charles to prorogue Parliament on June 9.[78]

When Parliament next reassembled on October 13, the same anxiety about English soldiers serving abroad in the French army and the same stratagem of exploiting the fear of a standing army to dis-credit the policies of the king reappeared. The opposition in the House of Commons used gossip, histrionics, and sensationalism and threw two men into the Tower to dramatize the fact that English soldiers were still serving in the French forces. For almost a month, members of the House of Commons focused their attention on an inelegant verbal and literary altercation involving their own mem-bers, William Cavendish (who became the first duke of Devonshire and marquis of Hartington in 1694) and Meres, on the one hand, and Thomas Howard,[79] a Roman Catholic living in retirement, on the other. Cavendish and Meres allegedly insulted Howard's brother John, who had died serving in the French army, by saying that he deserved such a fate because he had joined the French army "against the vote of Parliament." To protest this slur on his brother's reputa-tion, Howard purportedly wrote and signed a letter which was distrib-uted in St. James's Park, in which he called the two M.P.'s "barba-rous incendiaries" and described them as "unworthy," "base," and "bold and busy." This letter was brought before the House of Com-mons by Sir Trevor Williams, who said his servant had found it in the park, because two members had been "shamefully traduced." Whether Cavendish schemed to use Howard's letter at the opening of Parliament to obstruct the king's business, as was charged, is not clear, but it is clear that opposition leaders Russell, Sacheverell, Powle, and Mallet seized the opportunity to avoid any serious discus-

[78]Haley, *Shaftesbury*, p. 380.

[79]Thomas Howard of Richmond and Carlisle was brother to the earl of Carlisle and distantly related to William Cavendish.

111

sion of Charles's demand for money. Ostensibly the issue was that the privileges of Parliament had been insulted by Howard, but no one could have been unaware that the fundamental reason for the episode was exasperation that English soldiers continued to serve in the French army in defiance of a vote of Parliament and a proclamation of the king.[80]

While this ruckus was going on, a relative of Howard's challenged Cavendish to a duel. The incident was used by the opposition to draw the attention of Commons to the dangers posed by the king's Guards. One member declared that the safety of the whole House was threatened by the challenge Cavendish had received and that "some course must be taken, or we shall be hectored by every life-guard man, and be obliged to fight him."[81]

With excitement over the Cavendish–Howard episode running high, Powle introduced a motion on October 23 for a bill to impose penalties on any English subject who joined the French forces. Legal experts in the House supported the idea and members agreed to bring in a bill. The concurrence of the Lords was not obtained, however, and the bill was lost.[82] But the effort in the fall of 1675 revealed the continued concern of members of the House to win some part in deciding where English soldiers might serve and thus indirectly to achieve a role in foreign policy and military command.

During these weeks, Shaftesbury and his circle in the House of Lords were fomenting dissension between the two Houses and distrust of the king's policies in an attempt to force the dissolution of the Cavalier Parliament. Again, the menace of standing armies was used. Tracts were printed. For example, the famous pamphlet, *A Letter from a Person of Quality to His Friend in the Country*, which recounted the arguments used in the debate on the Anglican Test in the spring, was circulating among members before Parliament opened.[83] By early November, it could be bought on the streets. That the House of Lords ordered the tract burned and a committee appointed to find out who wrote, published, and printed it indicates that the pamphlet had an impact.[84]

---

[80]The details of the episode may be followed in Grey, *Debates* 3: 290–92, 297–301, 312–16, 333, 337–39, 349–54, 417–19. Also, *The Bulstrode Papers* 1: 295, 315–16, 317, 318. Many members were in attendance for this session. See Folger Manuscripts, Newdigate Newsletters, L.C., 237.

[81]Grey, *Debates* 3: 337; cf. p. 339.

[82]Grey, *Debates* 3: 334–36, 435–36; *C.J.* 9: 263; *Bulstrode Papers* 1: 319, 322, 323.

[83]Louise F. Brown, *The First Earl of Shaftesbury* (New York, 1933), p. 233; Haley, *Shaftesbury*, p. 390.

[84]*L.J.*, 13: 13; *The Bulstrode Papers* 1: 322–23.

Another tract published anonymously, *Letter from a Parliament-Man to His Friend, Concerning the Proceedings of the House of Commons, This Last Sessions, Begun the 13th of October, 1675,* used the danger of a standing army to underscore the thesis that the greatest enemy to English law and liberty was "encroaching prerogative." The *Letter* recommended that religious liberty be given to dissenters, and scourged prelates as the "greatest friends to prerogative." The prelates were bound to support prerogative because "all their promotions, dignities and domination depends upon it." The pamphlet went on to identify a standing army with the prelates and the militia force with the dissenters! "The Militia must . . . be . . . for English liberty! . . . but a standing force can be for nothing but Prerogative, by whom it hath its idle living and substance."[85] By suggesting the unlikely equation of prelates and a standing army, the *Letter* cleverly used a common prejudice against professional soldiers to smear the reputation of the bishops. Further, this tract specifically asserted what the "Person of Quality" had suggested, namely, that the army was part of the corruption of government.

The revival of the *Shirley* v. *Fagg* case provided Shaftesbury with an opportunity to exacerbate tensions between the two Houses and obstruct the king's business. That case had been brought in the spring before the House of Lords on an appeal by Dr. Thomas Shirley, who had lost a suit in the Court of Chancery against Sir John Fagg, a member of the House of Commons. The issue was whether the House of Lords violated the privileges of the House of Commons in acting as a court of appeal in a case involving a member of the Commons. Shaftesbury and his friends had argued for the jurisdictional rights of the Lords, while Danby and others had supported the privileges of the Commons. The two houses had become deadlocked, and the case was one reason for the prorogation in June. In October, the case was deliberately reopened and exploited by Shaftesbury.[86] In a speech made on October 20, which appeared later in 1675 as a tract, Shaftesbury used the dangers of a standing army to support his plea to uphold the jurisdictional rights of the House of Lords. He argued that if the House of Lords abandoned its authority to serve as a court of final appeal, the consequence would be a standing army and arbitrary government. Declaring that it was in the interests of the entire nation that the Lords maintain their rights, the earl warned

[85] *A Letter from a Parliament-Man to His Friend, Concerning the Proceedings of the House of Commons this Last Sessions, Begun the 13th of October 1675* (London, 1675), p. 4.
[86] Haley, *Shaftesbury*, pp. 394-96; *L.J.* 13: 8, 9.

that "no Prince . . . ever Governed without Nobility or an Army" and drove home the point: "If you will not have one, you must have t'other."[87] If the nobility collapsed, the monarchy would go with it, or support itself by a standing army. To avoid a military tyranny, the jurisdictional rights of the Lords must be upheld.

The specter of a standing army was also used in the arguments for dissolving the Cavalier Parliament which Shaftesbury advanced in a speech in the House of Lords on November 20. This speech also appeared as a tract. The major thrust of Shaftesbury's remarks was that the king's refusal to call frequent and new Parliaments violated the ancient laws and customs of the nation. Such an unnatural situation as this, Shaftesbury warned, could only be maintained by force. Connecting the menace of a standing army with his political goal of dissolving the Cavalier Parliament, he declared that "a standing Parliament and a standing Army are like those twins that have their lower parts united, and are divided only above the navel; they were born together and cannot long out-live each other."[88] Such a warning must have been calculated to alarm members of Parliament and to persuade them to join in the effort to bring about a dissolution.[89]

These were not the only printed tracts that appeared in 1675 to discuss paid, professional soldiers. In a public letter to a friend in Amsterdam, Lord Holles approvingly referred to Machiavelli's dictum that money was not the sinew of war and asserted that mercenary soldiers "will ever be found much weaker than the Native Militia."[90] A more important publication was Henry Neville's translation of *The Works of the Famous Nicholas Machiavel, Citizen and Secretary of Florence*, which included *The Discourses, The Florentine History* and *The Arte of Warre*. Reprints of Machiavelli's works appeared in 1680, 1694, and 1695. Anyone who read *The Discourses* and the *Arte of Warre* would find persuasive assertion and historical proof to

[87]*The Earl of Shaftesbury's Speech in the House of Lords the 20th of October 1675*, in *A Collection of State Tracts* (London, 1689), p. 59 (the page is misnumbered p. 56). The speech was printed in late 1675, probably in England and not Amsterdam, as the title page indicated. See Haley, *Shaftesbury*, p. 403.

[88]*The Earl of Shaftesbury's Speech Delivered in the House of Lords on November 20, 1675*, in *Two Seasonable Discourses Concerning this Present Parliament* (London, 1675), in *A Collection of State Tracts*, p. 68.

[89]Probably at Shaftesbury's urging, Sir Harbottle Grimston, the septuagenarian, made a similar point on October 25 in the House of Commons. Grey, *Debates* 3: 341 and 341-43; Haley, *Shaftesbury*, pp. 398-99.

[90]Denzil lord Holles, *A Letter to Monsieur Van B — [Beuningen] de M — at Amsterdam Written Anno 1675 . . . Concerning the Government of England* (London, 1676), p. 3.

confirm and stimulate the conviction that professional, permanent troops were a menace.

Throughout the year, then, the antistanding army sentiment was exploited in Parliament. Critics of the king repeatedly raised the specter of standing armies. This tactic was partly responsible for frustrating the business of the court. On November 22, 1675, Charles again prorogued Parliament. Better furnished financially than ever before by a grant from Louis XIV and by the expectation of higher yield from current taxes as a result of Danby's reorganization and economy, Charles forfeited a grant from this Parliament and ruled without Parliament for fifteen months.

When Parliament reassembled in February 1677, the court's foreign and military policies again came under fire. Exasperation over the continued presence of English troops in the French army and the rumors of recruitment of men in Scotland and Ireland for that service (despite the vote of Parliament and the royal proclamation in 1675) was sharpened by the startling military success of Louis XIV.[91] On February 19, a strongly worded bill for the recall of English subjects was introduced. Severe penalties were laid on any soldier who remained in the French army after a certain time, and the power of the king to pardon such a soldier, except by act of Parliament, was denied. Despite the objection that the bill made service in the French army a crime greater than a sin against the Holy Ghost, the bill was read a second time on February 22 and handed over to a committee which included men who had long argued against Charles's military and foreign policies, Sacheverell, Sir William Coventry, Meres, and Lee.[92] On March 6, "country" members persuaded the House to address the king about the danger from France and to ask him to enter into alliances to secure England and preserve Holland. These anxieties were reinforced a fortnight later when an extraordinary episode relating to the English soldiers serving in France and reflecting most unfavorably on the king was revealed.

During the debate[93] on March 16, when it was resolved that anyone who had encouraged an English subject to serve in the French army should be declared an enemy to England, Sacheverell revealed that

---

[91]French armies took Valenciennes, Cambrai, and Cassel in the spring of 1677. For a brief narrative, see Ogg, *England in the Reign of Charles II* 1: 543–45; Browning, *Thomas Osborne* 1: 221 and n. 3.

[92]*C.J.* 9: 385, 387; Grey, *Debates* 4: 97–98, 131–34.

[93]Grey, *Debates* 4: 255–61; *C.J.* 9: 400–1.

a John Harrington[94] had secured an affidavit about dragooning of men from Scotland into the French service with the connivance of the duke of Lauderdale. Because the government, including Charles himself, was deeply implicated,[95] there was every reason for the government to arrest Harrington. When brought before the Privy Council and the king, according to some accounts, Harrington was rude to Charles and refused to answer questions. He was ordered off to jail, with personal instructions from the king that he be held "close prisoner." On his way to jail, Harrington was clever enough to sign a blank piece of paper and slip it to a friend, so that a petition for his release might be drafted and presented to the House of Commons.[96] Sacheverell had obliged. For two days, the details of this episode were recounted in the House. The procedure used in committing Harrington to jail was bitterly criticized. The House interrogated Harrington, one of the pressed Scotsmen, William Herriott, and Robert Murray, a confederate[97] of Shaftesbury's who had obtained an affidavit attesting to the dragooning of Scotsmen for Louis XIV's army. But members refused to support Harrington's petition, and on March 17, further debate on the matter was left *sine die*. Harrington's indiscreet dealings with foreign embassies, his radical political views, Herriott's retractions, and the general reluctance of most members to meddle directly with the king's power blunted the arguments that Sacheverell and a few other opposition leaders made on Harrington's behalf.

The "unhappy"[98] debates on March 16 and 17, 1677, however, were not the last of this incident. In June, Harrington's trial was postponed until the next term at the "express order from the King."[99] Around Christmas 1677, a tract appeared entitled *Mr. Harrington's Case*, which must have reawakened interest in the issue and spread news of it still further among the politically conscious public. The tract was

[94]John Harrington's pedigree has been worked out by Mr. J. P. Ferris of the History of Parliament Trust. Harrington was born about 1649, a second cousin to Shaftesbury. He was still living around 1696. *Miscelleanea Genealogica Heraldica*, new series, 4: 161, 192. For a brief account of this incident, see Haley, *Shaftesbury*, pp. 424–26.

[95]For evidence of this complicity, see K. D. H. Haley, "The Anglo-Dutch Rapprochement," *E.H.R.* 73 (1958): 622, n. 2.

[96]Andrew Marvell, *An Account of the Growth of Popery and Arbitrary Government*, in *A Collection of State Tracts*, pp. 96–97.

[97]See letter from Robert Murray to Shaftesbury dated May 1677 and signed "most humble, grateful, abused servant." P.R.O., PRO 30/24/6A/305. Haley, *Shaftesbury*, p. 425, refers to Murray's connection with Shaftesbury during the fall of 1676.

[98]Grey, *Debates* 4: 265.

[99]*C.S.P.D., 1677–1678*, p. 233; Roger Morrice, "The Entr'ing Book Being an Historical Register of Occurrences from April, Anno 1677, to April 1691" 1: 58.

said to have caused Danby great alarm.[100] Someone felt sufficiently concerned to draft a reply, which was not published. Entitled "Worse and Worse, or the Case alter'd in some short Reflections upon a late Scurrilous and Seditious Paper intituled Mr. Harrington's Case," the undated draft declared that the issue was much in "coffee House chatt" and that *Mr. Harrington's Case* contained "poison of a most pernicious Nature."[101] When Harrington came to trial in January 1678, it was not for contempt but for his comments about the government being in three estates and rebellion being no rebellion unless directed against all three. He was heavily fined and jailed.[102]

Although Harrington's petition had been argued on legal grounds in the House of Commons, no member could have been unaware that the basic issue was the connivance of the government at the continued pressing of men for the French service in the face of parliamentary vote and royal proclamation.[103] If the petition had been taken up and the questions it opened thoroughly investigated, it could have created an acutely embarrassing situation for the government. That Harrington's case was not championed by the House underscored the fundamental conservatism of most members. Even so, the debates in March 1677 further tarnished the reputation of the court and suggested that it was connected with practices that directly defied parliamentary sentiment. Although proof is lacking, it seems evident that opposition leaders in the House of Commons, and perhaps Shaftesbury himself, were aware of the political capital to be won from introducing the petition and thereby exposing the activities of the government.[104] Andrew Marvell did not fail to include a scathing account of the episode in his famous tract, *An Account of the*

[100]Grey, *Debates* 4: 283n. The matter is not mentioned in Browning's biography of Danby.

[101]The paper is in B.M., Add. Mss., 28,092, f. 42.

[102]Morrice, "Entr'ing Book" 1: 61; Grey, *Debates* 4: 283n. There is a discrepancy in the date of the trial in the two accounts. The January date given by Morrice is probably the correct one, for Harrington, free on bail, was distributing copies of his tract, *Mr. Harrington's Case*, around Christmas. See *C.S.P.D., 1677-78*, p. 683. Harrington was released in June 1680. In August 1681, he was "apprehended by a Messenger," but released on "Security." Around that time he was staying at a Mr. Morton's, a tailor on Pantin Street, and received there an unsigned and undated letter asking him to take certain steps in preparation for Shaftesbury's trial. See Morrice, "Entr'ing Book" 1: 261, 321; P.R.O., PRO 30/24/6B/433/5.

[103]Sir Thomas Clarges remarked, "One great Conspiracy you have found out against the Court, viz. levying men, contrary to the King's Proclamation." Grey, *Debates* 4: 279; cf. pp. 267, 269, 281.

[104]There is no direct proof that Shaftesbury was connected with this episode. See Haley, *Shaftesbury*, p. 426. Shaftesbury was in the Tower during these weeks.

Growth of Popery and Arbitrary Government, which appeared within a year. Sincere apprehension, principle, and propaganda were mingled in the opposition's revelations of the Harrington episode.

Intensified criticism of the army in 1678 and 1679 reflected genuine alarm and confusion over the purpose of the king's foreign policy. As before, the parliamentary leadership used the antistanding army sentiment to discredit the king and win partisan political goals, especially the dissolution of the Cavalier Parliament. The complexity and duplicity of Charles II's foreign policy from the spring of 1677 through 1679 may be followed elsewhere.[105] The question was whether Charles intended to make war on France or not.[106] Many men sincerely feared that the king, with the connivance of Louis XIV, was pretending to prepare for war with France as an excuse to raise men and money. Thus freed from Parliament, Charles and Louis would arrange a peace.

Genuine anxiety over this possibility led the parliamentary leadership to establish contact with the French ambassador, Paul Barrillon, marquis des Branges, in February and March 1678 to find out if war was intended or if an agreement had been made. Assurances were conveyed that no agreement had been made. In the course of the contacts, an identity of interest between the French king and the leaders of the opposition emerged: for vastly different reasons both wanted to dissolve the Cavalier Parliament and disband the army. Parliamentary and French spokesmen agreed that the way to accomplish these ends was to frustrate Charles's policies in Parliament so effectively that he would turn to Louis, who would then advise him to dissolve Parliament. To show their good faith, the French offered money to bribe members of Parliament to vote against supply and the army. Although Shaftesbury is said not to have accepted money from the French, Russell, Cavendish, Hotham, Sacheverell, and others did.[107] The fact that many of the parliamentary opposition accepted

[105]See Ogg, *England in the Reign of Charles II* 2: 544-58; Haley, "The Anglo-Dutch Rapprochement," pp. 633-48; Browning, *Thomas Osborne* 1: 225-27, 262-83.

[106]For example: H.M.C., *Finch MSS*, 2: 38, 41; A. Browning, ed., *Memoirs of Sir John Reresby* (London, 1936), pp. 131, 135, 142. Conversations with confederate ambassadors confirmed the suspicion that Charles was secretly promoting French interests. See Haley, *Shaftesbury*, p. 437 and n. 4. The enthusiasm of the duke of York for war was seen as sinister. The preparations for war may be followed in the *C.S.P.D., 1677-78*, pp. 566, 572, 610-11, 616-17, 627; *ibid., 1678*, pp. 2, 6, 12-13, 24-25, 38, 55, 63.

[107]See Dalrymple, *Memoirs* 2: 129, 132-33; Von Ranke, *History of England, Principally in the Seventeenth Century* 4: chapter 4, for a narrative account and Clyde Grose, "Louis XIV's Financial Relations with Charles II and the English Parliament," *J.M.H.* 1 (June 1929), 179-99; Haley, *Shaftesbury*, pp. 444-45

French bribes dilutes the disinterestedness of their opposition to standing armies and lends additional support to the thesis that the antistanding army sentiment contained ingredients other than fear and principle. Although the leadership was assured by Barrillon that no secret agreement existed between Charles and Louis to declare a sham war so that Charles might raise an army to make himself independent of Parliament, the parliamentary opposition persisted in describing the troops Charles was raising as a "standing army." Predicting that once established the army would not be disbanded, they objected to its proximity to Parliament, suggested that Catholics had penetrated it, and called for the nation to rely on the militia.[108]

A telling illustration of the way in which the parliamentary leadership disingenuously manipulated the antiarmy sentiment occurred in the debate on March 14, 1678, which followed close on the heels of the meetings with the French ambassador. At the opening of the debate, Sir Gilbert Gerrard moved that war against France be declared immediately to provide employment for the soldiers. Although it was apparent that some members enthusiastically supported the motion, Lord Russell, Shaftesbury's spokesman in the House of Commons, rose to offer a different motion, which would have turned the attention of the House away from foreign affairs to domestic matters. He wanted to "set the saddle on the right horse," and for him, the "right horse" was the "apprehensions we are under of Popery, and a standing Army."[109] The comment was consistent with the strategy that had been used before; it discredited the government by implying that the armed force would be turned against the nation. The remark was poorly received by members who wanted an aggressive policy against France, for obviously to discredit the army was no way to implement war, but Powle, Lee and Mallet, among others, made certain that the government's good faith was impugned by reiterating that newly raised regiments would be used at home, not abroad.

The menace of standing armies was also used in propagandist tracts to undermine confidence in the government. *A Seasonable Argument To Persuade All the Grand Juries in England to Petition for a New Parliament* linked the danger of standing armies and the goal of dissolving the Cavalier Parliament. The tract was a long list of men in the Commons who were said to be in the pay of the court and who, therefore, corrupted the deliberations of the House. These men had

---

[108]Grey, *Debates* 5: 119–22, 150–53, 223–48. See *C.S.P.D., 1678*, p. 122, for an anonymous tract charging that the term "standing army" was unfairly applied.

[109]Grey, *Debates* 5: 224, 223–48, for debate.

agreed, the lengthy title asserted, to "maintain a Standing Army in England under the Command of the Bigoted Popish Duke, who by the Assistance of the Lord Lauderdale's Scotch Army, the Forces in Ireland, and those in France, [would] bring all back to Rome."[110] It was effective propaganda. The title alone suggested that a standing army, like "placemen," was an instrument of corrupt court influence.

Andrew Marvell's *An Account of the Growth of Popery and Arbitrary Government* was plainly designed for propagandist purposes as well. *The Growth of Popery* so annoyed the government when it appeared that a warrant was issued to seize all copies and to apprehend the printer.[111] Showing remarkable affinities with the ideas and conclusions which the "Person of Quality" had advanced two-and-one-half years before, Marvell strove to demonstrate that a conspiracy had long existed to draw England into the French orbit, establish an absolute government, reintroduce Catholicism, and rule by a standing army. In terms of the antiarmy ideology, Marvell's most important contribution was to make explicit that military officers who served in Parliament were a major element in the corrupt influence which the court exercised. They and other "placemen" would always support an increase in the standing army, or the levying of heavy taxes by illegal means, or indeed any bill the court desired. The presence of army officers in Parliament disrupted the normal functioning of government and unbalanced it in favor of the king. Sensitive as Marvell was to the army as a weapon to impose tyranny, he was equally alarmed over the army as an instrument of political corruption.

Another significant feature of the debates of the spring of 1678 was that the terms of the argument were radicalized. An implicit challenge to the king's command of the military had occurred in January when some members claimed that Parliament should nominate the officers of the new regiments.[112] Later "some murmuring" was heard against individuals who had been appointed officers, and at another time it was stressed that all officers in the army, with no exceptions, should be required to take the Test Act.[113] No steps were taken by Parliament (as in 1641–42) to appoint men conformable to their views, but as distrust of the king deepened, the king's prerogative to raise what soldiers he wished so long as he paid them was directly

---

[110]The tract is conveniently available in Andrew Browning, ed., *English Historical Documents, 1660–1714* (London, 1953), 8: 237–49.

[111]Haley, *Shaftesbury*, p. 438 and n. 2. [112]*Ibid.*, p. 437, quoting Barrillon.

[113]*C.S.P.D., 1678*, p. 66; Morrice, "Entr'ing Book" 1: 71; Grey, *Debates* 5: 234, 241–42.

challenged. In the debate of May 7 Vaughan, Hotham, Clarges, and Cavendish asserted that the only time the king could legitimately raise forces other than the militia was in time of war. The Petition of Right was called upon to support this contention, and the House was reminded of previous resolutions that any force besides the militia was a grievance.[114] At the end of the month, the theme surfaced again. In the discussion, Vaughan emphatically asserted that according to English law, "no men can be raised but for foreign service."[115] Williams was even more unequivocal. Friends of the court, among them Sawyer and Winnington, promptly and indignantly replied. It was suggested that Williams's remark be written down, but Williams apologized and the matter was passed over.[116] The exchange revealed, however, the increasingly radical thinking about the king's military prerogative.

The king's Guards came in for criticism, too. Meres felt it would be better for the king to live without any guards, as kings before him had done. He and Lee favored paying off and disbanding the Guards along with the other regiments raised for the war.[117]

Such actions testified to the Commons's hardened determination to have some say in military and foreign affairs. Defying the king's recommendations, the members decided, after a "strong debate" the end of May, to disband the army.[118] Throughout June, days were devoted to examining the accounts of the army, questioning the commissary and paymaster of the Army, agreeing to postponing the date of disbandment, and deciding to raise money by a land tax for disbanding the army.[119] But, despite their efforts, Charles did not disband the army. For reasons of personal diplomacy, Charles committed his soldiers, in the summer of 1678, to several battles against Louis XIV and, even after the Treaty of Nijmeguen was signed, English troops continued to be sent abroad. Not until September 8 were the ships for transporting the men discharged. Secretary Williamson was deeply concerned over Parliament's reaction to the news that the army had not been dismissed.[120] Thus, with his army still intact, Charles met Parliament on October 21, 1678, amid much speculation and many rumors about a "Popish Plot."[121] It may be presumed that even if there had been no Popish Plot, an effort would have been made to

---

[114]Grey. *Debates* 5: 325, 326; *C.S.P.D., 1678*, p. 159.   [115]Grey, *Debates* 6: 42.
[116]*Ibid.*, pp. 44–46.   [117]*Ibid.*, p. 39.   [118]Morrice, "Entr'ing Book" 1: 85.
[119]*C.J.* 9: 485, 487, 493, 508–9; *L.J.* 13: 260, 288; *C.S.P.D., 1678*, pp. 204–5, 224, 237, 271; Grey, *Debates* 6: 68–70, 80–82, 85–86, 94, 97–98, 100–1, 109–11.
[120]*C.S.P.D., 1678*, pp. 345, 347, 358, 360, 397, 415.
[121]The latest study is J. P. Kenyon, *The Popish Plot* (London, 1972).

G. Kneller Eques pinxit.   Geo. Vertue Lond. Sculp 1737.

HENRY POWLE Esqr
Speaker of the House of Commons & Master of the Rolls

Henry Powle (1630–1692) (*left*) and Sir Thomas Lee (1635–1691) (*right*) were prominent leaders against the standing army in the House of Commons in the 1670s and in the Convention Parliament of 1689.

123

WALTER MOYLE *of* Bake *in Cornval Esq.*
obijt 9ᵉ Jun. 1721. æt. 49.

Andrew Fletcher.

From an Authentick Portrait, in the Collection of the Earl of Buchan.

Among the major pamphleteers in the standing army controversy in 1697–99 were Walter Moyle (1672–1721) (*left*) and Andrew Fletcher (1655–1716) (*right*).

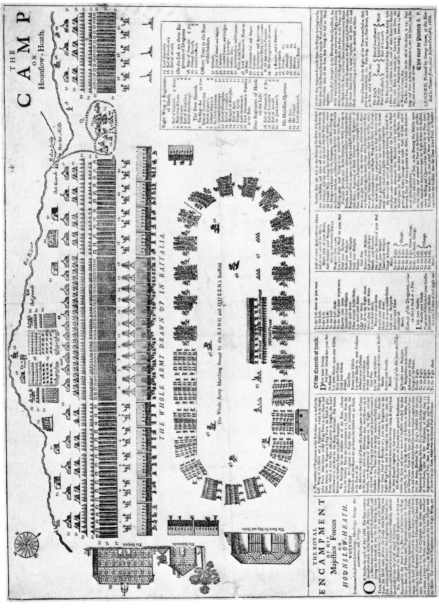

This diagram, showing King James II's whole army drawn up in battalia on Hounslow Heath, twelve miles from London, was printed in 1686.

disband the army. But in the mounting excitement generated by the successive revelations of Titus Oates and by the murder of Sir Edmund Berry Godfrey, the opposition to the army took on an emotion that matched the panic over the plot. "No Popery" and "No Standing Army" became slogans which aroused almost every country gentleman to anger and fear.

Charles and the Lord Chancellor Finch opened Parliament with speeches that attempted to justify the government's failure to implement the Disbanding Act and asked for further supply.[122] The king's plea, however, was ignored in the preoccupation with Titus Oates's testimony about the plot. Parliament's response was to call for disbanding the king's army and calling up the local militia. What better way was there to underscore their distrust? Great activity to achieve that end followed. Overtures were made to the duke of York.[123] It was resolved, on November 18, to ask the king to put the entire militia in readiness and raise one-third of it on a rotating basis for a fortnight. The basic purpose of the motion was to train the militia to be guards to the king, that the "King might have no farther use of an Army."[124] It took a fortnight to achieve agreement between the two Houses about the militia, but by November 28, a bill was agreed to which empowered the deputy-lieutenants to keep the militia embodied for forty-two days.[125] Whatever the ultimate purpose of the House, the effort to embody the militia to defend the nation carried great psychological and propaganda significance for underscoring the distrust of the king.

This Militia Bill brought to a head the fundamental question at stake in the standing army issue—ultimate control of the military. Like his father before him, Charles regarded the matter as an altogether "fit subject" for a king to quarrel about. He said he would "consult and advise" with the Lords before he returned an answer.[126] Apparently none of the king's friends in either House spoke against the bill when it was debated.[127] Burnet credited himself with pointing out to the king the dangerous implications of the bill and declared that Charles thanked him for his advice.[128] On November 30, Charles II, for reasons similar to those his father had used nearly forty years before,

---

[122]Grey, *Debates* 6: 112; Cobbett, *Parliamentary History* 4: 1019, for Finch's speech, which is not reported in Grey's *Debates*.

[123]Browning, *Thomas Osborne* 1: 297 and n. 1.   [124]Grey, *Debates* 6: 214.

[125]*C.J.* 9: 545, 548; Grey, *Debates* 6: 270; Burnet, *History of My Own Time* 2: 171.

[126]*C.J.* 9: 548.   [127]H.M.C., *Ormonde Mss.* 4: 257–58.

[128]Burnet, *History of My Own Time* 2: 171.

rejected the bill and announced that he would veto any legislation that put the militia out of his hands "but for half an hour."[129]

The opposition members of Parliament protested the king's answer and denied categorically that it was their intent to invade the royal prerogative.[130] In response, the king invited the House on December 4 to frame another Militia Bill and promised assent to any legislation for readying the militia so long as the royal authority over it was left intact.[131] In a very thin House, the invitation was rejected. The difficulties of circumventing the prohibition on introducing two bills for the same thing in a session were stressed.[132] The basic conservatism of most members acted as a brake to avoid actions which would have repeated 1641–42. In the meantime, a parallel effort was made to disband the army. A most effective way to discredit the army and to provoke the king to dismiss it was to identify it with Catholicism, a tactic which had been employed before, but not stressed. On November 18, the same day that the resolution about the militia was passed in Commons, Sacheverell charged that in the last month at least sixty Catholics had been commissioned by Secretary Williamson. The minister's excuse that he did not have time to read every paper he signed and that the men had been dismissed and sent off to Ireland was ridiculed out of hand, and Williamson was thrown into the Tower.[133] In the course of the attack, Cavendish made a significant remark which underscored the growing interest in stripping the king of the right to keep soldiers in peacetime if he paid them. Reflecting a sentiment voiced earlier in the year by Vaughan and Williams, Cavendish declared that he was of the opinion that a "standing Army, in time of peace, whether the Officers be Popish or Protestant, is illegal."[134]

As details about the Popish Plot continued to be revealed, the effort to disband the army took another form. On November 27, a full-scale debate on disbanding the army was held in the House of Commons. There was much reiterative comment, but one suggestion was new.

[129]Grey, *Debates* 6: 301.

[130]*Ibid.*, pp. 306, 307, 311, 314; H.M.C., *Seventh Report*, part I, appendix, p. 495.

[131]Grey, *Debates* 6: 316–17; *C.J.* 9: 552; H.M.C., *Ormonde Mss.* 4: 257–58; *C.S.P.D., 1678*, pp. 554, 563–64.

[132]Grey, *Debates* 6: 317–18.

[133]*Ibid.*, pp. 216–25, 236; cf. *C.S.P.D., 1678*, pp. 508, 511. A modern study of the army would show how many Catholics were in the Guards and new regiments at various times. Ninety-one Catholics were dismissed from the duke of Monmouth's regiments.

[134]Grey, *Debates* 6: 218.

Members insisted that the money appropriated for the disbanding of the army should be placed in the Council Chamber in London (rather than in the Exchequer) where specially appointed commissioners would supervise its disbursement and assure that it was spent this time to disband the army and not to maintain it. The opposition intimated that Danby had been responsible for misappropriating the funds so that Charles could keep his army over the summer. Unanimously, the House resolved that all the forces raised since September 29, 1677 and all still abroad should be dismissed.[135]

To implement this resolution, the House of Commons applied itself for the next several weeks to the details of the Disbanding Bill. Exasperation, temper, and extremism overwhelmed some members. For example, on December 9, Sir George Hungerford wanted a proviso to the Disbanding Bill that would have made it treason to use the money for any purpose other than dismissing the army, and this idea was dropped only after the astonished speaker urged members to consider making an action treasonable by a rider to a bill.[136] More liberally bribed by Barrillon at this time than at any other, opposition leaders framed a Disbanding Bill which granted more than £200,000 to disband the army and which specifically outlawed the billeting of soldiers on *any* subject who did not consent to it. On December 17, the bill was sent to the House of Lords where it was debated at length. The Lords were unable to agree that the money for the disbanding should be placed in the Chamber of London instead of in the Exchequer. On the grounds that such a step would be an invasion of the king's military prerogative, the Lords, with twenty-one members dissenting (including Shaftesbury, Holles, Wharton, and Buckingham) amended the Disbanding Bill to place the money in the Exchequer.[137]

Another aspect of the standing army issue in the fall of 1678 was its connection with attacks on the king's ministers. The most important target was Danby.[138] A move against the lord treasurer was delayed until mid-December in part to allow time for the Disbanding

---

[135]*C.J.* 9: 548; Grey, *Debates* 6: 278-85; Morrice, "Entr'ing Book" 1: 98.

[136]Grey, *Debates* 6: 335-37; cf. p. 328 for an account of an abrupt adjournment following a noticeably inane debate. *C.J.* 9: 550, 552, 557, 558. Some urgency must have been added by reports of misbehavior by the soldiers. See Morrice, "Entr'ing Book" 2: 102.

[137]*L.J.* 13: 420, 422, 423-26, 428, 443.

[138]Browning, *Thomas Osborne* 1: 310-21; Roberts, *The Growth of Responsible Government in Stuart England*, pp. 211-18. The articles of impeachment and Danby's speech to the Lords in his defense may be found conveniently in Browning, *English Historical Documents* 8: 198-203.

Bill to be framed so that Danby would not have an army to defend himself.[139] Then, using letters that Danby had written in 1677, Parliament appointed a committee to draw up articles of impeachment.[140] Article II specifically charged Danby with raising a standing army under specious pretenses and keeping it up with funds designed by Parliament to disband it.[141] Commons resolved to impeach the minister on that article. Although Danby was surely guilty of the charge, the House of Lords, impressed by his defense and persuaded that none of the charges amounted to treason, refused to send him to the Tower as the Commons wanted.

For many reasons, not just to save Danby, Charles prorogued Parliament on December 30. This, of course, meant that the king forfeited the supplies for paying the army that were part of the Disbanding Bill. Nonetheless, the king insisted to Parliament, his council, and the lord mayor and aldermen of London that he would see to it that the army was dismissed.[142] Over the next three weeks, private meetings among Danby, representing Charles, and Lord Holles, and a small number of Presbyterian leaders were held. In the negotiations,[143] Holles and his friends promised to moderate the attack on Danby, persuade the London gold- and silversmiths to lend money to the government for disbanding the army, and guarantee a supply from Parliament. In return, the king promised to disband the army and dissolve the Parliament that had sat for eighteen years. On January 24, Charles did dissolve Parliament. Thus, a political goal toward which many members of the opposition had worked for years was achieved. The antimilitary sentiment, directed as it was against the king and court, played an important role in bringing this about.

The disbanding of the army was less readily accomplished, however. Some of the army was still on hand when Charles opened his newly elected Parliament on March 6, 1679, with the announcement that he had dismissed as many soldiers as he could pay and that he hoped that more money would be granted to disband the rest.[144] The House of Commons, preoccupied for the first six weeks with other

[139]Haley, *Shaftesbury*, p. 488.   [140]*C.J.* 9: 560.   [141]*Ibid.*, p. 562.

[142]*L.J.* 13: 447; H.M.C., *Ormonde Mss.* 4: 495.

[143]The best account of these negotiations is Lacey, *Dissent and Parliamentary Politics*, pp. 95–98.

[144]For the election of 1679, see Dorothy M. George, "Elections and Electioneering, 1679-1681," *E.H.R.* 45 (October 1930): 552–78; Jones, *The First Whigs*, pp. 35–48; Lacey, *Dissent and Parliamentary Politics*, pp. 112–20. For Charles's speech opening Parliament, *L.J.* 13: 449; Grey, *Debates* 6: 400. The precise number of soldiers still on hand in March is not known. See Morrice, "Entr'ing Book" 1: 106; *C.S.P.D., 1679-80*, pp. 15–16.

matters, ignored the army. Then, on March 25, Shaftesbury delivered a speech in the House of Lords that played upon old fears: Popery in government, the Scottish Militia Act of 1669, and the presence of Catholic officers in the army. Probably, there is a connection between Shaftesbury's speech and the motion introduced by Cavendish a few days later in the House of Commons that the disbanding of the army be taken into consideration.[145] Lengthy debates about the army followed, familiar arguments were recited and the story of past efforts to be rid of the soldiers was reviewed. Garroway, Lee, and Sacheverell were truculent. On April 1, 1679, Commons resolved that the continuing of any standing forces other than the Militia was illegal and a grievance and vexation to the people.[146]

For the next few weeks, members attended to the details of disbanding the army and finally on May 2 passed the Disbanding Act, notable for its enormous bulk, which granted, as the Act of December 1678 had done, over £200,000 to pay off all the forces that were raised since September 29, 1677.[147] The delay was explained by a contemporary: "Other things take up the time," he wrote. Besides, the army was not "in number sufficient to give any fear."[148] A week later, on May 9, the House of Lords agreed to the legislation to disband the army.[149] Although rumors circulated that the army would not be disbanded, all the soldiers who had been raised the year before to fight against the French were reported to have been dismissed by the middle of June.[150] Thus, although new levies were immediately required for the specific purpose of putting down the uprising of the covenanters in Scotland, the army that had been the object of such bitter contention was removed.[151] Moreover, a proposal to raise a new guard of gentlemen to protect the king was rejected, possibly because the court feared that such a step would provoke Charles's critics "to question" the guards he already had.[152]

At the same time progress was being made on disbanding the army, some attention was being given to the militia. Members, however,

[145]Cobbett, *Parliamentary History* 4: 1116-18, for Shaftesbury's speech; Haley, *Shaftesbury*, pp. 510-12, for comment; *C.J.* 9: 579, and Grey, *Debates* 7: 64, for Cavendish's motion.

[146]Grey, *Debates* 7: 67-73.

[147]*C.J.* 9: 595-610 *passim*; Morrice, "Entr'ing Book" 1: 163-64. The Disbanding Act was so swollen by the Commissioners' names that one man could hardly carry it. See H.M.C., *Ormonde Mss.* 5: 76.

[148]H.M.C., *Ormonde Mss.* 4: 503.   [149]*L.J.* 13: 561; H.M.C., *Ormonde Mss.* 5: 90.

[150]H.M.C., *Ormonde Mss.* 4: 510; Morrice, "Entr'ing Book" 1: 197.

[151]H.M.C., *Ormonde Mss.* 5: 128, 131, 132; *C.S.P.D., 1679-80*, pp. 170, 171, 173.

[152]*C.S.P.D., 1679-80*, pp. 176-77, 201; Morrice, "Entr'ing Book" 1: 208.

were not really serious about making the militia more useful. On April 14, Gerrard introduced a motion to take the condition of the militia into consideration, but the effort was deflected by Powle who wanted to review the state of the Navy. Despite Sir John Lowther's plea that the motion on the militia "not be stifled," members were intent on discussing the number of Catholic officers in the Navy and attacking ministers who were responsible for the deplorable state of the Navy.[153] At the end of the month, several changes in the militia were reported to be under consideration. Among them was the suggestion that Parliament nominate militia officers.[154] Danby, now in the Tower, wrote to Charles that the Commons's attempts to control the militia was consistent with their efforts to change the succession and showed that the House was aiming at nothing less than sovereignty in the state.[155] In May, the Commons resolved unanimously to petition the king to raise the Militia of London, Westminster, Southwarke and the Tower Hamlets, and the counties of Middlesex and Surrey.[156] The significance of these steps was polemical rather than substantive, for nothing concrete was done about the condition of the militia. What more might have been done was cut short on May 27 by Charles's proroguing Parliament to destroy the first Exclusion Bill, which would have disabled the duke of York from inheriting the crown.

By mid-1679, the uses of the antistanding army sentiment as a political weapon had been demonstrated. Genuine fear of soldiers had been exploited to embarrass the king, undermine the credibility of his ministers, and thwart his policies. Criticism of the army provoked Charles more than once to prorogue Parliament in the 1670s and was partly responsible for his decision to dissolve the Cavalier Parliament. It brought about the disbandment of forces he raised in 1677 and restricted the total number of his army. It helped to radicalize men's thinking about the crown's prerogative powers and encouraged an anachronistic, perhaps altogether rhetorical, devotion to the militia. The belief that James favored a professional, permanent force was one factor in the effort to exclude him from the succession.

It is curious, therefore, that the antiarmy issue did not play a more important role in the Exclusion Controversy. The standing army question was almost completely ignored in the last two Exclusion

---

[153]Grey, *Debates* 7: 108, 110.   [154]H.M.C., *Ormonde Mss.* 4: 506.
[155]Browning, *Thomas Osborne* 1: 338 and n. 2.
[156]*C.J.* 9: 617, 618; cf. H.M.C., *Ormonde Mss.* 4: 510, 514, 515.

Parliaments and in the many Exclusion pamphlets reprinted between 1679 and 1681.[157] Only at the time of the Oxford Parliament (so-called because Parliament was summoned to meet at Oxford in March 1681 in hopes that away from London it would be more sympathetic to the king), was appeal made to the antiarmy sentiment. Then, much concern (some of it real, some politically inspired) was expressed about the king's intentions of bringing his Guards to Oxford. Early in February, the Guards were protested in the Court of King's Bench as illegal because they had not been authorized by a statute. Nothing came of the protest.[158] About the same time, Shaftesbury sent members of the Oxford Parliament some instructions whose third point was that Parliament "should restore . . . that Liberty we and our Forefathers have enjoyd, untill this last forty years, of being free from Guards and Mercenary Soldiers."[159] A speech by Shaftesbury recommended that the goals the upcoming Parliament should endeavor to achieve were exclusion, annual Parliaments, and no standing armies.[160] The "addresses of instruction," which have been described as "the feature"[161] of the elections of 1681, indicate that the standing army issue continued to be used, although not ranked first in importance.

Early in 1681, Henry Neville's *Plato Redivivus* appeared in two editions.[162] It was the only tract from these years that dealt in theoretical terms with the question of military power. Harrington's protégé and Machiavelli's translator, Neville was deeply indebted to classical and seventeenth-century English libertarian traditions. Like the "Person of Quality," Neville rejected Harrington's view of the Middle Ages. In contrast, he idealized the medieval era, finding in it the origins of England's ancient mixed and balanced constitution, in which king, Lords, and Commons share sovereign power.[163] Under this arrangement, the disposal of the militia was "natural."[164] The peers served as a bulwark to the ambitions of kings and "so long as the peers kept their greatness, there was [sic] no breaches but what were immediately made up in Parliament."[165] The power of the sword

[157]O. W. Furley, "The Whig Exclusionists: Pamphlet Literature in the Exclusion Campaign, 1679-1681," *C.H.J.* 13 (1957): 19-36, for a survey of the literature and the arguments.

[158]Haley, *Shaftesbury*, p. 623. [159]P.R.O., PRO 30/24/6B/399.

[160]*Ibid.*, PRO 30/24/7/499.

[161]For the addresses of instruction, see Jones, *The First Whigs*, pp. 166-73; cf. Haley, *Shaftesbury*, p. 627 and n. 3.

[162]Robbins, *Two English Republican Tracts*, p. 67, n. 1.

[163]Neville, *Plato Redivivus*, ed. Robbins, pp. 112, 113, 119, 120.

[164]*Ibid.*, p. 125. [165]*Ibid.*, p. 122.

was exercised by the great men of realm and their freeholders acting under the commission of the king whose authority was "tacitly consented to."

Neville asserted that this happy state of affairs changed around 1485, when land shifted from the king and peers to the gentry and commonalty. Tenures were abolished, and the limits on the crown removed.[166] The situation in France well illustrated what can happen when the nobility is weakened. England could go in the same direction: the army kept in Scotland frightened many people.[167] To remedy the "distemper" in the English government caused by the shift of property, a change in the administration,[168] although not the nature, of the government was necessary. Steps should be taken to prevent the king from using his power for arbitrary purposes. He should be asked to hand over those prerogatives that touched his subjects' "lives, liberties and estates" to four councils composed of men appointed by and answerable to Parliament. Among the prerogatives was the "sole disposal and ordering of the militia by sea and land."[169] Although Neville denied that his proposal would give ultimate authority to Parliament, it is plain that by controlling the membership of the councils, Parliament would have predominant authority.

Neville's tract was of greater importance in the evolution of the antistanding army ideology than in the Exclusion Crisis. *Plato Redivivus* testified to the ongoing viability of classical, Renaissance, and seventeenth-century English libertarian ideas, especially about military power. It was reprinted in 1698 when the standing army issue reached a climax. Reissued four times in the eighteenth century, it continued to shape antimilitary notions. In 1681, Shaftesbury made no effort to use it in his campaign against the duke of York,[170] and it was the only tract printed that dealt with the standing army issue.

It may be that Shaftesbury and his friends thought it was an effective tactic to stress one issue, Exclusion, and not deflect attention from it by bringing in other questions. On the other hand, the downplaying of the standing army issue may have reflected Shaftesbury's failing health and a less acute political perception than he had shown before. For several years, the opposition had been trying to achieve some role for Parliament in the control of the military; if exclusion should be won by parliamentary bill, changes in military

---

[166]*Ibid.*, pp. 87, 89, 132–34, 157.   [167]*Ibid.*, pp. 143, 179, 186.   [168]*Ibid.*, p. 165.   [169]*Ibid.*, p. 186.   [170]Haley, *Shaftesbury*, p. 628.

command and organization might be achieved. The temporary lapse of the Licensing Act gave opportunity to discuss such basic political problems in ways that might have strengthened even more the pro-Exclusionist case. Who can say what might have happened if Shaftesbury had moved this issue, which had proved its capability of arousing country gentlemen to the point of hysteria, to the forefront of the Exclusion battle?

From another viewpoint, it may be that the question was soft-pedaled because it posed difficulties in persuading men that no basic change in the government was intended by excluding James from the succession. The pamphleteers avoided discussing sovereignty in general; so too they avoided discussing military prerogative.[171] The logical conclusion of the past criticism of the army and militia was an invasion of royal military prerogative as traditionally exercised and explicitly stated in Restoration laws. To justify that would have led men in 1679-81, as it had led Parker, Prynne, and others in 1642-43, to a theory of government in which sovereignty lay ultimately in the House of Commons. Whatever the indebtedness to Parker and Prynne, who were often quoted, and to republican theories, the Exclusion pamphleteers argued that barring York from the throne would preserve rather than change the ancient contractual constitution. Their problem in maintaining this fiction would have been infinitely compounded by discussing the standing army issue and royal military prerogative.

Charles's success in the Exclusion crisis, his refusal to call Parliament after 1681, the discovery of the Rye House Plot, which implicated many Whigs in an alleged scheme to murder Charles and James and to place Princess Anne on the throne, and the subsequent prosecution of many leading members of the opposition defused the interest in libertarian issues, the standing army among them. But in 1683, at the time of Russell's treason trial, the constitutionality of the Guards was questioned. One of the articles against Russell was that he planned to surprise and overcome the king's Guards, and this point was a major reason for his conviction.[172] Following Russell's execution, an anonymous tract, *A Defence of the Late Lord Russell's Innocency*,[173] appeared, arguing that the attainder should be reversed because the charge he had planned to attack the royal Guards should

[171]Furley, "The Whig Exclusionists," pp. 22, 27, 29.
[172]For the trial, see Howell, *Collection of State Trials* 9: 598-600, 625-35.
[173]*Ibid.*, pp. 730-31.

be thrown out. Treason must be an act against something that is legal. The Guards were not legal, because neither statute, lawbook, nor custom sanctioned them. Only the militia was a legal guard for the king. Ceremonial guards were acceptable, it was granted, but not the "armed bands, commonly now-a-days (after the French mode) called the King's life-guard, [which] ride about and appear with naked swords, to the terror of the nation." For them, there was no law whatsoever, and therefore, the conviction was illegal and the attainder should be reversed.

This tract was of some importance. It provoked an answer[174] and served as a basis for a pamphlet written in 1689 by Henry lord De la Mere entitled *The Late Lord Russell's Case, with Observations upon It* which declared that it would "be easier to find a world in the Moon, than that the Law has made the Guards a lawful Force."[175]

The antistanding army attitude was politicized in the 1670s. Principle, propaganda, and partisanship were joined. The parliamentary opposition took the initiative in criticizing the army and the king's military and foreign policies. With deepening fury, they attacked the soldiers raised for the Third Dutch War, the Scottish Militia, the English troops serving in Louis XIV's army, the men raised ostensibly for a war with France, and the king's Guards. Fearful of Charles's soldiers but also aware of the propaganda opportunities, "Country"-Whig spokesmen played upon the antiarmy sentiment to tarnish the reputation of the king, to discredit his ministers, to thwart his policies, and to achieve certain goals—the dissolution of the Cavalier Parliament and the reduction of the army. As bold as they were, they avoided a forthright attack on the king's military prerogative. In a few debates and tracts, however, the idea was expressed that the king cannot alone raise an army in peacetime, for neither law, legal commentary, nor custom sanctions it. By word and action, Whig proponents paved the way for further criticism of standing armies and of royal military prerogative.

[174]*Ibid.*, pp. 765–66.   [175]See the tract, p. 14.

CHAPTER VII

STANDING ARMIES:
1685-1689

 In the development of the antistanding army tradi-
tion, the reign of James II is important because on
two occasions in 1685—the rebellion in June of
Charles II's illegitimate son, James Scott, duke of
Monmouth, who sought to displace James, and the
parliamentary debates in November—antiarmy sentiments were sharply articulated. In neither case did
the protests alter the immediate course of events.
But the protests did testify to the continued viability
of antiarmy sentiments, and they were used as precedents in later
attacks on the army. At the Revolution of 1689, the Declaration of
Rights, which was read to William and Mary on February 13 when
they were proclaimed king and queen and was later that year given
statutory form as the Bill of Rights, asserted the principle that the
civilian legislature should have ultimate authority over the military
in peacetime, recognized the right of Protestant subjects to bear
arms and declared that there should be no billeting of troops upon
private citizens. The Mutiny Act of 1689 reaffirmed that a professional army was a constitutional force, dependent upon parliamentary approval. For the first time, the army was disciplined by provisions set out in a parliamentary statute.

When the duke of Monmouth landed in June 1685, a program-
matic statement of his principles, designed to rally people to his
cause, was published. Entitled *The Declaration of James, Duke of*

Monmouth,[1] written by Robert Ferguson, a radical Presbyterian minister, and approved by Monmouth while he was in Amsterdam, the *Declaration* stressed that England's government was a limited monarchy whose due bonds had been grossly violated by James II and whose religion, law, and liberties were threatened by a scheme to introduce arbitrary government and Catholicism. The tract called for the overthrow of James, labeled him a traitor and tyrant, and promised a catalog of changes.

Three clauses in the manifesto related to the military issue. First, it promised that Monmouth would shift military authority away from the crown. Second, it pledged that the Militia Act, passed at the time of Restoration, would be repealed. That step would have had the effect of removing the declaratory statement that the power of the militia was solely in the king. Third, the manifesto recommended two new laws relating to military power: one to "prevent all military standing force, except what shall be raised and kept up by Authority and consent of Parliament"; the other to put the militia under the local sheriffs who would be elected by the freeholders of each county. So far as can be determined, the latter scheme, which had obvious affinities to the recommendations of the Levellers, had never before been suggested. Taken together, the three points in the Declaration about the standing army and the militia show that earlier radical notions about military power were far from dead.[2]

It is difficult to judge how much enthusiasm was generated by the manifesto, specifically by the sections about the military.[3] With the defeat of Monmouth, the *Declaration* was declared treason by Parliament. But in many respects the manifesto accurately reflected the aspirations of the oppositional forces, and many of its recommendations remained the goals of that opposition. A comparison of the *Declaration* and the Bill of Rights readily reveals identities between the two documents.

[1]A copy of *The Declaration of James, Duke of Monmouth* is in B. M. Lansdowne Manuscripts, pp. 258-61, verso. It is reproduced in George Roberts, *The Life, Progresses and Rebellion of James, Duke of Monmouth* (London, 1844), 1: 235-50.

[2]It is worth noting that the republican Andrew Fletcher, of Saltoun, who was to develop an elaborate scheme for training the militia during the standing army controversy in 1697-99, was with Monmouth when the *Declaration* was being drafted. Although it has never been suggested that he had a hand in the manifesto, nor has any proof been found, it seems probable that he would have at least approved the sections on standing armies and the militia.

[3]James Ferguson, *Robert Ferguson, The Plotter* (Edinburgh, 1887), p. 220, declares the *Declaration* was enthusiastically received.

The second instance of publicly expressed antiarmy sentiment occurred in the debates of Parliament in the fall of 1685. In this case, it was no group of insurrectionists who had been directly influenced by republicanism who articulated dislike of a standing army, but a majority of the members of the most conservative Parliament that had sat in a decade. The criticism was provoked by James II's announcement of policies toward the army which plainly violated the Test Act, a parliamentary law. On November 9, James opened Parliament with a speech about standing armies, which, in effrontery and truculence, is unmatched by any speech Charles II or William III or any British monarch delivered on that subject. With unexampled provocativeness and arrogance, James declared that he had doubled the number of professional soldiers; he demanded a supply to pay them. The king asserted that the militia was "not sufficient" to protect England from domestic and foreign dangers; he trusted that no one would, in the light of recent rebellions (the reference was, of course, to Monmouth's rebellion and to an uprising in Scotland led by Archibald Campbell, earl of Argyll, in May and June 1685), think otherwise. Acknowledging that Catholic officers, who were obviously not qualified by the Test Act, had been retained in the army, James warned Parliament not to use that fact as an occasion for fomenting dissension. The officers were, he said, excellent soldiers who had served him faithfully and well. He knew them personally, trusted them implicitly, and would not dismiss them. "I will deal plainly with you," said the king. "I will neither expose them to Disgrace nor Myself to the Want of them."[4]

The policy of keeping a standing army officered by Catholics had been seriously considered at least since June. James had revealed his intentions to the French Ambassador, and on June 25, Barrillon reported that James seemed "very glad to have a pretence for raising troops" and concluded that Monmouth's rebellion would make him "more master" of England than he already was.[5] A fortnight later, on the day of the battle of Sedgemoor, where Monmouth was decisively defeated, James told Barrillon that he had armed Catholics in Ireland, appointed Catholics in Scotland to command the army and the militia, and given military commands in England to as many Catholics as he could.[6] At the end of July, Barrillon wrote that James

[4]Grey, *Debates* 8: 353.   [5]Dalrymple, *Memoirs* 2: 169.
[6]Two interviews with Barrillon on that day are recounted in J. C. Turner, *James II* (London, 1948), p. 285.

was determined to keep a standing army on hand, even if Parliament should contribute nothing to its support.[7] Barrillon thought that James made his truculent announcement to Parliament with the aim of achieving a revocation of the Test Act.[8] The simplest solution to the illegality of his actions was for Parliament to revoke the Test Act, a notion that is not implausible, since Parliament was generally sympathetic to James.

The confidence of James's opening speech testified to the king's satisfaction with the results of the court's extraordinary efforts in the spring of 1685 to return a Parliament agreeable to his interests.[9] That carefully managed campaign had succeeded in electing a House of Commons which contained no more than forty people unfriendly to the king. Of 513 men, 400 were new[10] to Westminster Hall and their docility and compliant attitude was demonstrated in the first session of Parliament. Moreover, to secure agreement with his plans for a standing army, James instructed his secretary of war to issue an order on November 3, 1685, less than a week before the second session of Parliament opened, that all army officers who were also members of Parliament should attend the session.[11]

Sir Thomas Clarges and Sir Thomas Meres[12] were the only men returned who had been leading spokesmen against the army in the 1670s. But two Dissenters, Sir John Maynard and Richard Hampden, were elected and played a part in opposing James's military policy. Sir Edward Seymour, the Cavalier and Tory leader, sat in this Parliament, as did Sir Richard Temple, who had played a prominent role in the Popish Plot. Neither one had been active in previous attacks on the army. Seymour, however, had proposed the resolution on March 29, 1679, to reduce all forces raised since September 29, 1677.[13] In 1685, both spoke out emphatically against James's standing force.

James's speech on the ninth of November had the effect of bringing together an opposition in the House of Commons led by Clarges, Hampden, Maynard, Seymour, and Temple, who found general sup-

---

[7]Dalrymple, *Memoirs* 2: 169-70. [8]*Ibid.*, p. 171.

[9]See R. H. George, "Parliamentary Elections and Electioneering in 1685," *Transactions of the Royal Historical Society*, 4th series, 19 (1936): 167-95 (hereafter cited as *T.R.H.S.*).

[10]David Ogg, *England in the Reigns of James II and William III* (Oxford, 1955), p. 143.

[11]Clode, *History of the British Army* 1: 79. It is not known how many army officers sat in this Parliament.

[12]Meres supported the king in this session. [13]Grey, *Debates* 7: 65.

port among the majority of members. It was said that the king's remarks met with a "great deiection of countinance in verie manie considereigne men in the House."[14] But as would be expected in a House whose election had been so carefully managed by the court, most men were less extreme than the major spokesmen against the army. The House, which was poorly attended on November 9,[15] declined a motion to return thanks for the king's speech and adjourned until the twelfth to have time to consider it.

Within those three days the Reverend Samuel Johnson claimed to have sent to "very many Members" a broadside entitled *Several Reasons for the Establishment of a Standing Army, and the Dissolving the Militia.*[16] Written with heavy sarcasm, the sheet listed nine reasons for keeping up a standing army. Among them were that the lords, gentry, and freeholders were incapable of guarding their own laws, estates, and liberty and required keepers; that the Irish Papists were the best soldiers and they were not in the militia (this a jab at James's emphasis on the superior military abilities of the Papists); that two standing armies, at least, were needed (a second army to protect the people from the first); and that, unless the army was established by an act of Parliament, it would be a "risk in law" and a "nullity," because the Papists who were to fill it were prohibited by statute from bearing arms and were restricted to an area within five miles of their house. So far as can be determined, this was the only printed statement against armies in the fall of 1685.

Members returned from the three-day recess well prepared to oppose James's military policy and his demand for money. Four major lines of argument were developed in the debates which took place on November 12, 14, and 16.[17] What most concerned the members of the House of Commons was that the king, in dispensing with

[14]John Bramston, *Autobiography* 32 (London [Camden Society], 1845): 210. The demands were characterized by Evelyn as "very unexpected and unpleasing to the Commons" (de Beer, *The Diary of John Evelyn* 4: 488).

[15]"Not very full," according to James; *C.S.P.D., James II*, vol. 1, February–December 1685, no. 1883. In the calendar for James II's reign, each entry is given a number.

[16]Reprinted in *The Whole Works of Samuel Johnson* (London, 1710), p. 151. The date given in the B.M. catalogue is in error. The next year Johnson published *An Humble and Hearty Address to All the English Protestants in This Present Army* (1686) in the *Works of Samuel Johnson*, pp. 160–61, for which he was degraded as a cleric. Johnson printed several tracts at the height of the controversy over standing armies in 1697–99.

[17]The identification of the speakers in these debates as reported in Anchitell Grey's account should be checked against the Lowther Manuscripts, "The Several Debates of the House of Commons, Pro et Contra Relating to the Establishment of the Militia, Disbanding of the New-raised Forces—And Raiseing [sic] a Supply for His

the Test Act so that Catholic officers could be appointed, had violated the law and integrity of Parliament. Clarges recalled that during the Exclusion controversy men had warned that a Catholic king would establish an army dominated by Catholics, but it had been said that the Test Act would be an effective bulwark against Catholics because James had promised to preserve the law. Now, in setting aside the Test, James had broken the law and breached the liberties of the people.[18] This point was echoed throughout the debate. The second line of argument was that in voting a supply for the army, Parliament would be establishing the soldiers on a legal basis. This, it was asserted, would have the effect of making the army all the more dangerous.[19] Members implied that they were in a stronger position to oppose an army if Parliament did not sanction its creation in the first place. This was in sharp contrast to the position taken later, at the Revolution of 1689, when the Convention Parliament was settling the government in the hands of a king in whom they felt much greater confidence. Then, parliamentary approval of a standing army in peacetime was a restriction imposed upon royal authority. But in 1685, the distrust of the king's intentions was so deep that an army, legalized by act of Parliament, was regarded as the ultimate folly.

The third concern of the men who opposed James's policy in the House was to reform the militia. This time-honored response of country gentlemen to the threat of a standing army under executive authority was stressed. Many speakers rose to defend the militia and to recommend that it be put into better shape. The most eloquent of them all on this topic was the former speaker of the House of Commons, Sir Edward Seymour. A staunch Tory who, it has been said, was "prouder of ruling Devon than controlling England,"[20] declared, "I had rather pay double to [the militia] from whom I fear nothing, than half so much to those [the army] of whom I must ever be afraid."[21] Another member emphasized that if military power were exercised by men who had an "interest in their Country," Parliament and law were safe and the king was secure, "for there is no

Matie. Beginning the 9th Day of November 1685 and Ending the 20th Day of the Same Month Being the Day of the Prorogation." I am grateful to the History of Parliament Trust for allowing me to use a photocopy of the manuscripts. The original is in the Cumberland Record Office.

[18]Grey, *Debates* 8: 356; cf. p. 358.   [19]*Ibid.*, p. 359.
[20]Feiling, *History of the Tory Party*, p. 142.   [21]Grey, *Debates* 8: 357.

such security of any man's loyalty, as a good estate."[22] The resolution to bring in a bill to make the militia more effective passed *nemine contradicente*.[23]

Finally, the traditional disadvantages of a standing army were recited. One member bitterly criticized an army on the grounds of its misbehavior and its use of free quarter. In what must have been a telling remark, the speaker reminded the House that strict laws had been laid down for the army by the king,[24] that the soldier's unseemly behavior proved that the king, himself, obviously was unable to govern the army and, if that were the case, all Englishmen were endangered.[25] Another speaker remarked that although James had ordered that no soldiers were to be quartered in private houses and that no free billets were to be allowed, the soldiers were quartered in private houses and paid nothing. Supplying an army was "maintaining so many idle persons to lord it over the rest of the subjects."[26] Another member stressed that a standing army was objectionable because it lured "ploughmen and servants" into its ranks and thus depleted the supply of manpower in the counties.[27]

Against these protests, James's military policy was ably defended by the earl of Ranelagh, Lord Preston, Sir John Ernle, William Blathwayt, and Sir William Clifton (rather than Sir Winston Churchill).[28] In contrast to James, these men were careful not to deprecate the value of the militia, but rather argued that, until the militia was remodeled and threats to England's security from abroad were removed, some additional professional forces were necessary. Changes in military technology necessitated training; soldiering was a "trade" that had to be learned.[29] Moreover, it may have impressed some men that Meres, who had in the previous decade worn out his voice criticizing Charles II's army, now joined these men. In urging that the army James wanted should be accepted, Meres said he would call them "Guards."[30] He implied that this word was inoffensive and

---

[22]*Ibid.*, p. 365.   [23]*C.J.* 9: 759.

[24]Two articles of war were issued, one in 1685 and the other in 1686.

[25]Grey, *Debates* 8: 365, where the speaker is given as Edmund Waller, the poet. Although Waller was returned, he probably did not attend the session of Parliament because of old age (he was 79) and illness; the three speeches attributed to him were made by William Wogan (ca. 1635-1708). See Lowther Manuscripts, "The Several Debates of the House of Commons, Pro et Contra," f. 40. For Waller and Wogan, see the unpublished biographies at the History of Parliament Trust.

[26]Grey, *Debates* 8: 358.   [27]*Ibid.*, p. 366.

[28]See Lowther Manuscripts, "The Several Debates of the House of Commons, Pro et Contra," ff. 9, 26, 40; cf. Grey, *Debates* 8: 354, 359, 364.

[29]Grey, *Debates* 8: 354-56, 359.   [30]*Ibid.*, p. 358.

could be used for a "considerable force." Meres's wordplay supports the thesis that the term "standing army" had been deliberately used in the past to arouse apprehension.

The leading spokesmen against the army were unable to bring the House to vote specifically to condemn a standing army. Moreover, the House agreed unanimously to grant a supply to the king and to bring in a bill to reform the militia. The fact that a supply of £700,000 was given the king suggests how ambivalent the attitude toward a standing army was in this Parliament. The sum was much less than what the court wanted (i.e., £1,200,000), but on the other hand, it was much more than what the antiarmy spokesmen wanted (£200,000). By settling on £700,000 members seemed to feel that they were giving the king enough money to secure the nation, but not enough to rule without calling Parliament again. There was much confused thinking. Political self-interest, fear of alienating the new king, and hope of professional opportunity for themselves or relatives in a professional army were considerations. Basically what concerned the majority of this Parliament was having a standing army officered by Catholics. Hampden, Clarges, and others argued for a law to remove the Catholic officers.[31] It was finally agreed that an Address be drawn up explicitly stating that by law Papists could not serve in the army and that this incapacity could not be removed except by act of Parliament. In other words, the king could not dispense with an act of Parliament. It was proposed that the Address contain the further statement that the king should remove those Catholic officers. The Address was written by Clarges, Seymour, and Maynard but was softened by the House to make it as inoffensive to James II as possible. The clause asking the king not to continue the Catholic officers was removed, and one was substituted for it that prayed the king to take steps so that no apprehensions would remain. It may be argued that if James had asked for a standing army officered by Protestants, he could probably have won it from this Parliament, which contained so many men, as already noted, who were friendly to him.

The Address about the Catholic officers was presented to James on November 16. The king, visibly angry,[32] returned a peremptory reply in which he said he had not expected such an address. The House took refuge in silence. The emotional intensity of the situation

[31]Bramston, *Autobiography*, pp. 213-14; Grey, *Debates* 7: 361.
[32]Dalrymple, *Memoirs* 2: 172-73; Morrice, "Entr'ing Book" 1: 496-98.

was revealed when in responding to a motion to take the king's speech into consideration another day, a member made a remark about Englishmen not being frightened by high words, which so offended the king's friends that, despite apologies, the individual was thrown into the Tower.[33]

In the House of Lords, "very great debates" took place on November 19 on the king's speech.[34] The same arguments as those made in Commons were taken up by the Lords. The most effective comments were offered by Henry Compton, bishop of London, who stressed not the dangers of a standing army but the illegality of appointing Catholic officers in the army, an act which he took as portending the Catholicizing of the entire government. Contemporaries thought that it was these debates in the House of Lords which led James, much to people's surprise, to prorogue Parliament the next day.[35]

By this rash act, the king lost the £700,000 supply which had been granted. But James had already told Barrillon that he would keep his army even if Parliament refused to give him money for it. Parliament's generosity in the spring session in granting the king a supply for life allowed James greater financial independence than his brother ever enjoyed. The prorogation scattered members and dissolved the forum where they might have continued to debate the king's military policy and to frame a bill to strengthen the militia. Some men who had spoken out against the king were punished. Bishop Compton was removed from the council, and military officers who had voted with the opposition in the House of Commons were dismissed.[36]

Although the debates of November 1685 accomplished nothing in the immediate circumstance, they were of importance in the evolution of the standing army issue. Contemporaries regarded these debates as significant. An account of the debates was reprinted in *The Faithful Register* in 1689,[37] possibly when the Convention Parliament was in session. Again in 1697 when the standing army controversy was reopened, the debates of 1685 were reprinted. The

---

[33]Grey, *Debates* 8: 369-70.

[34]Narcissus Luttrell, *A Brief Relation of State Affairs from September 1678 to April 1714* (Oxford, 1857), 1: 364. The best account of the debate with comments on the discrepancies in the earlier accounts is H. C. Foxcroft, *Halifax* 1: 458-59 and n. 5.

[35]Luttrell, *A Brief Relation* 1: 364; de Beer, *The Diary of John Evelyn* 4: 489.

[36]Luttrell, *A Brief Relation* 1: 367; Dalrymple, *Memoirs* 1: 88.

[37]*The Faithful Register; Or, the Debates of the House of Commons in Four Several Parliaments . . . wherein, the Points of Prerogative Priviledges, Popish Designs, Standing Army, County-Militia, Supplies . . . Are Fully Discuss'd* (London, 1689).

preface[38] to this edition insisted that there was much value in these earlier debates. The anonymous author praised the members of Parliament of 1685 for showing so much "free English spirit" and for striving to leave liberties, which they had inherited from their ancestors, "entire to succeeding Generations." By implication the preface exhorted men in 1697 to do the same and model themselves on their predecessors in the Parliament of 1685 who had argued against a standing army and for a militia.

During the next three years the army was a highly visible and irritating symbol of power. In 1686, James had thirteen thousand soldiers under the command of Louis Duras, earl of Feversham, stationed at Hounslow Heath, where daily mass was observed.[39] However unprepossessing and unmartial the men may have looked,[40] their presence so near London was a plain threat to the capital. Further, the use of martial law, including the death penalty for desertion in time of peace, which was set out in the Articles of War for the discipline of the army in 1686, offered further evidence of James's concern to assure the loyalty of the army and his willingness to use means of doubtful legality. Some high-ranking legal officers protested these steps, and at least two of them resigned.[41] In 1687, moreover, James further alienated the local aristocracy by dismissing many lord-lieutenants and their deputies and other local officers who were well liked and highly regarded in the counties. As a consequence of these purges of men of substance and social position, James lost the allegiance of the militia and, at the Revolution, was unable to count on its support. By 1688 James had a peacetime military establishment of over fifty-three thousand officers and men.[42] Many of the commands were given to Irish Catholics.[43] He also had secured, as a result of the efforts of his minister, Robert Spencer, earl of Sunderland, a subsidy from Louis XIV and a promise of mili-

[38]*The Several Debates of the House of Commons in the Reign of the Late King James II Pro and Contra, Relating to the Establishment of the Militia, Disbanding the New-Raised Forces* (London, 1697), preface to the reader.

[39]Ogg, *England in the Reigns of James II and William III*, p. 169.

[40]*Ibid.*; de Beer, *The Diary of John Evelyn* 4: 514; Margaret Verney, *Memoirs of the Verney Family from the Restoration to the Revolution 1660 to 1696* (London, 1899), 4: 414-15.

[41]Morrice, "Entr'ing Book" 1: 623, 625, 652; Ogg, *England in the Reigns of James II and William III*, pp. 182-83.

[42]A List of James II's Army, dated 1688, gives the total as 53,716 officers and men; 37,000 were infantry. See *C.S.P.D., James II*, vol. 3, June 1687-February 1689, no. 2124, and S.P. 8/2, part 2, fols. 99-100.

[43]*C.S.P.D., James II*, vol. 3, June, 1687-February, 1689, no. 1193.

tary assistance from the French king "pour opprimer ses ennemis et se faire obèir de ses sujets."[44]

But, as is well known, events fell out differently, and William of Orange, the husband of James's Protestant daughter, Mary, landed in England unopposed in November 1688. James's army, on the whole, transferred its allegiance to William, and a military contest was avoided.[45] In January 1689 a Convention Parliament met to settle the government. After long debate, it was agreed that James had abdicated, that the throne was vacant, and that the royal power should be vested in William and Mary. For two weeks, members labored to draw up a statement of constitutional guarantees. On February 13, in the palace of Whitehall, this statement, referred to then as a Declaration of Rights, was read by the Clerk of the House of Lords and presented to William and Mary in the course of the ceremony in which they were proclaimed king and queen.[46] This Declaration became a statute, commonly known as the Bill of Rights,[47] when it was signed by the king on December 16, 1689.

The presence in the Convention Parliament of so many former opponents of the army assured that the standing army question and the issue of militia reform would be considered. Birch, Boscawen, Clarges, Lee, Littleton, Maynard, Powle, Sacheverell, Seymour, Temple, and Williams were all elected to the Convention.[48] They took the initiative in introducing the military issue. All of them, except Powle, who was chosen speaker of the House, were appointed on January 29 to a committee of thirty-nine members charged with bringing in a list of measures to secure England from arbitrary government.[49]

Lee, Temple, and Williams raised the issues of reforming the militia and settling the army in the debate on January 29, 1689. Williams wanted the committee to review the Restoration Militia Act and, as he phrased it, "in whose hands you will put it should be our Head."[50] He was asking for a review of the crown's prerogative power

---

[44]Ogg, *England in the Reigns of James II and William III*, p. 192.

[45]Not all soldiers, however, willingly accepted William III, as the mutiny of Lord Dumbarton's regiment in March 1689 dramatically showed. Morrice, "Entr'ing Book" 2: 432, 449, reports reluctance among the soldiers as early as January.

[46]*C.J.* 10: 29.

[47]The Bill of Rights is conveniently found in Browning, *English Historical Documents* 8: 122-28. The present author projects a detailed study of the Declaration of Rights.

[48]For a study of that election, see John H. Plumb, "The Elections to the Convention Parliament of 1688-89," *C.H.J.* 5 (1937): 235-54.

[49]*C.J.* 10: 15. [50]Grey, *Debates* 9: 30, 31, 32, 33.

over the militia and implying that that power should be shifted to Parliament. Temple felt that the Convention should "provide against a Standing Army without consent of Parliament" in peacetime. Lee remarked that "There was an opinion formerly, of the Long Robe that must be exploded, 'that the king may raise what Army he pleases, if he pay for them.'" Plainly, he was calling for the repeal of a section of the Disbanding Act of 1660 and for the removal of a royal prerogative which the crown had always exercised. Lee went on to say that allowing the king such a right was tantamount to supporting slavery.[51] These comments in the debate on January 29 are the only recorded ones made on the army and militia questions. There is no specific evidence of what was said about the army and militia (or anything else) in the meetings of the committee that drafted the Declaration of Rights.

As for the press, many pamphlets were printed in 1689 to justify the Revolution, advise the Convention, or explain events. Few go beyond mere mention of the questions of the militia or the standing army.[52] An account of the debates about the militia and army in November 1685 was reprinted in *The Faithful Register* and several tracts written earlier by Shaftesbury's circle which criticized a standing army were reprinted, along with many other pamphlets, in *A Collection of State Tracts . . . Privately Printed in the Reign of King Charles II*. John Humfrey's *Advice Before It Be Too Late: Or a Breviate for the Convention* was distributed to members of the Convention before it was printed. It explicitly asserted that the "Power of the Sword" should be placed in the hands of Parliament. John Humfrey[53] was a prominent Presbyterian who had for years written pamphlets on current topics to persuade members of Parliament to a course of action, but his *Breviate* failed to move the Convention sufficiently to change the Militia Act or to state directly that the authority over the militia was not the king's.

The private correspondence and personal papers that remain[54] for the weeks around the Convention also fail to reveal an interest in the

[51]*Ibid.*, p. 35.

[52]Two examples of tracts that mention military questions are: *The History of the Late Revolution in England, with the Causes & Means by which It Was Accomplished* (London, 1689); and *A Letter to a Gentleman of Brussels, Containing an Account of the Peoples Revolt from the Crown* (Windsor, December 22, 1688).

[53]Lacey, *Dissent and Parliamentary Politics*, pp. 56, 65, 68, 69, 226-27.

[54]Many private and public papers were deliberately destroyed in this revolutionary period. *The Calendar of State Papers, Domestic Series, James II*, vol. 3, June 1687-February 1689, and the material still in manuscript in the Public Record

standing army issue as intense as that which consumed men's minds a decade before. Among the papers of Lord Wharton, the Presbyterian, was a proposal for remodeling the government which recommended that the freeholders should "nominate" the militia officers. Wharton specified that freeholders who had £20 a year or held a copyhold for life of £30 a year should nominate "all commission officers of the militia."[55] This idea was similar to that put forward earlier in the Duke of Monmouth's *Declaration* and also had affinities with still earlier recommendations offered by the Levellers. The point was to bring the control of the militia closer to the people in the local county and dilute the authority of the central government over the operation of the militia. There is no specific evidence that Wharton actually argued for this arrangement for the militia, but it may have been part of the thinking behind the clause on reform of the militia that was dropped from the final draft of the Declaration of Rights.

The first draft of the Declaration of Rights was reported from the committee on February 2 by Sir George Treby.[56] This draft included the suggestions about the army and militia which had been advanced on January 29. Article v asserted that the Militia Acts were grievous to the subject and implied that they should be reformed. Article vi declared that the consent of Parliament was required to raise and maintain an army in peacetime, and Article vii held that Protestant subjects should be allowed to keep arms for their own defense. These clauses relating to military matters were agreed to by the House on February 4 Morrice reported, "with great unanimity."[57] A copy of this draft of the grievances, entitled *The Publick Grievances of the Nation, Adjudged Necessary, by the Honorable the House of Commons To be Redressed*, was printed, presumably with a view to informing the politically conscious public and enlisting its agreement. There is no record of petitions to the Convention on the military questions.

Within less than a week, however, the article dealing with the militia had disappeared. On February 8, following debates which lasted into the night of the seventh, John Somers presented a new

---

Office (S.P. 8/1; 8/5; 32/16 32/17 44/98) are fragmentary and uninformative for the months of January and February 1689. In neither the calendar nor the manuscripts is the standing army issue referred to.

[55]Bodleian Library, Carte Manuscripts, 81, f. 766.   [56]*C.J.* 10: 17.

[57]Morrice, "Entr'ing Book" 2: 456.

draft which did not contain a reference to the militia.[58] Undoubtedly, it was removed at the insistence of the House of Lords, possibly because the proposed law would have curtailed the power of the lord-lieutenants. Morrice noted that some of the Lords failed in an attempt to persuade William to reject the stipulations that the House of Commons were framing and that afterwards they disagreed with the Commons in "a few articles." One of those articles concerned the militia, for Morrice went on to say the Lords "would have it not so very generally expressed about the Militia Clauses."[59] Apparently, the House of Commons dropped the clause about reforming the militia to avoid disagreement with the Lords.[60]

It should be noted, however, that later in March the oath in the Militia Act of 1662, which required a man to swear that he would not take up arms against the king or those commissioned by him, and which, it will be recalled, the Person of Quality had objected to so strenuously in 1675, was repealed.[61] Moreover, following a mutiny in the army, Parliament (the Convention was turned into a Parliament on February 23) made another abortive attempt in April 1689 to introduce legislation that would reform the militia. A committee which included Garroway, Musgrave, Sacheverell, and Somers brought in a bill which would have created a strong militia as a counterweight to the professional army.[62] But for diverse reasons, this further effort at reform of the militia was lost at the end of the session.

If the House of Lords sabotaged the clause about the militia in the draft of the Declaration of Rights, they strengthened the section about the standing army. They recommended that the phrase "and quartering soldiers contrary to Law" be added to the list of James's tyrannical acts.[63] The argument was that free quarter aggravated the general grievance of keeping a standing army in peacetime without the consent of Parliament and was a plain violation of the provisions of the Petition of Right of 1628. The addition was accepted by the Commons. By February 12, both Houses had agreed to the statement

---

[58]*C.J.* 10: 23–25, Grey, *Debates* 9: 79. Folger Manuscripts, Newdigate Newsletters, L.C., 1967, 1972.

[59]Morrice, "Entr'ing Book" 2: 464–65.

[60]The debate in the House of Lords on February 2 was so violent that Morrice (*ibid.*, p. 454) reported that "all sober and thinking men were affraid they [the Lords] were resolved to put it to a decision by the sword."

[61]1W & M, cap. 8, s. 11; *Statutes of the Realm* 6: 59.

[62]See Western, *The English Militia in the Eighteenth Century*, pp. 85–89.

[63]*L.J.* 14: 722; Folger Manuscripts, Newdigate Newsletters, L.C., 1973, 1974.

of rights, both accepting the clauses that there should be no standing army in time of peace without the consent of Parliament and that Protestant subjects might have arms for their defense "suitable to their conditions and as allowed by law." By the end of the year, the statement had become a law, the Bill of Rights.

So far as the standing army issue is concerned, the Bill of Rights was a revolutionary document. In the first part which listed James's illegal acts, it declared (quite inaccurately and without regard to common law and practice or the clause in the Disbanding Act of 1660) that it was illegal for the king, on his own, to raise and maintain an army in peacetime. In the section which reaffirmed the rights of Englishmen, Article VI asserted that it was ancient right and law that there should be no standing army in time of peace without Parliament's consent. Far from this being ancient law, it was a revolutionary assertion, which reflected parliamentarian and republican thinking since 1641-42.[64]

In terms of the prerogative powers of the king, Article VI was the most important clause in the Bill of Rights. It was drafted, so far as the record shows, with no discussion in the Convention or the press about its implications for the theory and practice of government. The Militia Acts of the Restoration giving the king sole military command were not repealed, and the monarch remained the commander-in-chief of the army and militia in war and peace. The limits of the crown's authority over the military forces were not explored or spelled out. Parliamentary control of the army in peacetime was simply asserted, and in that assertion, sovereignty was shifted from the crown to Parliament. Struggles between crown and Parliament would recur in the future, but by Article VI, the king was stripped of his most important prerogative, to raise as many soldiers as he wanted in peacetime so long as he paid them.

This first Parliament of the Revolution dealt with another military-related question that had long been a contentious issue between king and Parliament; that is, the discipline of the army. This was handled in a way that reflected the revolutionary principle in the Declaration of Rights, that Parliament should have ultimate power over the army in peacetime. The first Mutiny Bill, passed by the House of Commons on March 28, 1689, was a response to the mutiny in Lord Dum-

---

[64]Cf. Thomson, *Constitutional History* 4: 175; G. N. Clark, *The Later Stuarts* (Oxford, 1934), p. 140. Curiously, Holdsworth does not comment on Article VI.

barton's regiment which had been reported on the fifteenth of that month.[65] Regulation of the discipline of the army was long overdue, and even before the mutiny, a committee composed of Lee, Sacheverell, Somers, and Sir John Holt had been asked to bring in a bill to punish mutineers and deserters from the army.[66] The projected war with France and the threat from Ireland added urgency. Surely the bill reflected the influence of the court. William simply had to have the means to discipline the large army that was necessary to carry out his plans.

Clode regards the Mutiny Act as the "great divide" in the history of martial law.[67] By its terms, martial law, as distinguished from civil law, was established by a statutory regulation. The Act reaffirmed that a standing army in peacetime without the consent of Parliament was illegal. For the first time, statutory sanction was given to capital punishment for mutiny, sedition, or desertion. Procedures were spelled out. It was specified that the act was not to extend to the militia forces and that no soldier or officer was to be exempt from the "ordinary process of law." In other words, "the soldier was to remain a citizen."[68] Significantly, in terms of Parliament's intentions to limit the power of the crown over the army, the Act was to be in force for only six months. Thereafter, a Mutiny Act was passed each year, with few exceptions. The Mutiny Act and certain clauses in the Declaration of Rights had the effect of assuring that the king, if he was to keep an army, would not be able to function without Parliament.

One can only speculate about why there was an absence of theoretical talk about military power in the spring of 1689. As already indicated, there is no evidence that the implications of Article vi in the Declaration of Rights for the principle of sovereignty in the government were explored. A radical act was performed in taking from the king his most important prerogative, of raising and keeping an army in peacetime so long as he paid them, as the Disbanding Act of 1660 had allowed. Why did not members of the Convention thoroughly discuss the significance of what they were doing? Possibly, members felt that discussion about Article vi would have led them

[65]The Mutiny Bill is in Browning, *English Historical Documents* 8: 812–13; for the debate on the mutiny in Lord Dumbarton's regiment, see Grey, *Debates* 9: 164–69; *C.J.* 10: 49, 69.

[66]*C.J.* 10: 47, 52, 53, 67.

[67]Clode, *The Administration of Justice under Military and Martial Law*, p. 9.

[68]Thomson, *A Constitutional History of England* 4: 292–93.

into a labyrinthine examination of the beginnings and nature of government, which in another connection Sir William Williams counseled them to avoid.[69] In fact, avoidance of careful definitions of ultimate military power and lengthy discussions about it may be regarded as a mark of political astuteness. Ignore what is being said around London, advised Maynard. Stick to the "obvious and apparent."[70] Too much discussion about limiting the king can only lead to confusion, warned another member.[71] Prince William would not have tolerated the explicitly stated assertion that the military power of the crown had been diluted. Further, the Convention Parliament was not a radical assembly. Two hundred members from the Parliament of 1685 were returned to the Convention Parliament, and 183 had never before sat in a Parliament.[72] Morrice noted that there were proportionately as many members in the House of Commons as in the House of Lords who favored the idea that the throne was not vacant, which suggested their basic conservatism.[73] If the Lords were successful in eliminating the article citing the militia laws as a grievance, possibly they blocked any discussion of the implications of Article VI. Besides, the members of the Convention were more interested in other matters than they were in the army and the militia. Settling the throne in a formula that both Houses could accept was of overriding importance. There was a sense of urgency: Prince William and some members urged the Convention to complete quickly the Declaration of Rights.[74] So an illegal assertion and a revolutionary principle were inserted in the Declaration of Rights without a searching examination of the implications or a stirring declaration that Article VI marked a transfer of sovereignty in the government from king to Parliament.

Finally, the general question of whether there should be a standing army at all in peacetime was not raised. The lack of anxiety about the army suggested trust in William whom the Convention was preparing to crown king. Further, the majority of members had become more comfortable with a professional army in peacetime so long as it was Protestant and agreed to by Parliament. In 1689, when there was a chance to insist, as men had so often done before, that responsi-

---

[69]Grey, *Debates* 9: 15; cf. Morrice, "Entr'ing Book" 2: 444, who reports that "many thought they [members of the Convention] would never have disentangled themselves nor have got to a question."

[70]Grey, *Debates* 9: 32-33.   [71]*Ibid.*, p. 34.

[72]Plumb, "The Elections to the Convention Parliament of 1688-89," p. 244.

[73]Morrice, "Entr'ing Book" 2: 459.   [74]Grey, *Debates* 9: 35, 70-71, 79-80.

bility for the military defenses of the nation should be borne by a remodeled militia and a very limited number of Guards, this was not done. So far as the record of the Convention debates shows, it was never said that England should be without any standing army during peacetime, nor that the militia was sufficient for the defenses of the land. Indeed, in the next month, Sir Christopher Musgrave, a man who was no lover of standing armies, remarked in the House, "I believe that England can never be without some standing force."[75] Thirty years of a standing army, which had offered opportunity for careers for members of the upper classes, had generated more acceptance than has been granted, so long as Parliament had a part in the army's control and the Test Act was operative. In sum, the antiarmy sentiment had been somewhat "tempered."

Revolutionary in basic character, but unjustified by theoretical exposition in debate or tract, Article VI of the Declaration of Rights set the constitutional position of England's armed forces on a basis which would have delighted the Parliamentarians of 1641-42 and gratified the republicans of the Interregnum. It established the principle of civilian control of the military and testified to the conviction that restrained in this manner the monarchy could be kept from developing into a tyranny. Article VI was the most important step that the Convention took to secure the nation's laws, liberties, and rights. The principle that it articulated was to be tested by King William III ten years later.

---

[75]*Ibid.*, p. 179. But note Morrice's comment ("Entr'ing Book" 2: 455): "There ought immediately be a Reform of that Army, not much less then a disbanding of it."

CHAPTER VIII

THE CLIMAX OF THE STANDING
ARMY ISSUE IN PARLIAMENT
AND PRESS: 1697–1699

 The climax in the history of protests against maintaining professional soldiers in peacetime occurred between the fall of 1697 and the spring of 1699, following the Treaty of Ryswick. The immediate practical question was what to do with King William's large, victorious army. The ideological issue at this time was not whether Parliament had the right to approve the military force in peacetime (that had been established at the Revolution), but whether the king would accept Parliament's decision on the size of the army and abide by it. For about eighteen months, William III and his supporters fought over this issue against a Tory coalition in the House of Commons, which was supported by a group of radical Whig pamphleteers. The confrontations in Parliament and press illuminate the continuing struggle for power between the king and the House of Commons. The question of maintaining a standing army in peacetime also reached a crescendo in the press in 1697–99. For the first time, the issue was discussed directly and fully, instead of in connection with some other question.

Both sides regarded the contest as one of special importance; the parliamentary debates were notably stormy and the pamphlet literature contentious and voluminous. For King William there was no question during his reign which touched his interest more deeply or involved him more directly in English domestic politics. For his opponents, the issues were the historic, decisive ones of many generations. What was the relative power of king and Parliament? Would not a standing army threaten law, liberty, and Parliament? Would military power in the court control the power of party groupings in Parliament? The whole combined was further complicated because it exacerbated the deep division in the Whig party between court or ministerial Whigs and so-called "Old Whigs," men who did not hold office and who represented the interests of country members.

For several reasons, the king lost his battle to keep a large standing army in peacetime. This outcome was never seriously in doubt as the strength of the two sides was disparate. Parliament voted to reduce the army to ten thousand men in 1697, to cut it further to seven thousand natural-born subjects in 1698, and to deny the king his Dutch Guards in 1699. Still, a contest did take place, and as the votes on the motions about the army prove, sometimes the court made a very respectable showing. A compromise was reached in the end, and a small force was allowed. By the end of the century, no one in Parliament suggested that England could be safe with no standing force at all.

Planning and decision in this controversy were concentrated in the king's hands.[1] Like his predecessors, William felt that the military establishment of the nation was the "fittest" of all subjects for a king to quarrel about. If he had been blessed with a more outgoing or winning personality, his dealings with his Parliament and ministers on the army issue might have been more effective. He was never a popular king. He was regarded as too "solemn and serious," too cool and withdrawn. His Dutch favorites, his obvious preference for Holland, and his European rather than English orientation (in a reign of thirteen years, he was away from England about five years) were resented by many Englishmen. He was brusque in manner and never suffered fools gladly. He was never in robust health. He shared his thoughts and emotions with very few men, and these not Englishmen. This habit, combined with his view that foreign affairs should be conducted by the king as an undoubted prerogative of the crown, led him to exclude Englishmen close to him in government from the secrets of international negotiations.[2] He favored neither Whig nor Tory and was

---

[1]Lois G. Schwoerer, "The Role of King William III of England in the Standing Army Controversy—1697-1699," *J.B.S.* 5 (1966): 74-94, where part of this chapter appears in different form. Dennis Rubini treats the disbandment of the army in his *Court and Country 1688-1702* (London, 1967), chapter 6.

[2]Gilbert Burnet, *History of My Own Time*, ed. Earls of Darmouth and Hardwicke, Speaker Onslow, and Dean Swift (Oxford, 1833), 4: 2-3, 25, 219, 286, 562, 563; Paul Grimblot, ed., *Letters of William III and Louis XIV and Their Ministers, Illustrative of the Domestic and Foreign Politics of England from the Peace of*

willing to use as his ministers men from either party, so long as they would support his foreign policy of resistance to Louis XIV.[3] For an English monarch to rule above party groupings is not novel, but in William's case it is pertinent to understanding the failure of his military aims. There was no group of men who were committed, as a party, to his general interests or to his specific goal of a sizable army.

The standing army issue was not argued in 1697–99 with innuendo that William wanted an army to Catholicize the nation or bring England within the French orbit, as had been the case with his predecessors. But William was suspected of holding as high notions about royal prerogative as any Stuart king. His rule as Stadholder of Holland had demonstrated such convictions, and in England he made it plain that he had not come "to establish a commonwealth."[4] But there is no evidence of a calculated ulterior motive of using a standing army to set up an absolute government in England behind William's military policy. He candidly told Camille d'Hostun, duc de Tallard, Louis XIV's ambassador, that "if he proposed and insisted on retaining the troops, it was not for any private interest or to uphold his authority, or to make himself master; that such ideas might occur to him if he had children or if the crown were to remain in the hands of some member of his family, but that he was alone; and, therefore, it was the affair of the nation rather than his. . . . "[5] William undoubtedly wanted as large a force as he could get, but he seems to have been willing to think in realistic terms of an army of around thirty-five thousand men, a reduction of almost two-thirds of the total number on hand in October 1697.[6] Such an army would have been small indeed in comparison to Louis XIV's huge establishment. Even so, William plainly was insensitive to the real possibility of danger to English liberties which

---

Ryswick to the Accession of Philip V of Spain, 1697 to 1700 (London, 1848), 1: 454, 416, 345. For William's absences from England, see Ogg, *England in the Reigns of James II and William III*, p. 332. The best of several biographies of William is Stephen Baxter, *William III* (London, 1966), which is especially strong on his rule in Holland.

[3]Feiling, *History of the Tory Party*, pp. 256, 275.   [4]*Ibid.*, p. 256.

[5]Grimblot, *Letters of William III and Louis XIV* 2: 31–32; but cf. *ibid.* 3: 236, in which Tallard reported that Portland told him William might have handled things differently if he were younger and his passion more ardent.

[6]The total number of land forces, exclusive of officers, on hand in October 1697 was 90,172 (*C.S.P.D., 1697*, p. 454). The size of the projected army was reported variously (*ibid.*, pp. 484, 512); Narcissus Luttrell, *A Brief Historical Relation of State Affairs from September 1678 to April 1714* (Oxford, 1857), 4: 281, 284; Grimblot, *Letters of William III and Louis XIV* 1: 133–34, 137–38; Northamptonshire Record Office, Delapré Abbey, Shrewsbury Correspondence, vol. I, letter no. 154.

an army implied, and could write that "people here only busy themselves about a fanciful liberty."[7]

William III's interest, with single-minded intensity, was focused on the vexing problem of Louis XIV's ambition. He had no illusions about the need for England to maintain a strong military posture. His personal correspondence with his two closest confidants, Anthony Heinsius, grand pensionary of Holland, and William Bentinck, earl of Portland, provides a backdrop for the progress of the several army bills. His letters repeatedly reflect anxiety, lament, anger, frustration. He was certain that Louis was planning to resume the war, that Parliament had weakened his hand in the Partition Treaty[8] negotiations and embarrassed him before the world, that the army reductions were encouraging France to formulate plans she had not even thought of before, that England *must* commit herself to a continental role, that Englishmen were so fatuous that "one would say, either this island is the only thing on the face of the earth or that it has nothing to do with the rest of the world."[9] More effectively than anything else, these letters reveal William's acuteness in plumbing Louis's motives and explain William's persistence in the standing army controversy.

Further testimony to William's determination to win a sizable army was his effort to make himself more ingratiating during the standing army contest. An observer noted that "upon this occasion . . . [the king] behaved himself much different from the haughty character he had all along maintained."[10] Another wrote that "the King is more than usually pleasant and shows outwardly no resentment."[11] In view of his private correspondence and of recurrent poor health during this time, one can imagine what it cost him to convey an impression of "extreme patience" and "imperturbability," and to appear never "to be hurt at any resolution which may have been taken."[12] The modification in the king's demeanor underscores the seriousness of his purpose.

[7]Grimblot, *Letters of William III and Louis XIV* 1: 148.

[8]For a brief account of the Partition Treaty negotiations see Baxter, *William III*, chapter 26.

[9]Grimblot, *Letters of William III and Louis XIV* 1: 184, and cf. 133, 143, 211, 218, 311, 321, 324, 348, 349, 359, 363, 431; 2: 209, 210, 213, 214, 219, 229, 233, 238, 248.

[10]*Political Remarks on the Life and Reign of William III*, in *Harleian Miscellany* 10: 560.

[11]H.M.C., *Hastings Mss.* 2: 310.

[12]Grimblot, *Letters of William III and Louis XIV* 1: 355; 2: 27, 238. F. Bonnet (the ambassador from Brandenburg) notes recurrent indispositions: B.M., Add. Mss., 30,000 A, ff. 379, 411.

William found support for his position in varying degress of enthusiasm and conviction. John lord Somers, who had recently been appointed lord chancellor of England, was the most prestigious man who defended the king's need for a standing army. On April 22, 1697, he was appointed lord high chancellor and on December 2 was raised to the peerage. The consequence of this recognition was that Somers was removed from the House of Commons where the battle of the land force was most bitterly fought. Tallard reported that Somers was the only Englishman who had any "real share in public affairs" and described him as "very honest, and much esteemed by all parties."[13] At the same time, however, Tallard noted that he had no part in international policies. Respected as he was by all parties, Somers was a Whig. A contemporary styled him a few years later as "the life, the soul and the spirit of his party."[14] As a minister of the king, Somers must have felt some reluctance in supporting a measure which violated a traditional Whig principle and, one suspects, his own convictions. His major contribution was to write a tract defending the king's policy entitled *A Letter, Ballancing the Necessity of Keeping a Land-Force in Times of Peace: With the Dangers that May Follow on It*, which will be discussed below.

In addition to Somers, a few of the king's ministers and officeholders argued William's case in the House of Commons. Sir Thomas Littleton, who held a post as lord of the Admiralty, was described as "the best and most artificial advocate against disbanding . . . [the army] at all."[15] Charles Montague, formerly chancellor of the Exchequer and in 1697 first lord of the Treasury (in 1701, earl of Halifax), was singled out as an effective speaker for the king's project. He countered the attack on the army by using ridicule and suggesting that William's critics should take the advice of men wiser than themselves.[16] Others, like William Blathwayt, the secretary of war, Richard

---

[13]Grimblot, *Letters of William III and Louis XIV* 1: 467.

[14]Philip Yorke (second earl of Hardwicke), ed., *Miscellaneous State Papers from 1501 to 1726* (London, 1778), 2: 446 (Robert Spencer, earl of Sunderland to King William, September 11, 1701). Professor William Sachse's biography of Somers is awaited. Henry Maddock, *An Account of the Life and Writings of Lord Chancellor Somers* (London, 1812), may be consulted.

[15]*Considerations upon the Choice of a Speaker of the House of Commons in the House of Commons in the Approaching Session* (London, 1698), in *A Collection of State Tracts Publish'd during the Reign of King William III* (London, 1706), 2: 652.

[16]G. P. R. James, ed., *Letters Illustrative of the Reign of William III from 1696 to 1708 Addressed to the Duke of Shrewsbury by James Vernon, esq., Secretary of State* (London, 1841), 2: 239-40. Also B.M. Bonnet, Add. Mss., 30,000 A. f. 397 verso; 30,000 B, ff 8 verso, 9; 30,000 C, f. 3 verso.

Jones, earl of Ranelagh, the paymaster-general of the army, and Thomas Coningsby, earl of Coningsby and in 1698 paymaster of the forces in Ireland, were also mentioned as participating in debate.[17] As the votes on some of the motions about the army show, there were a number of men in the House of Commons who voted with the king, some undoubtedly from sincere agreement with his proposal and others, as the antiarmy pamphleteers charged, probably from fear of losing their credit with William. Further, a majority of the members of the House of Lords and the Judges of the Circuit supported the policy of a large land force.[18]

Outside the government several paid and volunteer pamphleteers wrote to vindicate the king's policy. Arguing for William's position were chiefly Daniel Defoe and, less significantly, Matthew Prior and Richard Kingston. That there were more pamphlets justifying a paid army than attacking it and that some tracts were written by private citizens suggest more unorganized, general sympathy for the king's policy than hitherto recognized. Some members of the army tried to exert their influence in favor of William's proposal. According to one source, "thousands of . . . subjects of enlightened intellects and considerable fortunes"[19] concurred with William's judgment.

Strong reasons, more fully discussed below, were presented in debates and pamphlets for William's project. It was argued that the continued threat from France made a standing army essential. England could no longer rely upon the fleet and the old militia and count upon her island fortress to protect her from such a menace. Despite the recent treaty, the French king continued to threaten the peace of Europe, Protestantism everywhere, and England. The changes in warfare, which required professional training to master, and the threat of Jacobitism were offered in justification of an army. Further, a standing army would not endanger England's free institutions, because it would be paid by Parliament and its size annually reviewed by Parliament in relation to the requirements of the international situation. Such points as these won adherents, changed votes and, at least in one case, persuaded an individual who was closely connected with the antiarmy pamphleteers that the army should not be entirely dis-

---

[17]*C.S.P.D., 1697*, pp. 506-7, where still other supporters are named.

[18]For judges, see H.M.C., *Mss. of the Earl of Westmorland and Others*, p. 334.

[19]Richard Kingston, *Cursory Remarks upon some Late Disloyal Proceedings in Several Cabals* (London, 1699), in *Somers Tracts* (London, 1809-15), 11: 176.

banded.[20] But they failed to persuade a majority of the members of the House of Commons.

Opposing William's project was an increasingly important coalition of Tories and Whigs, which had begun to form as early as 1693 under the leadership of former Whigs Paul Foley and Robert Harley: the latter to become the earl of Oxford and lord treasurer under Queen Anne. Sometimes called "The New Country Party," this coalition had by 1695 established close connections with Tories such as John Granville, Sir Christopher Musgrave, and Sir Edward Seymour, the former speaker of the House of Commons and, as noticed before, a champion of the militia under James II. It also attracted "Old Whigs," men who wished to be distinguished from court or ministerial Whigs, such as Simon Harcourt, Harley's cousin (later Viscount Harcourt), John Grubham Howe, known as "Jack Howe," Sir William Williams, Sir Charles Winnington, former solicitor-general, and his son Salway.[21] The "New Country Party" had tested its power on various measures against the Whig Junto[22] in previous parliamentary sessions and, in 1697 and 1698, it could count on men of various political interests, Jacobites and republicans, to vote with it against the army. All of these men had experienced the standing armies of Charles II, and James II and could remember the arguments against the army and the political uses to which the army issue had been put in those decades. Although most of the former spokesmen against the standing army (Powle, Birch, Lee, Sacheverell, and Clarges) were dead, Musgrave, Seymour, and Williams had earlier opposed standing armies, and might be expected to show special sensitivity to the question in 1697. Among the strengths of the "New Country Party" in the contest against the army in 1697–98 were the remarkable political and parliamentary skill of Foley and Harley, their ubiquitous social and family connections in the House of Commons and in the shires, and their talent for marshalling arguments that would appeal to different elements in Parliament.

The opposing coalition had developed identities on other questions, but the issue of the army served to bind it together more firmly,

[20]James, *Letters to Shrewsbury by Vernon*, 1: 444; Luttrell, *A Brief Historical Relation* 4: 313.

[21]Robert Walcott, *English Politics in the Early Eighteenth Century* (Cambridge, 1956), pp. 66–68, 86–89, 214–15, 225–26; Feiling, *History of the Tory Party*, pp. 289, 291, 310, 315, 331.

[22]The term refers to the group of men who directed affairs between 1694 and 1698. See Ogg, *England in the Reigns of James II and William III*, pp. 337–39.

even as that issue had united earlier Whigs in the 1670s. Political opportunism figured in the opposition to the standing army. For almost thirty years, the cry "No Standing Army" had proved its efficacy in rallying opponents of the court. Despite the genuine apprehension and the distaste that the idea of a peacetime standing army aroused, William's friends correctly charged that some of the men who protested the army did so because they were unfriendly to the government, not because they disliked a standing army on principle.[23] Indeed, there is evidence that Foley and Harley had been prepared not to oppose William's military proposal on a *quid pro quo* arrangement with the king but backed away from such a deal when they gauged that sentiment in the House was running predominantly against the army.[24]

Harley and his friends maintained that a standing army in peacetime would endanger the liberties of Englishmen, enlarge the already swollen power of the monarchy, and threaten the country's form of government.[25] In theory, they wanted no standing army at all; in practice, they were willing to accept a small army. They gave lip-service to the idea that the nation would be safe with a remodeled militia. In both sessions of Parliament, the coalition introduced bills to reform the militia, but failed to push them. At the same time, under Harley's leadership the House of Commons slashed the size of the army and forced the king to send back to Holland his beloved Dutch Guards. They justified these actions by arguing further that England was at peace, that a standing army was costly, and that paid soldiers were morally irresponsible and a threat to the sanctity of property. They expressed deep resentment that William's army contained so many foreigners and that in the reductions the court proposed so many foreigners were retained while Englishmen were dismissed. As will be shown, these and other points were more fully articulated in the press by such pamphleteers as John Trenchard, Walter Moyle, and Andrew Fletcher, of Saltoun.

Weeks before debate opened in Parliament, in December 1697, king and court were aware of mounting resistance to the army. As

[23]*C.S.P.D., 1697*, pp. 487, 494.

[24]Feiling, *History of the Tory Party*, pp. 326–27. A contemporary described the antistanding army sentiment as a "fixed" principle among country gentlemen (P.R.O., S/P 32/11/87).

[25]A. McInnes, "The Political Ideas of Robert Harley," *History* 50 (1965): 309–22. McInnes stresses that Harley was preeminently a country gentleman who in this period of his career was concerned to fetter royal power because it imperiled England's mixed and balanced constitution (especially pp. 319, 320–22).

early as September 28, 1697, James Vernon, secretary of state, predicted that the counties will "press their members to make haste to disband" the army. Two days later, it was observed that members of Parliament were "almost jaded with giving" and may hold their hands this session.[26] In October, a pamphlet, *An Argument, Shewing That a Standing Army Is Inconsistent with a Free Government, and Absolutely Destructive to the Constitution of the English Monarchy,* appeared, the first blast in the pamphlet warfare which was to continue for many months. Written by John Trenchard, it was widely circulated in London and the counties and was popular enough to require a second printing within a month. The army issue rapidly became the "common topic," "the talk of the town," and was hotly debated on both sides. It was generally known that the majority of the Western members, indeed the country gentlemen as a whole, were staunchly opposed. It was believed that Parliament would be well attended and that many members would be on hand at the opening.[27]

William took steps to counteract this growing anxiety. He allowed rumors to spread in London as early as September 21 and throughout October that a substantial disbandment would take place and that regiments of French Protestants and Dutch soldiers would be sent to Holland.[28] On October 18, William, still at Loo, approved the earl of Galway's plan for keeping certain troops in Ireland and confided his intentions of making some reductions "to remove all jealousy in England."[29] In October and November, several regiments were dismissed to "sweeten people" as Robert Harley put it, and some public dissatisfaction was noted at a meeting of the lord justices because English regiments were broken while regiments of foreigners were kept up.[30] On November 17, the very day after his triumphal return,[31]

[26] James, *Letters to Shrewsbury by Vernon* 1: 409, 414.

[27] H.M.C., *Portland Mss.* 3: 592, 593; H.M.C., *Mss. of J. J. Hope Johnstone*, p. 102; *C.S.P.D., 1697*, pp. 474, 479, 483, 498; Grimblot, *Letters of William III and Louis XIV* 1: 137-38; B.M. Bonnet, Add. Mss. 30,000 A, 391.

[28] Luttrell, *A Brief Historical Relation* 4: 280-81; *C.S.P.D., 1697*, pp. 429, 434; Grimblot, *Letters of William III and Louis XIV* 2: 81.

[29] Grimblot, *Letters of William III and Louis XIV* 1: 129.

[30] *C.S.P.D., 1697*, pp. 445, 446, 447, 466; H.M.C., *Portland Mss.* 3: 593; Luttrell, *A Brief Historical Relation* 4: 313.

[31] He was received with unusual warmth. See Luttrell, *A Brief Historical Relation* 4: 269-306 *passim*; H.M.C., *Mss. of Lord Kenyon*, pp. 422-423; de Beer, *The Diary of John Evelyn* 5: 273; B.M., Bonnet, Add. Mss. 30,000 A, 376. Many of the laudatory sermons and congratulatory poems written for the occasion are at the Houghton Library, Harvard University.

William met with his council at Kensington in anticipation of the "warm debates" in Parliament. Two days later, his decision was reported to prorogue Parliament in order to gain more time to formulate plans. At the same time, the court newsletter made the point that the king wanted the army matter to be "regulated according to . . . [Parliament's] resolution." Toward the end of November, William confessed to Heinsius that the idea of keeping up troops "will meet with more difficulties in Parliament than I had expected" and complained of the "infinite pains" taken to discredit the policy "in the eyes of the public by speeches and by pamphlets." But, he went on, "nothing is neglected to oppose this notion."[32]

Before Parliament convened, at least three tracts appeared to answer Trenchard's *An Argument*. One, already referred to, was Somers's "Ballancing Letter." The author's reputation, his position as lord chancellor, his dignified, reasonable style must have lent the pamphlet uncommon importance. Another came from the ready pen of Daniel Defoe. His *Some Reflections on a Pamphlet Lately Publish'd, Entituled, an Argument Shewing That a Standing Army Is Inconsistent with a Free Government, and Absolutely Destructive to the Constitution of the English Monarchy* went through two editions before Parliament opened. The third tract, *Some Remarks upon a Late Paper, Entituled, an Argument Showing, That a Standing Army Is Inconsistent with a Free Government, and Absolutely Destructive to the Constitution of the English Monarchy*, was anonymous. The fact that William and the court were able to meet the challenge of Trenchard's pamphlet so promptly and effectively says much for the king's understanding of the power of the press and his ability to move swiftly.[33]

On December 3, William opened Parliament with a speech that dealt with a standing army in the most circumspect terms. The words "standing army" were not even used. Instead, he mentioned the "circumstances of affairs abroad" and declared himself "obliged" to convey his "opinion" that for the moment England would not be safe "without a land force." This reference to the army was buried between a comment on the size of the navy and a promise to employ his "thoughts in promoting trade," remarks designed to appeal to the interests of the members of Parliament. Probably with the same kind

---

[32]Grimblot, *Letters of William III and Louis XIV* 1: 139-40; *C.S.P.D., 1697*, pp. 479, 483.

[33]William's adroit use of pamphlets at an earlier stage in his political career has been detailed by Haley, *William of Orange and the English Opposition, 1672-74 passim*.

of calculation, William did not specify the size of the "land force" that he felt was necessary. Such euphemism and discretion were not lost on the contemporary diarist, John Evelyn, who thought it "an handsom speech" and the king wise not to mention a standing army.[34] When compared to the address on the same topic delivered by James II in 1685, just twelve years before, it is extraordinarily discreet. But unhappily for William, the House, according to Burnet, did not "like the way the King offered them his opinion."[35] Men opposed to the army seized the initiative, and on December 10, with the House sitting as a committee of the whole, Harley opened the debate with a resolution that the army be reduced to the size it was in 1680. The acid-tongued Howe followed and a debate of four hours ensued. It was a noisy affair. Friends of the court tried to introduce another motion that the question should be whether a land force was not necessary for the public safety. Upon their own account, they could not make themselves heard, and with sentiment running in favor of Harley's motion, they gave up the effort.[36] The king's ministers, Ranelagh, Montague, Coningsby, and others, argued in vain that the consent of Parliament for a temporary force to meet the necessity of the times could not be regarded as a breach of the Bill of Rights. The resolution to reduce the army to its size in 1680 was carried with "a cry" by three-to-one that afternoon.[37] It was calculated that in 1680 the army had numbered around 6,500 men, but no specific figure was allowed to be mentioned in the debate.[38]

According to a contemporary, the "sudden and unexpected vote did amaze and astonish" the king and his friends.[39] One foreign observer attempted to explain the vote by the xenophobia of the members present and by the absence of some others,[40] but the fact was that men who were known to be for William such as Sir Herbert Crofts, Sir Richard Onslow, and Sir William Strickland abandoned him on the standing army issue. They were joined by others whose emotions carried them along with the popular antiarmy sentiment. The debate had been carried on with vigor and violence enough to arouse the members to a high pitch.[41] But, after the resolution about the army had passed by a majority of only thirty-seven on December 11, it was

---

[34]De Beer, *The Diary of John Evelyn* 5: 278. William was always careful not to offend the prejudice for the navy and the militia.

[35]Burnet, *History of My Own Time* 4: 376.   [36]*C.S.P.D., 1697*, p. 507.

[37]*Ibid.*, p. 506.   [38]*Ibid.*, pp. 506, 507.

[39]H.M.C., *Mss. of Duke of Buccleuch and Queensberry* 2 (parts 1-2): 593.

[40]B.M., Bonnet, Add. Mss., 30,000 A, 399.

[41]*C.S.P.D., 1697*, pp. 506-7, 512. A duel was narrowly averted.

observed that the vote on December 10 was the "effect of the gentlemen's first heat and aversion to a standing army" and that "many who were so hot have grown easier."[42] The large vote was also explained as an attack on the king's ministers. It was reported that a "peak of country gentlemen against Mr. Montagu [sic] occasioned that hot resolve."[43] Some members plainly regarded the vote on the army as a means of destroying Robert Spencer, earl of Sunderland, who was widely blamed for the army policy.[44] It was suggested, too, that the rumors about disbandment and the shifting of regiments exacerbated rather than allayed English fears about a standing army.[45] However explained, the vote on December 10 was a staggering setback for the king. Yet, large as Harley's majority was, the diverse nature and motivation of the opposition gave hopeful opportunity to the king's continuing efforts.

The king grasped every opportunity to assure as large and effective an army as possible. His efforts reveal a political adroitness. Throughout the session of 1697-98, he put pressure on members of Parliament and persuaded others of the wisdom of his army plans. The Brandenburg ambassador reported that ever since William's return he had been busy receiving peers and "deputés des villes," while Harley wrote home that "great endeavours have been used to make converts."[46] Trenchard complained that "members of Parliament were discoursed with as they came to town" and declared that threats were made: " 'twas whispered about that the Whigs would be turned out of imployments."[47] William summoned the duke of Devonshire "into his cabinet" and made "him some reproaches" because the duke's two sons had opposed him in the House of Commons.[48] Probably bribes were used and there is direct evidence that at least one man was omitted from a government job because of his antiarmy atti-

---

[42]*C.J.* 12: 5; *C.S.P.D., 1697*, pp. 512, 513, 516-17; H.M.C., *Bath Mss.* 3: 156.

[43]*C.S.P.D., 1697*, p. 517.

[44]*Ibid.*, pp. 521-23; James, *Letters to Shrewsbury by Vernon* 1: 439, 451-54; H.M.C., *Mss. of J. J. Hope Johnstone*, p. 102. See J. P. Kenyon, *Robert Spencer, Earl of Sunderland 1641-1702* (London, 1958), pp. 287, 293-95, 297-300.

[45]*C.S.P.D., 1697*, p. 512; Grimblot, *Letters of William III and Louis XIV* 2: 81; John Oldmixon, *History of England during the reigns of King William and Queen Mary* (London, 1735), p. 169.

[46]B.M., Bonnet, Add. Mss., 30,000 A, f. 377; H.M.C., *Portland Mss.*, 3: 600.

[47]John Trenchard, *A Short History of Standing Armies in England* (London, 1698), in *State Tracts during William III* 2: 666.

[48]Grimblot, *Letters of William III and Louis XIV* 2: 321; *C.S.P.D., 1697*, p. 513. The two sons were Marquis of Hartington and Lord Henry Cavendish. James, *Letters to Shrewsbury by Vernon* 1: 444, reports another interview.

tude.[49] There is also some evidence that William approached the most radically opposed men. On November 30, 1697, Robert Harley wrote his father about the efforts the Court was making and said "our friend in Essex Street is sent for at eleven tomorrow."[50] The remark probably referred to the Grecian Coffee House, located in Essex Street, where John Trenchard met with his friends to write pamphlets against the army. It is possible that William contacted his old friend, Trenchard, who at the Revolution had advanced William £60,000 to urge him to soften the literary attack. The next year, William refused to allow Montague to take Trenchard into custody for writing *A Short History of Standing Armies in England*.[51] Other maneuvers employed by the king included spreading rumors at opportune times to soften the resolve of the opposition, using his prerogative to delay the opening of Parliament in 1697 and 1698, and inducing Parliament to take a long Christmas recess in 1698, in each case to gain time to make converts to his cause.[52] Members on whom he could count were urged to attend Parliament.[53] Both Vernon and Harley mentioned that a political club was set up—"to retrieve ourselves" as Vernon put it.[54]

William was also at pains to prevent any incident by the soldiers, some of whom were opposed to being dismissed. Macaulay recounts that some veterans threatened reprisals for the insults hurled at the army in debates in the House of Commons, and that William, mindful that a single untoward episode could undermine his army project, ordered officers to their quarters and "succeeded in preventing all outrage." Some army officers, as members of Parliament, did create a stir.[55] But for the most part, the officers and men wisely enough seem to have made no effort to intrude themselves in the controversy raging about them.

In 1698, William resorted to subterfuge to maintain his army. His defiance of the parliamentary vote of January 11, 1698, to reduce

---

[49]James, *Letters to Shrewsbury by Vernon* 2: 149.   [50]H.M.C., *Portland Mss.* 3: 593.

[51]*Works of John Trenchard* (London, 1737), preface.

[52]Grimblot, *Letters of William III and Louis XIV* 2: 27. Tallard said he traced the rumor to Lord Godolphin. It was circulated in anticipation of Commons's request for a report on the army. Also, de Beer, *The Diary of John Evelyn* 5: 323.

[53]H.M.C., *Mss. of Earl of Lonsdale*, pp. 108–9.

[54]James, *Letters to Shrewsbury by Vernon* 2: 258, 262–63; H.M.C., *Portland Mss.* 3: 595; Northamptonshire Record Office, Delapré Abbey, Shrewsbury Correspondence, vol. 1, letter no. 162.

[55]Thomas Babington Macaulay, *History of England*, ed. Charles H. Firth (London, 1915), 6: 2747; Luttrell, *A Brief Historical Relation* 4: 501, 505; C.S.P.D., *1697*, pp. 512, 530; C.S.P.D., *1699*, p. 177. It is not known how many army officers were in this Parliament or the one elected in 1698.

the army to ten thousand men raised the constitutional question that the king was violating Article VI of the Bill of Rights and it was around this point that he was attacked. As early as December 27, 1697, Vernon wrote, "We are coming upon a ticklish point, which is the keeping up a greater number of forces than the Parliament seems yet to intend."[56] In his personal correspondence, William was quite candid about his scheme. On April 8, 1698, in a detailed letter to Heinsius, William wrote of his plan to enlarge the Mediterranean squadron and "hasten its departure." The troops already in the West Indies were to be joined by others and to remain there. "This will make a considerable squadron," he estimated. He also mentioned sending four or five regiments to Jamaica "under pretence of defending our possessions in those parts." He concluded that he felt he could "at least for some time. . . . put off any further reduction of troops."[57] In August 1698, he cancelled further reductions, awaiting news of the life-and-death struggle of the king of Spain. Skillfully, he avoided complying with requests for an accounting of reductions, and before leaving for Holland in 1698, left sealed instructions with his ministers that sixteen thousand men be kept up.[58] Throughout the months, he used lack of funds as an excuse for the slow disbanding and blamed disorders in the nation's coin and credit.[59] In making reductions, William kept the officers and dismissed the men, following the French fashion.[60] Thus, the regiments could more readily be re-formed. William was delighted when Parliament agreed in January 1698 to keep native (not foreign) officers on half-pay. He estimated their number at fifteen hundred and calculated that they would allow the speedy reassembling of a substantial army.[61] Later Vernon hoped that the Commons would not object that "so many officers are appointed to so few men."[62] William also kept up a greater proportion of cavalry than infantry, because he felt cavalry was more effective in an emergency, took longer to train and permitted more rapid regrouping.[63] In December 1698, the actual

[56]Delapré Abbey, Shrewsbury Correspondence, vol. 1, letter no. 171. Cf. Luttrell, *A Brief Historical Relation* 4: 318.

[57]Grimblot, *Letters of William III and Louis XIV* 1: 348–49.

[58]Burnet, *History of My Own Time* 4: 384.

[59]Grimblot, *Letters of William III and Louis XIV* 1: 322, 481; 2: 3, 29; cf. James, *Letters to Shrewsbury by Vernon* 2: 85.

[60]Northamptonshire Record Office, Delapré Abbey, Shrewsbury Correspondence, vol. 1, letter no. 154.

[61]Grimblot, *Letters of William III and Louis XIV* 1: 150–51.

[62]*C.S.P.D., 1699*, p. 73.

[63]H.M.C., *Portland Mss.* 3: 605; Grimblot, *Letters of William III and Louis XIV* 1: 149–50.

number of soldiers came to over thirty thousand men,[64] an army far larger than Parliament had intended.

Subterfuge gave way to supplication in late 1698. William confronted a recently elected House of Commons containing many new men who were bent on reducing the army. On November 25, Trenchard's *A Short History of Standing Armies in England* appeared, a tract which was so popular that it went through three editions before the end of the year and which, as already noted, incensed Montague so much that he wanted to take Trenchard into custody. On December 16, the House voted to reduce the army to seven thousand natural-born subjects of England.[65] The vote deeply upset William. "I am so chagrined," he wrote to Heinsius, "at what passes in the Lower House with regard to the troops, that I can scarce turn my thoughts to any other matter. I foresee that I shall be obliged to come to resolutions of extremity." This letter hinted at a threat to resign and return to Holland. William drew up a speech to deliver to Parliament and took into his confidence Somers, John Churchill. earl (later duke) of Marlborough, Montague, and Edward Russell, earl of Oxford, as well as "divers others," so Somers believed.[66] The threat became generally known, but there is no evidence that the knowledge created any apprehension in the House. William was dissuaded (principally by Somers), but he continued to rely heavily upon personal prestige and entreaty. Interestingly enough, there is no evidence that he entertained the idea of vetoing the Disbanding Bills, a fact which again testifies to his political sensitivity and respect for public opinion.[67]

In January 1699, the House of Commons made it plain that it was unwilling to include William's Dutch Guards in the establishment.[68] Hoping to arouse parliamentary sympathies for an aggrieved king, William twice made a direct plea that his Guards, of whom he was especially fond, be allowed to remain with him. On February 1, 1699, when he assented to the Disbanding Bill, he stressed that he regarded himself as "unkindly used." This speech made an impression on the Lords, but nothing came of their efforts to oblige him. Therefore, on

[64]For number of forces, *C.S.P.D., 1698*, p. 428; *C.J.* 12: 356-58; cf. Bonnet's estimate of 33,615 in B.M., Bonnet, Add. Mss., 30,000 B, ff. 191-97.

[65]*C.J.* 12: 359. Matthew Prior noted that many men in Parliament thought even that figure too high. See his *The History of His Own Time* (London, 1740), p. 44.

[66]Grimblot, *Letters of William III and Louis XIV* 2: 219, 220n, 233.

[67]Williams vetoed five public bills, none after 1696; Ogg, *England in the Reigns of James II and William III*, pp. 496-97.

[68]*C.S.P.D., 1699*, p. 6.

March 18 William made another personal effort. He had Ranelagh read a special message for him begging the House of Commons to keep on the Guards as a special favor to him. But the timing was poor, his friends lacked the courage to speak and the dramatic appeal misfired. To his embarrassment, the plea was rejected, the House returning what the king termed an "impertinent address." Wrote Vernon, wearily, "Nobody that heard of it could imagine that it would have any effect. However, his Majesty would have it attempted."[69]

Opportunities were missed, however, by both the king's spokesmen in Parliament and his friends in the press to turn to William's advantage the fact that the opposition was not serious about the bills to reform the militia which were introduced and then ignored in both the 1697 and the 1698 sessions of Parliament. It might have been argued from the history of those bills that national defense was being neglected by an irresponsible opposition, that the interest in the militia was perfunctory and that, therefore, the standing army recommended by the court was necessary. Two militia bills were introduced, one in December 1697, the other in December 1698. But nothing came of either of them.[70] In Parliament, where actions could have made a real difference, there were obviously few men who believed in the militia. The handling of the two militia bills well illustrates that the cry "Reform the militia," like the cry "No Standing Army," had propagandist rather than substantive meaning. For the politician, as opposed to the intellectual, the militia had become a sacred cow. In a measure, the standing army menace had become a bogey which could be invoked to discredit the court while the demand to reform the militia could be served up to assure the politically conscious that the defense of the nation was not being neglected. By the end of the seventeenth century, this tactic was assuredly a part of the antistanding army ideology. The friends of the court missed an opportunity to make this point in Parliament and press.

William's efforts were undermined by several fundamental factors. He confronted an antiarmy sentiment which over the century had become deeply rooted in English political and constitutional thinking.

---

[69]Grimblot, *Letters of William III and Louis XIV* 2: 309–10; James, *Letters to Shrewsbury by Vernon* 2: 268–70; B.M., Bonnet, Add. Mss. 30,000 C, ff. 70 verso, 71.

[70]The progress of the two bills may be followed in: *C.J.* 12: 12, 41, 147, 154, 160, 184, 197; *C.S.P.D., 1697*, p. 518; *C.S.P.D. 1698*, pp. 114–15; Luttrell, *A Brief Historical Relation* 4: 329, 330.

Besides this, he had no ministerial body which could effectively influence the House. Already weakened[71] before the standing army controversy, the Whig Junto had to deal with an acutely self-conscious House of Commons, markedly jealous of royal prerogative and sensitive to royal influence. William's ministers were asked to press a measure which they knew was repugnant to the majority of the House of Commons and to members of their own party. Their dilemma of reconciling their obligations to the king with the political realities in the House was never resolved.[72] Further, they were neither individually nor as a group properly informed about international affairs nor instructed on the details of William's army requirements. It was said that during the entire winter of 1697-98 William "would not speak to any in his Service about his affairs," because he wanted to see how things would turn out and which party would prove the stronger.[73] His willingness to use anyone who could help him was partly responsible for his ministers' lack of vigor in promoting his military scheme. In the fall of 1698, Lord Chancellor Somers, reputedly the king's closest English adviser, confessed that he was "entirely at a loss, what is to be aimed at." Somers declared the king had no real ministry and asserted that the consequence was that "everybody (seeing the little credit those have who serve him), is in a manner, invited to endeavour to ruin or expose" the men about him.[74]

So uncommunicative was William that his ministers lacked specific instructions about the size of the army he hoped to win and were, thus, at a disadvantage in the numbers game Harley played with the army establishment. In December 1697, the ministers were not authorized to aim for a specific size for the army. Hence, they offered no certain alternative to Harley's resolution of December 10, 1697, that the military establishment be reduced to the level of 1680. In December 1698, the ministers told the king they thought the House could be brought to give ten thousand men, but William felt this figure was grossly inadequate and refused to authorize them to propose it. Harley again took the lead in debate and proposed seven thousand men. It was felt that the members, not knowing what figure would be decided upon if the seven thousand was rejected, accepted Harley's

[71]Feiling, *History of the Tory Party*, p. 326; cf. pp. 313-22, 324.
[72]See Betty Kemp, *King and Commons, 1660-1832* (London, 1959), chapter 5 for ministers in this period.
[73]B.M., Add. Mss., 4224, f. 88.
[74]Hardwicke, *Miscellaneous State Papers* 2: 435 (Somers to Shrewsbury, undated, but written in the fall of 1698).

proposal.[75] If some of his ministers had been privy to the plans and secrets which William shared so generously with his Dutch confreres, his army policy might have been championed in Parliament with considerably more energy. Even so, plans were laid, and parliamentary counter-attacks were from time to time made on the army bill, which, as already indicated, never resulted in victory but did significantly cut majorities. On December 11, 1697, a motion to recommit was defeated by only thirty-seven votes; on January 8, 1698, the question was reopened by surprise, "contrary to all order," and the court was beaten back only after eight hours of debate by a majority of twenty-four. On December 23, 1698, an attack on the Disbanding Bill was lost after a two hour debate and another effort failed, but "not shamefully,"[76] in January 1699. On March 20, 1699, the decision to refuse the king his Dutch Guards passed by only six votes.

William was disgusted with the faltering way in which his ministers, as a whole, handled the army issue and blamed them for "their easy giving way."[77] It is true that more than once the ministers bungled the effort, remained silent, refused to divide, argued for one reason or another for accepting the Disbanding Bills and actually voted for them. As a result of their half-hearted efforts, they lost their standing with both king and Commons, were accused by the one of supporting an army and blamed by the other for failing to secure the establishment William wanted.[78]

A closely related weakness in the king's campaign was that he had no leader upon whom he could count as "manager" for the cause. Although several ministers were singled out by contemporaries as working for the king's project, no one took charge. Perhaps most disappointing to the king was the unenthusiastic activity of Somers, the lord chancellor. Nor did William find among members of the House of Lords resolute commitment to the army project. A majority among the lords, including Godolphin, Sir John Thompson, baron of

[75]James, *Letters to Shrewsbury by Vernon* 2: 235-236; B.M., Bonnet, Add. Mss. 30,000 C, f. 5 recto and 5 verso; Burnet, *History of My Own Time* 4: 399-400. The same kind of thing occurred in the authorization debate in January 1698 (*C.S.P.D., 1698*, pp. 23, 24). William told both Heinsius and Portland that he had not kept his ministers informed (Grimblot, *Letters of William III and Louis XIV* 1: 416, 434).

[76]P.R.O., S/P 32/11/124.

[77]James, *Letters to Shrewsbury by Vernon* 2: 241; 239-40, 245, 267-68, 277; H.M.C., *Portland Mss.* 3: 601.

[78]Grimblot, *Letters of William III and Louis XIV* 2: 232, 234, 244; James, *Letters to Shrewsbury by Vernon*, 2: 262-63, 270, 293-94; *C.S.P.D., 1699*, pp. 5, 6; de Beer, *The Diary of John Evelyn* 5: 309; B. M., Bonnet, Add. Mss. 30,000 B, ff. 8 verso, 279 verso; Burnet, *History of My Own Time* 4: 399-400, 406.

Haversham; Sir Thomas Osborne, earl of Danby and in these years duke of Leeds; John Sheffield, duke of Buckingham and Normanby; Portland; Laurence Hyde, earl of Rochester; and Forde Grey, earl of Tankerville, sincerely believed that peacetime troops were necessary. Their conviction was buttressed by their anger that the shrewd leaders in Commons had used the device of tacking the Disbanding Bill on to a money bill, a tactic which made it difficult for the Lords to change the terms of the disbanding at all.[79] But the Lords were unwilling to press the issue because they feared the consequences of a rupture with the House of Commons. Their dilemma is illustrated in the passage of the Disbanding Bill in 1699.[80] Plainly, the several props which supported the king lacked cohesiveness, resoluteness, and courage.

William's effort was further weakened by the many pamphlets arguing against a standing army in peacetime which appeared in 1697-99.[81] Taken together these tracts formed a carefully woven, eloquently written statement of antimilitary ideas that had appeared in bits and pieces throughout the seventeenth century. The themes these pamphlets explored were derivative, revealing the inheritance of earlier works that had dealt with the evils of standing armies. The reprinting of some of that earlier literature in the decade of the 1690s shows how immediate the influence was. For example, Neville's translation of all the works of Machiavelli was reissued in 1694 and 1695 and Neville's *Plato Redivivus* was reprinted in 1698. The tracts written by Shaftesbury and his circle and Shaftesbury's speeches from the fall of 1675 were made readily available in 1693 in the reprinting of *A Collection of State Tracts . . . Privately Printed in the Reign of Charles II*. In that volume, Samuel Johnson's *Several Reasons for the Establishment of a Standing Army* was included which, with such heavy sarcasm, had urged members of the Parliament of 1685 to oppose James II's demand for an army. The account of the debates in November 1685 about the army were also printed in 1697. James Harrington's *Oceana* and his other works, which were freely drawn on by all the writers against the army, were edited by John Toland and republished around the time of the controversy, in 1700.

---

[79]Grimblot, *Letters of William III and Louis XIV* 2: 240-41.

[80]*L.J.* 16: 377-78; H.M.C., *Mss. of the House of Lords* 3: 284; *Mss. of the Earl of Lonsdale*, p. 112; James, *Letters to Shrewsbury by Vernon* 2: 251-52, 254-55, 257-59; *C.S.P.D., 1699*, p. 34; Burnet, *History of My Own Time* 4: 432-33.

[81]Lois G. Schwoerer, "The Literature of the Standing Army Controversy, 1697-1699," *H.L.Q.*, 28 (1965): 187-212, where part of this chapter appears in different form.

Edmund Ludlow's *Memoirs,* which criticized Cromwell's New Model Army, and Algernon Sidney's *Discourses Concerning Government,* one of whose principles was the need to protect a free government from the tyranny of a standing army, were both printed in 1698. In December 1693, Robert Molesworth's *An Account of Denmark As It Was in the Year 1692* appeared: five editions of this work published before 1696 testifies to its widespread popularity. It had a deep impact upon the ideas of the major pamphleteers.

John Trenchard was the most important of the men who opposed the army in the press. He was involved in politics or polemical writing all his life. Born in 1662, the son of Sir William Trenchard and a distant relative of Sir John Trenchard, King William's secretary of state, he was educated at Trinity College, Dublin, and studied law in London. By inheritance and marriage, Trenchard became wealthy enough to be able to support the Revolution of 1689, as already noted, by lending William £60,000.[82] Although not elected to Parliament until 1722, Trenchard was appointed in 1699 by the Commons to investigate the forfeited Irish estates and was among the four commissioners who signed the report which sharply criticized the king and his ministers.[83]

Described by Thomas Gordon, with whom he collaborated in the 1720s in writing *Cato's Letters* and other polemical tracts, as the "great tutor,"[84] Trenchard was well qualified by his wide knowledge and able pen to inspire individuals with intellectual and political interests. He was widely read in ancient and modern historians, and had been profoundly influenced by Machiavelli, Bacon, and Harrington. He was deeply obligated to Molesworth, Sidney, Ludlow, Milton, Locke, Neville, and William Molyneux. Plainly his thought had been nurtured in the liberal traditions of the seventeenth century. There is no evidence, however, that he was influenced by Leveller tracts which had sought, it should be recalled, to restrict the military obligations which a government could impose upon an individual. Nor was he touched in any way by the Renaissance tradition of Christian universalism and pacificism.

---

[82]*The Works of John Trenchard,* preface. He referred to his wealthy background in *A Letter from the Author of the Argument against a Standing Army to the Author of the Ballancing Letter* (London, 1697), preface, in *State Tracts during William III* 2: 590.

[83]The report and other papers are reprinted in *State Tracts during William III* 2: 709-773.

[84]Quoted in C. H. Realey, "The London Journal and Its Authors, 1720-1723," *Bulletin of the University of Kansas Humanistic Studies* 5 (Lawrence, 1935): 4.

Trenchard possessed an attractive and compelling personality which also helped him to win the affection and respect of men. It was said that he never wrote himself, but declaimed while standing or walking about while another person took down his words.[85] Possibly the young Walter Moyle served as Trenchard's amanuensis. Gordon, who knew Trenchard well, said that he was "one of the worthiest, one of the ablest, one of the most useful Men that ever any Country" could have.[86] Discounting the personal prejudice, this remains high praise indeed.

Although Trenchard was not himself a member of Parliament in 1697-99, his friends Moyle and Molesworth were. He was also close enough to Harley to ask him for some information about the development of the army under Charles II and James II.[87] Although there is no direct evidence, it seems likely that the connection between Trenchard and the parliamentary opposition was close enough to allow for coordination between the appearance of the pamphlets opposing William's project and the motions in the House of Commons calling for the disbandment of the army.

It was Trenchard who initiated the pamphlet warfare[88] in October 1697 with *An Argument, Shewing*. He was busy again in December 1697 with *A Letter from the Author of the Argument against a Standing Army, to the Author of the Ballancing Letter and the Second Part of an Argument . . . with Remarks on the Late Published List of King James's Irish Forces in France*. When it became evident that the army was not being reduced to the limits set by the parliamentary vote, he was responsible in November 1698 for reopening the pamphlet controversy with *A Short History of Standing Armies in England*. *An Argument, Shewing* and *A Short History* provoked prompt replies from Somers, Defoe, and others. Both tracts gave such offense that the secretary of state, James Vernon, ordered the printer, John Darby, to appear before him to identify the author.[89] At a meeting of

---

[85]Richard Baron, an eighteenth-century dissenter and literary heir of Thomas Gordon, noted on the flyleaf of his copy of *Essays on Important Subjects* (London, 1750), now at the Houghton Library, Harvard University, that Trenchard declaimed while others took down his words.

[86]Thomas Gordon, *Cato's Letters, or Essays on Liberty, Civil and Religious* (London, 1733), preface, p. xi; cf. *An Historical View of the Principles, Characters, Persons, etc., of the Political Writers in Great Britain* (London, 1740), p. 15.

[87]B.M., Loan, 29/282. I am indebted to Professor Henry Horwitz for this reference.

[88]For the sequence of tracts, see Lois G. Schwoerer, "Chronology and Authorship of the Standing Army Tracts, 1697-1699," *Notes and Queries* [New Series, 13] (1966): 382-90.

[89]Luttrell, *A Brief Historical Relation of State Affairs* 4: 313, 455.

the king's council, Montague argued that Trenchard should be taken into custody for writing *A Short History*, but as already noted, William would not permit this. There is no evidence that any of the other anti-army pamphlets agitated the court to such an extent.

The other men associated with Trenchard were also wealthy intellectuals and reformers, interested in political theory, history, the classics, languages and economics. Walter Moyle, the young scholar among them, was the most familiar with the life and thought of the ancients and possibly contributed the classical allusions in *An Argument, Shewing*.[90] It is unlikely that he alone wrote *The Second Part of an Argument*, but the fact that the authorship was disputed underscores his reputation. As already noted, he sat in the House of Commons during the height of the controversy, as a member for Saltash (1695-98) and served on one of the committees relating to disbandment. At the same time, he was busy translating ancient texts and publishing his own essays on classical governments.[91]

The Rev. Samuel Johnson, who, it will be remembered, had protested James II's demand for a standing army in 1685 and in 1686 had urged the king's forces to desert, was asked[92] by Trenchard's circle to respond to John Somers' *Letter, Ballancing*. Accordingly, *A Confutation of a Late Pamphlet Entituled, A Letter Ballancing the Necessity of Keeping a Land-Force in Times of Peace, with the Dangers That May Follow on It* was published in early 1698 and was followed in 1700 by *The Second Part of the Confutation of the Ballancing Letter, Containing an Occasional Discourse in Vindication of Magna Charta*. Johnson was steeped in the thinking of constitutional and legal authorities, such as Bracton, Fortescue, Gerson, and Grotius. Because of this theoretical background, and because of his connection with the trial of Lord Russell, he was especially interested in the question of resistance to constituted authority. Despite Johnson's experience in pamphleteering, his erudition, his interest in the history and complexities of a theory of resistance, and his discursive style make heavy reading of his two contributions to the controversy. They are, to the twentieth-century reader, the least effective of the tracts which were written.

[90]Anthony Hammond, ed., *The Whole Works of Walter Moyle* (London, 1727), p. 5, states that Trenchard and Moyle collaborated in writing the tract.

[91]*C.J.* 12: 8. Fink, *Classical Republicans*, p. 174, refers to Moyle as "the last truly authentic" classical republican. Robbins, *Eighteenth Century Commonwealthman*, pp. 105-8 *et passim*, discusses Moyle's work.

[92]Kingston, *Cursory Remarks*, in *Somers Tracts* 11: 167.

Andrew Fletcher, of Saltoun, the famous Scottish patriot, is re-membered in this controversy for his keen grasp of history, his perceptive analysis of the decay of liberty in Europe around 1500, and its implications for peacetime armies, and his scheme for improving the militia.[93] Published in London in 1697, and then in Edinburgh in 1698 under a different title with a few minor changes, his *A Discourse concerning Militias and Standing Armies, with Relation to the Past and Present Governments of Europe, and of England in Particular,* enjoyed a long history of reprints. John Toland, pensionary of Molesworth and Shaftesbury and known in 1697 for his unorthodox views on religion, was concerned in this debate like Fletcher with formulating a practical scheme for revitalizing the militia. His ideas were presented in *The Militia Reformed; Or an Easy Scheme of Furnishing England with a Constant Land-Force, Capable to Prevent or to Subdue Any Foreign Power; and to Maintain Perpetual Quiet at Home, without Endangering the Publick Liberty,* which he said he wrote partly at the "request of the person I honor."

In the standing army controversy, these men and their friends were a closely knit group which met for conversation, pamphleteering, and drink at coffee houses in London. Most often the scene of their conversations was the Grecian Coffee House in Devereux Court off Essex Street, but if a contemporary can be believed, they also met at the Old Devil at St. Dunstan's, The Young Devil, the Long Dog, and Tom's Coffee House in Newgate. It was widely alleged that the pamphlets were resolved upon by the "club" as the result of these meetings.[94] The "club" was ridiculed for "affecting as zealous a look as if every man were a Machiavel," and for using "the grave nod, the solemn face, the whisper, the wise and politick forehead."[95] Luttrell reported that Edmund Waller gave *An Argument, Shewing* to the ded-

[93]See Caroline Robbins, "Causes of the Renaissance," *History of Ideas News Letter* 1 (no. 2): 7-10; W. C. Mackenzie, *Andrew Fletcher of Saltoun* (Edinburgh, 1935) is the best biography; Robbins, *Eighteenth Century Commonwealthman,* pp. 180-84 *et passim.*

[94]*The Whole Works of Walter Moyle,* pp. 5, 75; Kingston, *Cursory Remarks,* in *Somers Tracts* 11: 166, 167, 169, 187; Daniel Defoe, *A Brief Reply to the History of Standing Armies in England* (London, 1698), preface, pp. 3, 22-25; Luttrell, *A Brief Historical Relation* 4: 313; James, *Letters to Shrewsbury by Vernon* 2: 216; *Reflections on the Short History of Standing Armies in England* (London, 1698), p. 25; *A View of the Short History of Standing Armies in England* (London, 1698), p. 18; *An Argument Proving, That a Small Number of Regulated Forces Established during the Pleasure of Parliament, Cannot Damage Our Present Happy Establishment* (London, 1698), p. 15; and others.

[95]Kingston, *Cursory Remarks,* in *Somers Tracts* 11: 181, 190.

icated republican, Isaac Littlebury, who in turn took it to the printer. The tracts were printed almost always by John Darby in Bartholomew-Close and sold by Andrew Bell at the Cross-Keys and Bible in Cornhil and Andrew Baldwin in Warwicklane, near Oxford Arms Inn. Baldwin advertised himself as the book seller "of whom may be had all the pamphlets against a standing army."[96] Some of the tracts appeared just before the opening of Parliament in 1697 and 1698, in time to influence the course of debate, and were widely circulated between sessions. It was complained that the pamphlets were "so industriously handed about" that they appeared in the "remotest counties" before they were seen in London, where they were "bagged" about the streets.[97] Partly because of the tracts, the views and votes of members of Parliament were changed.[98]

The court's response to these pamphlets was made largely by Somers and Daniel Defoe. As already noted, Somers wrote *A Letter, Ballancing* in November 1697, a dignified and restrained plea for William's proposal, which must have assumed uncommon importance because of the author's position. The very reluctance which Somers expressed in recommending a standing army made the point of necessity all the more convincing. Yet, Somers made no sustained effort in Parliament or the press on behalf of the king's cause.

Defoe was a more enthusiastic and faithful advocate. During the decade of the 1690s he had served the court as a paid pamphleteer.[99] His interest in military affairs enabled him to write convincingly on military requirements for national safety. Travel abroad and information from the court circle gave him an intimate knowledge of international affairs. Defoe wrote three highly effective tracts: *Some Re-*

[96]Luttrell, *A Brief Historical Relation* 4: 313. Edmund Waller, related to the poet, was Member for Amersham, Bucks (*The Victoria History of the Counties of England-Buckinghamshire* 3: 151, 159, 161, 163, 164). Also, James, *Letters to Shrewsbury by Vernon* 1: 444. John Darby is described as a "true asserter of English liberties" in *The Life and Errors of John Dunton* (London, 1828), p. 247. For Baldwin, see *An Answer to a Letter from a Gentleman in the Country* (London, 1699), p. 15.

[97]Defoe, *A Brief Reply*, p. 25; Kingston, *Cursory Remarks*, in *Somers Tracts* 11: 163, 164. William complained of the "infinite pains" taken to "discredit the army by 'speeches and pamphlets'" (Grimblot, *Letters of William III and Louis XIV* 1: 139).

[98]Matthew Tindal, *A Letter to a Member of Parliament Showing That a Restraint on the Press Is Inconsistent with the Protestant Religion and Dangerous to the Liberties of the Nation* (London, 1699), p. 28; *A Letter to a Member of Parliament Concerning Guards and Garrisons* (London, 1699), in *State Tracts during William III* 2: 679.

[99]John Robert Moore, *Daniel Defoe, Citizen of the Modern World* (Chicago, 1958), especially chapters 10, 16. Moore estimates that during William's reign Defoe wrote at least twenty-seven tracts or poems to win support for court policies. Defoe was not the close intimate of king and court that Moore implies.

flections, already mentioned, *An Argument Shewing, That a Standing Army, with Consent of Parliament, Is Not Inconsistent with a Free Government,* which was printed in early 1698, and *A Brief Reply to the History of Standing Armies in England,* which appeared in November 1698.[100] The second tract is the most persuasive. Written with conviction and precision, it is a rapidly paced, hard-hitting statement, directed to the "English freeholder" and urging a reasonable, sensible course.

In addition to Somers and Defoe, men of lesser political and literary reputation argued for a standing army in peacetime. Matthew Prior, the poet and diplomat, was well aware of the international probabilities, distressed over the parliamentary attitude, and interested enough to send the earl of Galway a paper on the standing army.[101] Possibly his friend, Montague, encouraged him to write a poem, *A New Answer to an Argument against a Standing Army,* which was printed in 1697. Richard Kingston was a paid political pamphleteer who had been employed by the government since 1689. In 1698, his *A True History of the Several Designs and Conspiracies, against His Majesties Sacred Person and Government, as They Were Continually Carry'd On from 1688 to 1697* was printed to persuade people of the dangers facing England so that they would not voluntarily "drop the sword out of [their] hands." In 1699, *Cursory Remarks upon Some Late Disloyal Proceedings in Several Cabals* appeared.

Further, William's cause was justified by a score of nameless writers. One tract was written by a man proud to call himself a Whig,[102] another by a military man,[103] two others by private individuals, writing out of a sense of civic responsibility,[104] another by a man

[100]Defoe is identified as the author by John Robert Moore, *A Check-List of the Writings of Daniel Defoe* (Bloomington, 1960), and Donald Wing, *Short-Title Catalogue of Books Printed in England, Scotland, Ireland . . . 1641-1700* (New York, 1945), 1: 435.

[101]Prior's correspondence and a "Journal of the Proceedings at Ryswick, 1697" are in H.M.C., *Bath Mss.* vol. 3, *passim,* 186-87.

[102]*Some Remarks upon a Late Paper, Entituled, an Argument, Showing, That a Standing Army Is Inconsistent with a Free Government, and Absolutely Destructive to the Constitution of the English Monarchy* (London, 1697).

[103]*A Short Vindication of Marine Regiments, in Answer to a Pamphlet, Entitled, a Letter to a Member of Parliament, concerning the Four Marine Regiments* (London, 1699).

[104]*Reflections on the Short History of Standing Armies in England, In Vindication of His Majesty and Government. With Some Animadversions on a Paper, Entituled, Considerations upon the Choice of a Speaker* (London, 1699). *Some Queries concerning the Disbanding of the Army: Humbly Offered to Publick Consideration, Which May Serve for an Answer to Mr. A,B,C,D,E,F,G's Argument* (London, 1698).

who insisted his indignation compelled him to write with undue haste.[105]

The antiarmy argument reflected a radical Whig philosophy. For Trenchard and his friends the issue was a political one. They equated a standing army in peacetime with absolutism and argued that an army would alter the separation and balance which they saw among the parts of government—king, Lords, and Commons. In this balance lay the excellence of England's government. The English monarchy was strictly limited, not only by law, but also by the right of the people to resist tyrannical acts of the prince. Those limitations demanded vigilance. Already the balance of government was overweighted in the king's favor by his vast prerogatives, and a standing army apart, the nation was challenged to protect itself against the power of the court. If a standing army in peacetime were added, the possibilities for patronage would be increased, Parliament would be corrupted by the presence of army officers who would have only the interest of the court at heart, the power of the king's ministers would be enlarged, and the mixed and balanced government (the old Gothic constitution) would be destroyed. Fletcher argued that professional armies are composed of men whose trade is war, and that "no well-constituted Government ever suffered any such men in it."[106] Trenchard believed that a "deluge of tyranny" was overspreading the world, and that English liberty had been preserved only because of the absence of a standing army.[107]

The antiarmy writers belabored the idea that the right to resist, which had justified the Revolution and was an important point in the thought of the radical Whigs, would be nullified by a standing army. Trenchard reminded his readers that if Charles I had had an army the Grand Rebellion would never have been fought, and that if James II had not united the nation against him in opposition to his Catholicizing policy, his army on Hounslow Heath would have enslaved the country. It was also predicted that a standing army would inevitably destroy Parliament as a free and effective force. The history of Denmark and of England during the rule of Cromwell illustrated the fate of representative institutions. Trenchard, Fletcher, and Johnson adopted the extreme position that Parliament could not control the army through its control of appropriations and Trenchard went even further saying that an army established by act of Parliament was

---

[105]*A View of the Short History of Standing Armies in England* (London, 1698).
[106]Fletcher, *Discourse Concerning Militias*, pp. 16, 17.
[107]Trenchard, *An Argument*, pp. 3, 4.

more, rather than less dangerous, because it thereby became part of the constitution.[108] This point was one of the weakest in the antiarmy argument.[109] But it permitted the pamphleteers logically to reject the assertion that Parliament would fetter the army and was consistent with their position that an army, no matter the restraints imposed upon it, was dangerous to liberty.

History was freely used to confirm the relationship between absolutism and a peacetime army. Trenchard declared that history offered incontrovertible proof that "in all ages and all parts of the world a standing army has been the never-failing instrument of enslaving a nation."[110] Fletcher's analysis of the decay of liberty around 1500 was directed to the same point. Luxury, made possible by economic and social changes, led to the abandonment of the old, frugal, feudal military way of life. The defense of the realm thus slipped into the hands of kings who eliminated ancient freedoms and rights. England should learn that "nothing" can prevent her "from following the fate of all the other kingdoms in Europe" unless she avoids a standing army in peacetime.[111]

The antiarmy writers were ill-informed about international affairs. Trenchard asserted that with a peace just concluded "we can never disband our army with so much safety as at this time." Fletcher agreed that England was in no danger from France.[112] In none of the antiarmy tracts is there evidence of a sense of responsibility for the liberty and religion of the continent or understanding that what happened there would affect England. These men were the isolationists of the seventeenth century, interested in the fleet, colonies, and overseas dominion. They were not willing, beyond engaging the fleet, to use England's strength to contain the power of France. Trenchard reasoned that should war occur, "'tis our interest to let the Dutch and Germans manage it, which is proper to their situation, and let our province be to undertake the sea." Should England be forced to maintain troops

[108]Trenchard, *An Argument*, p. 17; Fletcher, *Discourse Concerning Militias*, p. 8; Johnson, *A Confutation*, in *Works*, p. 326; Trenchard, *The Second Part of an Argument*, in *State Tracts During William III* 2: 580, 583.

[109]It is paradoxical that these radical Whigs who were champions of parliamentary authority should not have found merit in the court's proposal to place the standing army under parliamentary authority. See MacKenzie, *Andrew Fletcher*, p. 340, n. 2.

[110]Trenchard, *The Second Part of an Argument*, in *State Tracts during William III* 2: 579.

[111]Fletcher, *Discourse concerning Militias*, pp. 9, 12, 28.

[112]Trenchard, *An Argument*, p. 15; cf. *A Short History of Standing Armies*, in *State Tracts during William III* 2: 674; Fletcher, *Discourse concerning Militias*, pp. 15, 16; Johnson, *A Confutation*, in *Works*, p. 325.

abroad, then "we may hire men from Germany for half the price we can raise them here and they will be sooner ready."[113] Such an attitude by no means weakened the thrust of the antiarmy argument; it reflected the opinion of most Englishmen, whose disinterest in international affairs was the king's frequent complaint.

With the exception of Fletcher, Toland and the nameless author of *The Late Prints for a Standing Army*, the antiarmy writers were as little informed about modern warfare as they were about foreign affairs. Political theorists rather than military strategists, they dealt with the question of defense in perfunctory fashion. One writer went so far as to recommend that the royal Guards be reduced to twelve hundred men. He argued that the militia could defend the Tower by turns and declared, quoting Aristotle and Machiavelli, that guards were an insult to a free people.[114] This pamphleteer also believed that the marine regiments should be dismissed. He scored a telling point, charging that the marine regiments were really designed as a land force, but were called marines "to deceive unthinking Men."[115] The sea was regarded by all the writers as England's natural empire and the fleet as capable of giving "laws to the universe."[116] While making passing reference to the need to strengthen the navy, they seem to have been unaware of the navy's tangled financial and administrative affairs, and of the sharp criticism levelled at it, especially since 1695, by other pamphlet writers.[117] Unwilling to entertain the idea that another nation could be superior to England in naval power, they discounted the growth of the French navy. The same kind of optimism was reflected in their attitude toward the militia. Admitting that the militia was in deplorable shape, they blamed its condition on proarmy men, whom they charged with refusing to remodel it so as to have an excuse for a standing army. Trenchard and his colleagues categorically averred that a trained militia, from the technical as well as the political point of view, was a superior military instrument. They dismissed the idea that war had become so complex technologically that professional soldiers were necessary. Revealing a surprising naïveté,

---

[113]Trenchard, *A Short History of Standing Armies*, in *State Tracts during William III* 2: 676; cf. Fletcher, *Discourse concerning Militias*, p. 27.

[114]*A Letter to a Member of Parliament concerning Guards and Garrisons*, in *State Tracts during William III* 2: 678–79.

[115]*A Letter to a Member of Parliament Concerning the Four Regiments Commonly Called Marines* (London, 1699) in *ibid.*, 2: 683.

[116]Trenchard, *An Argument*, p. 18.

[117]John Ehrman, *The Navy in the War of William III (1689–1697): Its State and Direction* (Cambridge, 1953) especially chapter 14.

Trenchard wrote that the technical advances in warfare "are as much gained in the closet as in the field,"[118] and that the militia organization was quite competent to deal with their instruction.

Of the three pamphlets offering detailed plans for reorganizing the militia, Fletcher's is the most significant. Developed in the 1698 edition of his *Discourse concerning Militias*, the plan reveals close affinities to Harrington's ideas. None but propertied men were to be included in the militia. Their service would be compulsory, lasting from one to two years, depending upon financial ability. The militia would be divided into four camps, and the techniques of marching, provisioning, strategy, and tactics would be taught by moving the camps every eight days. The strictest discipline would build character as well as train soldiers, and the knowledge and training would be kept fresh by a kind of reserve training program, involving exercises fifty times a year and attendance at a local summer camp. The radical idea of foreign service on a rotating basis was suggested. Such a blueprint for creating an alternative to a standing army had no practical significance at the end of the seventeenth century, but such schemes were recalled at various times in the eighteenth century, and as Fletcher's biographer has pointed out, Fletcher's plan, without the element of compulsion, has been realized today in the formation of the territorial forces.[119]

Trenchard and his colleagues were not unaware that social and economic prejudices were at the root of many a country gentlemen's fear of a standing army. Social and economic themes thread through their pamphlets, but on a subordinate level. Trenchard is plain that he "purposely" neglected the "lesser inconveniences" of a standing army because he felt they were "trivial" compared to those he wrote about "which strike at the heart's blood of our constitution."[120] Even so the various tracts deal with the lesser dangers: depletion of the labor market, cost of quartering and maintaining troops, unfortunate social composition and moral implications, and threat to the sanctity of property. Indeed, Fletcher stressed the economic implications of a standing army in a tract entitled *The First Discourse concerning the Affairs of Scotland*, printed in 1698. Fletcher asserted that, so far as Scotland was concerned, a standing army would increase the poverty of the country and reduce it to total desolation. No country endeavoring to establish manufacturing and advance trade should spend her substance on soldiers. The money could be more effectively used in

---

[118]Trenchard, *An Argument*, p. 24.　　[119]MacKenzie, *Andrew Fletcher*, pp. 135–36.
[120]Trenchard, *An Argument*, pp. 28–29.

promoting various economic enterprises. Finally, the sons of the nobility were far better off in trade than in war.[121]

In response, the royal writers had to deal with two formidable challenges: one was to answer Trenchard's central charge that a standing army meant the overthrow of a balanced government and the end of English freedom. The second was to persuade the reader that an army was necessary without antagonizing the widespread pride in the fleet and faith in the militia. One way they blunted the thrust of the antiarmy argument was to offer their proposals in circumspect fashion. Insisting upon a fine distinction which Trenchard did not hesitate to ridicule, Somers wrote, "When I seem to prepare you to consider the necessity of keeping a land-force, I am far from the thought of a standing army." He confessed that if international and military conditions were different, he would "reject the proposition with horror."[122] Or again, the proarmy writers insisted the standing army they envisioned would be different from past or present examples. For example, the standing army would be in the hands of Parliament and by this device rendered harmless. Somers asked for a "reasonable force from year to year" whose size would be determined annually by Parliament according to the demands of the international situation. Such annual reviews would make it impossible for the army to violate the constitution. Other writers pointed out that the army would be unlikely to attack Parliament, its paymaster. Defoe maintained that the consent of Parliament made the army legal, and thus standing troops, established by law, could not logically be inconsistent with a free government.[123] This kind of logic, convincing to some, failed to dispel the objections of Trenchard and his friends.

Another way the proarmy writers dealt with the equation of an army and tyranny was to appeal to England's devotion to freedom. Paid troops, Somers said, could do no harm so long as the country was dedicated to the principles of liberty and willing to protect its constitution.[124] Some royalist writers insisted that far from harming freedom, the army would protect English liberties which otherwise would be swallowed up in a French conquest.[125] Another argument was that the army's past behavior was exemplary. Readers were reminded that

---

[121]In *The Political Works of Andrew Fletcher* (London, 1737), pp. 91, 92, 93, 98.

[122]Somers, *A Letter, Ballancing*, in *State Tracts during William III* 2: 585, 586.

[123]Defoe, *An Argument*, pp. 10, 13, 18, 23, 25-26.

[124]Somers, *A Letter, Ballancing*, in *State Tracts during William III* 2: 598.

[125]*Some Queries*, p. 11; *The Case of Disbanding*, p. 8; *Reflections on the Short History*, p. 14.

James II's army had taken sides for the Protestant religion and political freedom and saved the country from a Catholic tyranny. Still another answer was the flat rejection of the "club's" use and interpretation of history. The royal pamphleteers charged Trenchard and his friends with deliberate misstatement, omission, misunderstanding, and useless display of pedantry.[126] Unfortunately for their cause, however, they never dealt systematically with the "club's" theory of mixed, balanced government. Only Defoe and the author of *A Letter to A,B,C,D,E,F,G, etc.* came to grips with the question of Gothic government. Defoe denied out of hand that the Gothic arrangement provided a true balance and a protection for liberty, arguing that the true balance was for the king to hold the sword and the people the money and for no war to be made without both concurring.[127] *A Letter to A,B,C,D,E,F,G, etc.* extended the analysis. Admitting that the outward form of government was threefold, the author argued that the "collective body of the people . . . with a King at the head of them" was the real government.[128] Rejecting the theory that the constitution and English liberties were protected by any mechanical method of balance among the parts of government or by any military arrangement, the author argued that freedom had been preserved by the power of the people and by God.

The major writers were more successful in meeting the second challenge: exposing the weakness of the fleet and militia as the only instruments of national defense. One argument stressed the manifest changes in the art of war. Defoe was the most effective in handling this point. He wrote that professional soldiers were necessary because war "has become a science and arms an employment," and "requires people to make it their whole employment." Paid troops, he reminded his readers, could be sent abroad (the militia could not), thus protecting England by keeping the fighting away from her shores.[129] Somers was the most sensitive to the general prejudice in favor of the militia. Lacing the "Ballancing Letter" with compliments for this force, he averred that he would never "disparage" or "derogate from" the mili-

[126]The references are numerous. For example, Somers, *A Letter, Ballancing*, in *State Tracts during William III* 2: 587; *A Brief Reply*, p. 6; *An Argument Proving That a Small Number of Regulated Forces*, pp. 20, 23; *A View of the Short History*, pp. 8-9.

[127]Defoe, *An Argument*, pp. 14, 15, 18.

[128]*A Letter to A,B,C,D,E,F,G, etc., Concerning Their Argument about a Standing Army; Examining Their Notions of the Supposed Gothick, or Other Balance, by the Constitution and Interest of the English Monarchy* (London, 1698), pp. 2, 9-14, 16, 21, 23-24.

[129]Defoe, *Some Reflections*, p. 21; *A Brief Reply*, p. 14; *An Argument*, pp. 5, 6.

tia, that he regarded them as "much the best in the world." But, the methodology of war and the tense international situation could not wait upon the necessary training of the militia. None of the royal pamphleteers exploited the opportunity to show from the history of Charles II and James II that there was always much talk and little action about revitalizing the militia, just as they neglected to mention that the committee set up by the House of Commons in 1697 to bring in a bill to reform the militia was poorly attended and made no progress. Somers and Defoe must have known this—certainly Vernon did.[130]

Another argument was that international affairs required a strong defense. Somers argued that "the best guaranty of a peace is a good force to maintain it."[131] Despite the sufferings of the last war, France was extremely strong. Not only did she have an army on hand, but she had retained strategically important places, such as Strassburg and Alsace, enjoyed untouched sources of wealth such as the church lands, and had enlarged the size of the French fleet. It was argued that Louis was shrewdly playing upon the jealousies of the former members of the League to make another coalition as difficult as possible, and that his ambitions were nothing less than to be a universal monarch. One pamphlet, *The Argument against a Standing Army Rectified, and the Reflections and Remarks against It in Several Pamphlets, Consider'd* treated with deepest insight the relationship between France and Spain and the implications for England. The author stressed that Louis's determination to unite the crown of Spain and France and the delicate health of the Spanish king, Charles II, made a stable peace impossible. If France should win the Spanish crown upon the death of Charles II, she would then have an excellent title to Flanders, which meant that England would be "blockt up on all sides, our trade must everywhere be at their mercy, and we are liable to their invasions without any prospect of relief."[132]

In addition, the threat of Jacobitism was offered as justification for a standing army. Somers and Defoe underplayed the threat of the Jacobites, but the lesser pamphleteers insisted that the exiled James, supported by Louis's army and by traitors at home, presented an immediate danger.[133] The most persuasive pamphlet was *A List of King*

---

[130]James, *Letters to Shrewsbury by Vernon* 2: 35.

[131]Somers, *A Letter, Ballancing,* in *State Tracts during William III* 2: 585-86; cf. Defoe, *An Argument,* preface; Defoe, *Some Reflections on a Pamphlet,* p. 16.

[132]*The Argument against a Standing Army rectified* (London, 1697), p. 10.

[133]*The Case of a Standing Army Fairly and Impartially Stated* (London, 1698), p. 24; *Reflections on the Short History of Standing Armies,* pp. 8, 10; *An Argument Proving, That a Small Number of Regulated Forces,* p. 1.

James's Irish and Popish Forces in France, Ready (When Called for), in Answer to an Argument vs. a Land-Force, Writ by A,B,C,D,E,F,G, or to Whatever Has Been, or Ever Shall Be, Writ upon That Subject. This was an exaggerated statement of James's military forces. It must have had an impact because two answers were immediately forthcoming from Trenchard's group.[134] Although there were many compelling qualities about the proarmy argument, it failed to move the majority of the people in and out of Parliament. Few of the tracts were reprinted, testimony to lack of organization among the writers and lack of enthusiasm for their message. Yet the evidence shows more general, unorganized agreement with the king's policy than has been granted.

The antiarmy pamphlets had a significant influence at the height of the controversy. They generated and maintained more interest in the question than might otherwise have existed, and they changed views and votes in Parliament. They are a major factor in explaining why William's proposal failed. Moreover, taken as a group, the pamphlets by Trenchard and his friends marked a climax in the history of the antistanding army ideology. Although the themes they explored were derivative, these tracts made an important contribution to political and intellectual history by summing up and fully articulating the antistanding army attitude which had been stated in fragments before, and by emphasizing the political dangers inherent in a professional, permanent military force. Further, the tracts played a vital role in the transmission of this attitude to eighteenth-century England and the American colonies. The antistanding army attitude became an intellectual tradition which, in modified form, still exists. At the same time, of course, the royal proposal of a small standing army in peacetime under the control of Parliament actually triumphed; it was this arrangement which was accepted in eighteenth-century England and in general terms has been followed ever since in England and in the United States.

[134]*A List* appeared probably between October and December 1697, not in 1699 as noted in *Somers Tract* 11: 473. It was answered by Trenchard in "Remarks on a Late Published List," appended to his *The Second Part of an Argument*, printed in December 1697, and *Some Queries for the Better Understanding of a List* (London, 1697).

CHAPTER IX

CONCLUSION: EIGHTEENTH-CENTURY ECHOES

 The general inclination to disparage the professional soldier, which was discernible at the opening of the seventeenth century, became by the eighteenth century a political and constitutional principle of enduring significance. In 1578, a little-known pamphleteer wrote that Englishmen had the "faute" of underestimating the value of the professional soldier. In 1697, John Trenchard asserted that a standing army in peacetime was a threat to freedom and a menace to the English constitution. Over these years, successive political and constitutional confrontations between the king (or protector during the Interregnum) and his critics in Parliament and the press resulted in a full development of the antiarmy attitude and profound constitutional changes. Men of all political persuasions came to believe that a professional, permanent army in the hands of the central government was undesirable, but the most persistent and articulate opponents were intellectuals and reformers on the left, who had been deeply influenced by seventeenth-century libertarianism and republicanism. The tracts they wrote stimulated and reflected what was said in Parliament and were of enormous influence in spreading and continuing the antimilitary tradition. The parliamentary contests were of near equal importance because they articulated and disseminated ideas and were decisive in the achievement of constitutional changes.

As early as 1628, country gentlemen protested Charles I's policy of keeping in England the troops he had raised for expeditions against

Spain and France. Appealing largely to precedential law and history, these men drafted the Petition of Right, which, for the first time in English history, challenged the monarch's authority to billet soldiers in private homes without the consent of the owner and to impose martial law without observing certain restraints. The Petition also reflected anger at the intrusion of an armed central government, through the agency of the deputy-lieutenant, into local affairs. Anti-militarism was, in part, the jealous parochialism of the parliamentary and county gentry. Throughout the century, the Petition of Right served as a precedent in arguments against the central government's armed force. In 1642 and 1643, radical Parliamentarians and pamphleteers took on the task of justifying Parliament's assumption of command of the militia. Thereafter, legislative control of the military became, no matter the discretion and circumspection with which it was handled during the Restoration, a central assumption in the anti-army attitude. The cry "No Standing Armies" became politicized in the 1670s by the parliamentary opposition which attacked every army Charles II raised and fulminated against English soldiers serving in the French army, the militia in Scotland, and the king's Guards. Dislike of a standing army was one reason for the Revolution of 1689. Parliament's control of a peacetime army was spelled out in Article VI of the Bill of Rights.

The military settlement at the Revolution was a watershed in the evolution of the antiarmy sentiment. Many of the major reasons for criticizing a paid, professional army were dealt with in the Bill of Rights. Thereafter, billeting, martial law, and the right of Protestant subjects to bear arms ceased to be the burning issues that they had been. Article VI marked a genuinely revolutionary change; it established that there could be no standing army in peacetime without the consent of Parliament. The power of the monarchy had been broken in its most essential feature. Although the king retained many prerogatives, and struggles between crown and Parliament recurred, the effect of Article VI was to transfer sovereignty to Parliament. The point was tested a decade later when the standing army controversy reached a climax in Parliament and press. From 1697 through 1699, the question was skillfully argued on both sides. Although William's army project received more support than usually credited, the outcome of the confrontation was never in serious doubt. The principle of Article VI was reaffirmed. Parliament reduced the army first to ten thousand men, then to seven thousand native-born subjects and sent home William's favorite Dutch Guards.

In Parliament, the motives of the army's critics were always mixed. Principle, propaganda, partisanship, parliamentary tactic, parochialism, and personal advantage played a part. The issue was seen on every level of understanding. At any point in its evolution, the argument contained a cluster of considerations—social, economic, moral, and political. But for most men, the most important element was political—the fear that permanent soldiers would destroy Parliament, law, and liberty, would impose tyranny, and would disrupt England's mixed and balanced government either by force or by corruption through patronage and influence.

The pamphlet controversy in 1697–99 seeded a tradition, whose echoes were heard for another century in England and the American colonies. The pamphlets which Trenchard, Fletcher, and Molesworth, in particular, had written were regarded as the repository of antimilitary ideas and were used to persuade eighteenth-century Englishmen of the dangers of paid soldiers in peacetime and the advantages of relying upon the fleet and a remodeled militia. They were reprinted many times. Trenchard's *Short History* went through three editions in 1698, and it or the preface to it were reprinted in whole or part eight times in the eighteenth century,[1] the last time in 1782 under the auspices of the Society for Constitutional Information. Fletcher's *Discourse concerning Militias* appeared six times (London, 1732, 1737; Glasgow, 1749; London, 1755, 1792, and 1798). Molesworth's *An Account of Denmark* was published in part or whole ten times, the last in 1814.[2] Trenchard personally helped to maintain the vitality of the antiarmy attitude by continuing to write tracts against standing armies. In the 1720s, he collaborated with Thomas Gordon[3] in writing a series of tracts, *The Independent Whig* and *Cato's Letters*, which were bitterly critical of government on many counts. In *Cato's Letters*, the menace of standing armies to liberty and a free government whether established by king or Parliament, the corruption of Parliament by army officers, and the overweighting of the power of king and ministers were stressed in terms so close to those Trenchard had used twenty years before that a critic charged "Cato" with adding

[1]London, 1703, 1706, 1731, 1739, 1749, 1751, 1782. Trenchard's *An Argument, Shewing*, was reprinted in 1698, 1703, 1706, 1726, 1727, 1728, 1750, 1751, and 1817.
[2]Robbins, *The Eighteenth-Century Commonwealthman*, pp. 393–94.
[3]*Ibid.*, pp. 115-25. Realey, *The London Journal and Its Authors, 1720-1723*, University of Kansas Humanistic Studies 5: 1-34. *Cato's Letters* appeared in *The London Journal* and *The British Journal* as essays and then in 1724 in book form.

nothing new.[4] *Cato's Letters* were many times reprinted in England, going through at least six editions before 1754.[5] Other seventeenth-century works dealing with questions of military power and organization that were reprinted in the eighteenth century were Harrington's *Oceana*, Henry Neville's *Plato Redivivus*, and Ludlow's *Memoirs*.[6]

The reprints were often made around the time when questions concerning the army were being most heatedly debated in Parliament. There the danger of standing armies was used by the opposition to embarrass the Hanoverian monarchy, the Whig minister, Robert Walpole, and the Whig oligarchy. Just as in the seventeenth century, the outcry against the standing army was used as a propaganda tool and a parliamentary tactic to frustrate the "establishment." Regularly, the debates on the size of the land force, on the passage of the Mutiny Act (especially in 1717), and on the Hessian troops afforded opportunity for the critics of the government to raise the specter of a standing army. "Long and warm" debates were the rule.[7] Some men repeated with monotonous regularity the identical arguments which Trenchard and his friends had advanced.[8] They referred admiringly to the figures which the parliamentary sessions of 1697 and 1698 had fixed, warned of the dangers to law and the constitution, and offered once more the "club's" favorite example, Denmark's Revolution of 1660, to illustrate the folly of allowing a large standing army.[9] Reflecting the same kind of xenophobia that had marked the earlier debates, these critics of the Hanoverian monarchy were especially hard on the Hessian troops, introducing time and time again motions that they be disbanded. Archibald Foord maintains that the issue of standing armies was "manufactured" by the Tories as a debating point.[10] Assuredly, there was more propaganda than principle in the

---

[4]*Censor Censored; or Cato Turned Cataline* (London, 1722), p. 23. *Cato's Letters, or Essays on Liberty, Civil and Religious* (London, 1733), nos. 25, 33, 59, 62, 63, 64, 65, 94, and 95, especially deal with political power, liberty, and armies.

[5]Robbins, *The Eighteenth-Century Commonwealthman*, p. 392.

[6]*Oceana* in 1737, 1771; *Plato Redivivus* in 1737, 1758, 1763; Ludlow's *Memoirs* in 1721, 1751 (2 eds.), 1771.

[7]For example, Cobbett, *Parliamentary History* 8: 46, 377; 9: 870.

[8]For one example, the staunch Tory, William Shippen. He was committed to the Tower for a speech he made in 1717 against a large standing army in peacetime (Cobbett, *Parliamentary History* 7: 505–12). Shippen apologized for the repetitions (*ibid.*, 8: 497, 771; 11: 249).

[9]*Ibid.*, 7: 536; 8: 61, 383, 405, 677, 678, 890, 1255; 9: 525; 10: 376.

[10]Archibald S. Foord, *His Majesty's Opposition, 1714–1830* (Oxford, 1964), pp. 78–79; cf. pp. 71, 94, 98–99, 138–39, 173, 176. A brief account of the demise of the Tory

regular attacks on the army in the eighteenth century. Significantly, no one seriously suggested that England could do with no professional army at all. At the very least, the establishment of 1697–99 was recommended, which testifies to the acceptance in principle of the need of some permanent force. Compared to continental armies, the English peacetime military establishment in the first half of the eighteenth century was always pitifully small, averaging around twenty thousand men. Although the government wanted a larger army, it did not violate the constitutional reforms that had been achieved in the seventeenth century—annual review of the army's size and appropriation by Parliament and civilian control in peacetime of the military. On the other hand, the Whig oligarchy stood guilty of the charges that the army, a source of royal and ministerial patronage, corrupted Parliament and enlarged the influence of the crown. Government spokesmen had no convincing response to allay the fear that an army under parliamentary control was still a potential menace to the country's liberties and form of government. Who is to say that there was no genuine anxiety reflected in the charge that the army would "alter the frame of government from a legal and limited monarchy to a despotic,"[11] by corruption if not violence? Whatever the proportion of principle and propaganda, which were always intermingled in the attacks on the armed forces, the menace of a standing army was regularly raised in parliamentary debates by the Tory opposition, and thus the antiarmy attitude was kept alive.

While the Tories criticized the military establishment in Parliament, the most famous of Tory writers of the early eighteenth century, Henry St. John, first viscount Bolingbroke, attacked Walpole's government.[12] His contributions to *The Craftsman* during the years 1726–36 and his *Letters* reveal how heavily indebted he was to Trenchard's and Gordon's views about armies.[13] Stressing the corrupting influence of the military, Bolingbroke insisted that a standing army, by its

---

party is Geoffrey Holmes, "Harley, St. John and the Death of the Tory Party," *Britain After the Glorious Revolution 1689-1714*, ed. G. Holmes (London, 1969), pp. 216-37.

[11]Cobbett, *Parliamentary History* 8: 61.

[12]Isaac **Kramnick**, *Bolingbroke and His Circle* (Cambridge, Mass., 1968), especially chapters 1 and 6.

[13]*Ibid.*, pp. 243-60. The point was established earlier by Bernard Bailyn, *The Ideological Origins of the American Revolution* (Cambridge, Mass., 1967), pp. 39 and n. 22, 50, a revision of the introduction to his *Pamphlets of the American Revolution, 1750-1776* (Cambridge, Mass., 1965). See Pocock, "Machiavelli, Harrington and English Political Ideologies in the 18th Century," pp. 552, 572, 578 for general identities of seventeenth- and eighteenth-century "country" attitudes.

nature an institution separate from society, promoted factions in society.[14] In *A Dissertation on Parties*, he declared that history showed that a standing army inevitably destroyed liberty. Arguing that a military coup d'état was more difficult to execute than men realized, he explained that he feared more the slow and sure corruption of Parliament by an army. When that happened, he warned, the whole edifice of government would crumble, because the integrity and independence of Parliament was the keystone of the constitution.[15] Another theme Bolingbroke reiterated was that luxury had an enervating effect, which led men to accept mercenary soldiers instead of shouldering the burden themselves of providing for the defense of the country. Reflecting Bolingbroke's broader political and philosophical assumptions about society and government, these strictures about standing armies testify to the continued viability of the antimilitary tradition.

Many other eighteenth-century tracts of less importance argued against the size of the military establishment, oftentimes referring to tracts by Trenchard and Fletcher, or to *Cato's Letters*. Some pamphlets are so deeply indebted to Trenchard as to be guilty of plagiarism. For example, *Reasons against a Standing Army*, printed in London in 1717, is nothing more than a piecing together, with connecting sentences and paragraphs appropriate to the situation in 1717, of Trenchard's *An Argument, Shewing* and *A Short History of Standing Armies*. William Harris's history of the reign of Charles II was heavily dependent upon Trenchard's *Short History* for an account of the army during the Restoration.[16] The fact that such tracts and books appeared throughout the eighteenth century[17] and that in 1793 David Buchan should entitle a pamphlet *Letters on the Impolicy of a Standing Army, in Time of Peace* testifies further to the continued appeal of the antiarmy sentiment throughout the century.[18]

The antiarmy tradition was also spread through the works of many eminent eighteenth-century constitutional writers and historians.

[14]*The Works of Henry St. John, Lord Viscount Bolingbroke, Selected from the Best Authorities* (Philadelphia, 1841), 1: 339.

[15]*Ibid.*, 2: 92-93.

[16]William Harris, *An Historical and Critical Account of the Life of Charles the Second* (London, 1766), 2: 310-21 *passim*.

[17]In the United States, the largest number of the less important eighteenth-century tracts on standing armies and the militia is in the Houghton Library, Harvard University.

[18]Another late eighteenth-century example is John Hampden, *Some Short Considerations Concerning the State of the Nation* (London, 1792).

Roger Acherley, who published *The Britannic Constitution* in 1727, found after a leisurely examination that a standing army in peacetime was inconsistent with England's mixed and balanced government.[19] In *The Constitution of England: Or an Account of the English Government* (1739), J. L. DeLolme praised the "astonishing subordination" of the military to the civil power in England and explained that although the king was commander-in-chief of all the forces, his military power was strictly limited. Each year, he said, Parliament must decide not whether the army should be disbanded, but whether it should be established anew.[20] The famous jurist, William Blackstone, whose *Commentaries* appeared from 1765 to 1769, regarded the militia as the "constitutional security" of the nation. He asserted that the laws of England knew no such state as a perpetual standing army, and declared that peacetime troops were wholly dependent upon the annual judgment of Parliament. Blackstone regarded the navy as England's "greatest defence," as "an army from which however strong and powerful, no danger can ever be apprehended to liberty."[21] James Burgh hoped that his *Political Disquisitions: Or, an Enqui·· into Public Errors, Defects, and Abuses, etc.* (1774) would prove the point that a standing army in peacetime imperils liberty. He stated flatly that it is "one of the most hurtful and most dangerous of abuses."[22] He followed Trenchard and Gordon in arguing that a free Parliament and a standing army were incompatible and declared that the corruption of Parliament could invalidate Article VI of the Bill of Rights. An army was always the "creature of the court," and every officer increased the influence of the king and his ministers. The proper security for a free island people was the navy and the militia, but the militia must be in the hands of men of property, otherwise "it is . . . but a mungrel army." Lamenting the enervating effects of luxury, Burgh declared that the possession of arms was the "distinction between a freeman and a slave."[23] Contemporary historians David Hume and William Robertson had the gravest misgivings about paid troops and believed that despotic power in Europe flowed from their introduction. G. Dyer's *Four Letters on the English Constitution* (1789, 1812, 1817) drew heavily on the pamphlet literature of 1697–99

---

[19]Roger Acherley, *The Brittanic Constitution* (London, 1727), pp. 50–57, 108–13.

[20]J. L. DeLolme, *The Constitution of England: Or an Account of the English Government* (London, 1739), pp. 71–76, 89, 91, 390.

[21]William Blackstone, *Commentaries on the Laws of England* (Philadelphia, 1908), 1: 411, 417.

[22]James Burgh, *Political Disquisitions* (London, 1774), 1: preface, 2: 341.

[23]*Ibid.*, 2: 346–48, 352, 356, 389–90, 396–97, 401–2.

in an effort to persuade readers that Parliament must be reformed or a military government will result. By the end of the century, the view that a standing army was incompatible with freedom was so deeply imbedded in the national consciousness that Mary Wollstonecraft, who wrote an important feminist tract, *Vindication of the Rights of Women*, printed in 1792, used the analogy of soldiers in a standing army to illustrate the existing plight of women.[24]

In England, the antistanding army attitude which Trenchard, Fletcher, Molesworth, and Gordon had promulgated had some practical effect. Opposition politicians in Parliament were vigilant in their efforts to keep the size of the nation's regular forces small. Their annually reiterated warnings acted as a brake on the military plans of the government, and England remained militarily weak in comparison to other European states. Throughout the century, moreover, politicians and pamphleteers argued for militia reform. Tracts appeared which offered the old arguments, chastized the gentry for not taking on their responsibilities to lead and revitalize the militia, and asserted that the militia would allow the army to be drastically reduced, if not eliminated.[25] Between 1745 and 1757, when threats from Spain, France, and the Young Pretender strained the nation's defenses, a serious attempt at reform of the militia was made. That effort and the arguments in Parliament and press have already been studied by J. R. Western, who concludes that the attempt was "the only serious political movement" in mid-eighteenth century England.[26] Although the militia act of 1757 was the product of complicated international tensions, it also reflected the ongoing influence of the antistanding army ideology.

The antistanding army bias was transmitted to the American colonies in the eighteenth century, where it was enthusiastically received. There the sentiment became a basic assumption of almost every political leader. Contemporary scholars have shown that the seventeenth- and early eighteenth-century English libertarian tradition was the most important intellectual force shaping the thought of the Ameri-

[24]Mary Wollstonecraft, *Vindication of the Rights of Women* (1792), ed. Charles W. Hagelman, Jr. (New York, 1967), pp. 45, 55.

[25]Two examples are: *An Essay for Regulating and Making More Useful the Militia* (London, 1701); *Observations upon the Subject-Matter Relating to the Militia and Recruit-Bills* (London, 1711).

[26]Western, *The English Militia in the Eighteenth Century*, p. 125 and chapters 5 and 6 *passim*. An example of a tract is Charles Sackville, *A Treatise concerning the Militia in four sections* (London, 1735) which repeats the major themes of Trenchard's *Short History*.

can colonists.[27] For reasons peculiar to the American circumstance, this tradition had special relevancy.[28]

From the early 1720s, the tracts that had put forward the radical Whig philosophy, which included the antiarmy sentiment, were circulating in America. Trenchard's and Gordon's *Cato's Letters*, Bolingbroke's *The Craftsman* and his *Letters*, and Trenchard's *An Argument, Shewing* and *A Short History of Standing Armies* were read, along with many other classical, legal, and reformist tracts by Aristotle, Polybius, Machiavelli, Coke, Harrington, Neville, Sidney, Burnet, and Burgh.[29] In the middle of the eighteenth century, the radical tradition was designedly carried to the American colonies, largely through the efforts of Richard Baron and Thomas Hollis, both of whom sent many pamphlets and books to Harvard.[30] The holdings in university, public and private libraries reveal the popularity and availability of the works in the Whig canon.[31] The tracts from the 1697–99 controversy were included. A catalogue (dated 1817) of Hollis's books to be sold contains such titles as "Army: 13 tracts relating to the army in the reign of William III," "Trenchard's *A History of Standing Armies in England*," "Fletcher's *Political Works* (1737 edition)," "Molesworth's *An Account of Denmark*," and "Rev. Johnson's *Works* (1710)."[32] *Cato's Letters* were especially popular, being "quoted in every colonial newspaper from Boston to Savannah," and exercising an "incalculable" influence in spreading ideas about government, liberty, and military authority.[33] They created what Bailyn calls a "Catonic"[34] view, one of

[27]Bailyn, *The Ideological Origins*, especially pp. 35, 43, 53–54; H. Trevor Colbourn, *The Lamp of Experience: Whig History and the Intellectual Origins of the American Revolution* (Chapel Hill, 1965), pp. 9, 49, 60, 86, 87 and *passim*; Clinton Rossiter, *Seedtime of the Republic: The Origin of the American Tradition of Political Liberty* (New York, 1953), especially pp. 141, 386, 494, n. 149.

[28]Bailyn, *Ideological Origins*, pp. 51–52, for a summary explanation. See also Bernard Bailyn, *The Origins of American Politics* (New York, 1968), especially chapter 2.

[29]Bailyn, *Ideological Origins*, pp. 22–54 *passim*.

[30]Caroline Robbins, "The Strenuous Whig, Thomas Hollis of Lincoln's Inn," *W.M.Q.*, 3rd series, 7 (1950); 406–53; "When it is that Colonies May Turn Independent," *ibid.*, 11 (1954): 214–51; "Library of Liberty—Assembled for Harvard College by Thomas Hollis of Lincoln's Inn," *Harvard Library Bulletin* 5 (1951): 5–23, 181–96.

[31]Colbourn, *The Lamp of Experience*, appendix 2, for a useful list of the holdings in colonial college, public, and private libraries.

[32]Harvard University Library, *A Catalogue of the Very Valuable and Highly Interesting United Libraries of Thomas Hollis and Thomas Brand Hollis. To be Sold by Auction by Mr. Samuel Sotheby on Tuesday, April 22, 1817*, pp. 7, 22, 31, 35, 42, 62.

[33]Elizabeth C. Cook, *Literary Influences in Colonial Newspapers, 1704–1750* (New York, 1912), p. 81; Frederick B. Tolles, *Meeting House and Counting House* (Chapel Hill, 1948), p. 178.

[34]Bailyn, *Origins of American Politics*, p. 54.

whose principle elements was a fear of standing armies in peacetime. In 1788, James Iredell could flatly assert, "Our jealousy of this danger [i.e., of a standing army in peacetime] has descended to us from our British ancestors."[35]

These readings nourished an aversion to standing armies which was confirmed by experience and events. The appointment of military governors illustrated the warnings.[36] Some colonists publicly expressed their indignation over the quartering of soldiers.[37] The annual oration memorializing the Boston Massacre was aimed at preserving "in the Minds of the People a lively sense of the Danger of standing Armies."[38] In 1773, the town of Boston testified that its citizens had not forgotten that lesson by declaring "standing armies have forever made shipwreck of free states" and by asserting that the militia was the natural and best defense. The letters, pamphlets, newspaper articles, and orations of American colonial figures including John Adams, Samuel Adams, John Dickinson, Elbridge Gerry, Thomas Jefferson, George Mason, and Josiah Quincy, Jr. reiterated the conviction that a standing army in peacetime was inimical to liberty, destructive of a mixed and balanced constitution, dangerous—no matter the restraints imposed on it—susceptible to corruption, and morally indefensible. All these men believed that the defense of the country should be in the hands of the militia.

This point of view had a practical political effect on the American colonies. The dislike of standing armies figured in the indictment of Great Britain. The Declaration of Independence complained that a standing army in peacetime had been kept up among the people, that troops had been quartered in the houses of unwilling civilians, and that an effort had been made to "render the military independent of and superior to the civil." The same ideas appeared in state constitutions, such as those for Virginia and Massachusetts. In Jefferson's several drafts of the Virginia constitution, it was explicitly provided that there should be no standing army except in time of actual war

---

[35] James Iredell, *Answer to Mr. Mason's Objections to the New Constitution* (1788), in *The Bill of Rights: A Documentary History*, ed. Bernard Schwartz (New York, 1971), 1: 455.

[36] See Stephen S. Webb, "The Strange Career of Francis Nicholson," *W.M.Q.*, 3rd Series, 23 (1966): 513–48, for military governors.

[37] For example, Joseph Galloway, *Letter to the People of Pennsylvania* (1760), in Bailyn, *Pamphlets of the American Revolution* 1: 269, 702, n. 11.

[38] Quoted in Rossiter, *Seedtime of the Republic*, p. 331 and n. 13. See also John Shy, *Toward Lexington: The Role of the British Army in the Coming of the American Revolution* (Princeton, 1965), pp. 19–83; Bailyn, *Ideological Origins*, pp. 116, 129, on the importance of the Boston Massacre.

and that no free man should be debarred the use of arms.[39] In *A Report of a Constitution or Form of Government for the Commonwealth of Massachusetts*, one article asserted that the "military power shall always be held in an exact subordination to the civil authority, and be governed by it."[40] Members of the Continental Congress expressed reservations about giving the Congress the power to raise a peacetime army. In 1784, Samuel Osgood reported that there was "an inconquerable Aversion in many to any Thing that looks like a standing Army in Time of Peace."[41] At the Constitutional Convention held in Philadelphia in 1787, Gerry argued against giving the Congress the power to raise and finance armies because he feared that peacetime forces were implied in that authority. He also opposed vesting in the Congress ultimate power over the states' militias.[42] The erosion of the powers of the states as well as the traditional fear of a standing army in peacetime were part of his concern.

The federal Constitution attempted to limit the military authority of the executive. While making the president the commander-in-chief of the army and navy, the Constitution specified in Article 1, section 8, that the Congress should have authority to raise and support armies, to call out the militia, to discipline the forces, and to declare war. It was also stated that no appropriation of money for maintaining an army shall be for more than two years. But for many men, these restrictions were not enough. One of the main considerations prompting Jefferson, Mason, Gerry, Melancton Smith, and James Winthrop to argue that a Bill of Rights should be added to the federal Constitution was the conviction that security against a standing army in peacetime should be provided.[43] Article 2 of the Bill of Rights was designed to achieve that end. It read, "A well regulated Militia, being necessary to the security of a free State, the right of the people to keep and bear Arms shall not be infringed." Gerry stressed that the intent was to prevent Congress from passing laws that would prohibit the states from keeping militias. In his view, the purpose of a militia was "to

---

[39]Julian Boyd, ed., *The Papers of Thomas Jefferson* (Princeton, 1950), 1: 338, 344, 353, 356, 363, 378, 418. Also Paul L. Ford, ed., *Writings of Thomas Jefferson* (New York, 1892), 1: 445, 457.

[40]Charles Francis Adams, ed., *The Works of John Adams* (Boston, 1850-1856), 4: 227. Rossiter, *Seedtime of the Republic*, p. 398, notes that many declarations of rights adopted by new states contained articles affirming civil supremacy.

[41]Edmund C. Burnett, ed., *Letters of Members of the Continental Congress* (Washington, 1921-1936), 7: 415 and n. 5; cf. 287-88, 302, 391.

[42]See Charles Warren, *The Making of the Constitution* (Boston, 1937), pp. 482-84, 505, 517-20.

[43]Boyd, *The Papers of Thomas Jefferson* 12: 425, 440, 571; Schwartz, *The Bill of Rights* 1: 443, 446, 487, 573.

prevent the establishment of a standing army, the bane of liberty."[44]
It is worth noting that the original draft of the amendment included
the idea that a person might be excused from military service because
of religious scruples. The clause was dropped. Article 3 gave further
protection to the individual, asserting that soldiers might not be
quartered in private houses without the consent of the owner in
peacetime and only as prescribed by law in war.

Concern about standing armies did not end with independence and
the adoption of the federal Constitution. The opposition to peacetime
forces took on a decided partisan coloration, with the Jeffersonian
Republicans adopting the sentiment as their own. *The Debates and
Proceedings of the Congress of the United States* (the *Annals*) reveal
that in the 1790s familiar arguments about the dangers of a standing
army and the value of a militia were advanced. Some occasions were
in 1790 when Henry Knox, secretary of war, introduced his Militia
Plan; in 1792 at the time of the Whiskey Rebellion; in January 1793
when there was a motion to reduce the nation's military establishment to 2,128 men; in the spring of 1794 when a crisis with Great
Britain led to a series of proposals to increase the size of the army;
and finally, in January and February 1797, when the Republicans introduced a motion to reduce the army.[45] The justification which Knox
offered for his Militia Plan reflected all the arguments Englishmen
had crafted over the generations. Knox maintained that "an ener-
getic national militia" was the best security for a free republic. Arguing
that vice, laziness, and luxury made a standing army necessary, he
declared, "It is when public spirit is despised, and avarice, indolence
and effeminancy of manners predominate, . . . that a standing army is
formed and riveted for ever." Believing that the militia must not be
composed of substitutes, he asserted that men of means have an obligation to serve. Refusal to participate in the militia should be grounds
for denying a man the right to hold public office or receive public
honor. A militia made up of all male citizens, serving on a rotating
basis, would defend the nation, encourage love of country and obedience to laws, promote good health, and improve the national character.[46]

[44]Irving Brant, *The Bill of Rights, Its Origin and Meaning* (New York, 1965), pp.
486-87.

[45]*Debates and Proceedings of the Congress of the United States, 1789-1800* (Washington, 1834-56), 1: 975, 995, 1001; 3: 553-54, 781, 784-90, 792-93, 796-98; 4:
500-57 *passim*, 735-38; 6: 1979-2094 *passim*.

[46]*American State Papers. Documents, Legislative and Executive of the Congress of
the United States. Military Affairs (Class V)* (Washington, 1832), 1: 6-13.

The American colonists, then, inherited a tradition which had been developed in seventeenth-century England. That tradition played a part in the indictment of Great Britain, in the Declaration of Independence, in the coming of the Revolution, and in the creation of a constitution with a Bill of Rights. At the end of the eighteenth century, it acted as a brake on the power of the executive. The fear lingered on. In 1812, the second Federalist president, John Adams, wrote, "The danger of our government is . . . that the army possess [sic] more power than Congress. The people should be apprised of this, and guard themselves against it. Nothing is more essential than to hold the civil authority decidedly superior to the military power."[47]

That warning can still be heard from some quarters today. To men concerned about current public policy respecting military power and the relationship between the executive and legislative branches of the American government, the seventeenth-century English tracts and parliamentary debates which articulated an antistanding army ideology are still relevant. With all their anachronistic and elitist prejudices, they could serve to remind readers that luxury and indolence enervates, that citizenship in a free society imposes obligations, that history has lessons which free men ignore at their peril, that military power, even with constitutional controls, is inherently menacing, and that there is a danger in entrusting the defense of any free state to professional soldiers or to a volunteer army.

[47]C. F. Adams, *The Works of John Adams* 10: 17.

BIBLIOGRAPHICAL NOTE

Most of the primary source material for this study is in printed form, but there are a few manuscript sources in such libraries as the Bodleian, the British Museum Manuscript Room, the Folger Shakespeare Library, and the Public Record Office. The most important are: the dispatches of Frederick Bonnet, the ambassador from Brandenburg, in Add. Mss. at the British Museum; the Carte Papers at the Bodleian; Sir Simonds D'Ewes "Journal" in the Harleian Manuscripts at the British Museum and available on microfilm at the Folger Library; William Schilling, ed., "The Parliamentary Diary of Sir John Gell: 5 February–21 March 1659" (M.A. thesis, Vanderbilt University, 1961); Roger Morrice, "Entr'ing Book, Being An Historical Register of Occurrences from April, Anno 1677, to April 1691," a photocopy of which is in the possession of the widow of Professor Douglas Lacey; the Newdigate Newsletters covering the years from 1673-74 to 1715 at the Folger; "The Several Debates of the House of Commons Pro et Contra Relating to the Establishment of the Militia, Disbanding the Newraised Forces . . . [in] November 1685," in the Lowther Manuscripts, Cumberland Record Office, available in photocopy form at the History of Parliament Trust in London; the Shaftesbury Papers and some unprinted state papers from 1697 through 1699 at the Public Record Office; and the Shrewsbury Papers at Delapré Abbey, the Northamptonshire Record Office, the most important of which are printed.

The printed primary materials include parliamentary debates, journals and diaries, personal memoirs and letters, contemporary histories and biographies, and public papers. Full citations to these sources are in the footnotes.

Many tracts and pamphlets were used in this study. An abbreviated title of each tract is in the first citation in the footnotes. The pamphlets are most conveniently found in the United States at the Folger Shakespeare Library in Washington, D.C., the McAlpin Collection at Union Theological Seminary in New York City, and the Houghton Library, Harvard University. For authorship, dating, and location see: British Museum, department of printed books; *Catalogue of the Pamphlets, Books, Newspapers, and Manuscripts Relating to the Civil War, the Commonwealth, and Restoration, Collected by George Thomason, 1640-1661* (London, 1908); Donald Wing, *Short-Title Catalogue of Books Printed in England, Scotland, Ireland, Wales, and British America and of English Books Printed in Other Countries 1641-1700*, (New York, 1945); and Samuel Halkett and John Laing, *Dictionary of Anonymous and Pseudononymous English Literature* (London, 1926). For the authorship and sequence of the tracts in the 1697-99 controversy, see Lois G. Schwoerer, "Chronology and Authorship of the Standing Army Tracts, 1697-99," *Notes and Queries*, new series, 13 (no. 10): 382-90.

No attempt has been made to list the secondary works that have been consulted; reference to them may be found in the footnotes.

INDEX

THE JOHNS HOPKINS UNIVERSITY PRESS

This book was composed in PTS Baskerville type by the Jones Composition Company. It was printed on S. D. Warren's 60-lb. 1850 paper and bound in Joanna Arrestox cloth by Universal Lithographers, Inc.

LIBRARY OF CONGRESS CATALOGING IN PUBLICATION DATA

Schwoerer, Lois G
    The antiarmy ideology in seventeenth-century England.

    At head of title: "No standing armies!"
    Bibliography: p.
    1. Great Britain—History—Stuarts, 1603-1714. 2. Great Britain, Army—
History. 3. Standing army. I. Title.
DA375.S37   355.02'13'0942   73-19337

ISBN 0-8018-1563-0